Sustainability in Fashion

Claudia E. Henninger • Panayiota J. Alevizou • Helen Goworek •
Daniella Ryding
Editors

Sustainability in Fashion

A Cradle to Upcycle Approach

palgrave
macmillan

Editors
Claudia E. Henninger
University of Manchester
Manchester, United Kingdom

Helen Goworek
University of Leicester
Leicester, United Kingdom

Panayiota J. Alevizou
Management School
University of Sheffield
Sheffield, United Kingdom

Daniella Ryding
University of Manchester
Manchester, United Kingdom

ISBN 978-3-319-51252-5 ISBN 978-3-319-51253-2 (eBook)
DOI 10.1007/978-3-319-51253-2

Library of Congress Control Number: 2017935408

Printed on acid-free paper

This Palgrave Macmillan imprint is published by Springer Nature
The registered company is Springer International Publishing AG
The registered company address is: Gewerbestrasse 11, 6330 Cham, Switzerland

Acknowledgements

Support is one of the most important things that you cannot buy; thus, we would like to thank our family and friends for their continuous support and believe in our work. A special thanks to Panayiota, Helen, and Daniella for their dedication towards this book, their enthusiasm, and their hard work.

We would also like to thank each and every one of our amazing contributors, without whom this book would not have been possible. Thank you for being part of our book, for all your hard work, and your timely submissions. We believe that every chapter has added value to our book, making it a unique piece by providing a multifaceted lens to sustainability in fashion. Thank you! Danke! Ευχαρίστώ!

Contents

Notes on Contributors

Dr Phoebe Apeagyei is a Senior Lecturer in Fashion Technology and Anthropometrics at Manchester Metropolitan University. Her experiences and research interests lie in body scanning technology, anthropometrics, body image, sizing, plus consumer perceptions and attitudes towards fashion, innovation, and sustainability.

Dr Marsha A. Dickson is Irma Ayers Professor of Human Services in the Department of Fashion and Apparel Studies, and co-director of the Sustainable Apparel Initiative at the University of Delaware. Dr Dickson is internationally recognized for her research and teaching on social responsibility in the apparel industry. She is lead author of the book Social Responsibility in the Global Apparel Industry, has co-authored two books on fair trade, and has published on consumer and business practices in social responsibility in peer-reviewed journals such as *Business & Society, Journal of Business Ethics, Journal of Corporate Citizenship*, and the *Clothing and Textiles Research Journal.* She has conducted research on social responsibility in Bangladesh, Cambodia, China, Guatemala, Hong Kong, India, Thailand, Vietnam, and in the UK and Europe. For 14 years Dickson served an executive member of the board of directors of the Fair Labor Association (FLA), a non-governmental organization originally formed by President Clinton to improve working conditions in factories around the world. She is currently on the board of directors of the Fair Factories Clearinghouse. Dr Dickson has received several awards for her academic and industry contributions in social responsibility, including the All Star Award from Apparel Magazine and the International Textile and Apparel Association (ITAA) in 2009, ITAA Distinguished Scholar in 2011, and ITAA Fellow in 2016.

Dr Kirsi Niinimäki is an Associate Professor in Fashion research in Aalto University. Her research focuses on holistic understanding of sustainable fashion and textile fields and connections between design, manufacturing, business models and consumption. In Aalto University Niinimäki runs the Fashion/Textile Futures research group. The research group is involved in several significant research projects, which integrate closed loop, bioeconomy and circular economy approaches in fashion and textile systems. Her work is widely published in top scientific journals.

Sarah Netter is the Centre Manager at the Centre for Corporate Social Responsibility (cbsCSR) at the Copenhagen Business School (CBS) in Denmark. Prior to her appointment, Sarah has been a PhD fellow and a Post-Doctoral fellow at the Department of Intercultural Communication and Management at CBS. Her research focusses on the sharing economy, sustainable consumer behaviour, business model innovation, and the fashion industry. As part of her research, Sarah has conducted extensive fieldwork on the sharing economy in Europe and the USA. In her research, Sarah aims to explore this new phenomenon and to provide a more nuanced understanding of the opportunities and tensions that characterize the sharing economy. Sarah is affiliated with the MISTRA Future Fashion initiative. MISTRA Future Fashion is a large-scale, cross-disciplinary research initiative, which aims at promoting systemic changes towards sustainability in the fashion industry.

Dr Helen Goworek is MSc Marketing Programme Leader at University of Leicester, UK, and Chair of the British Academy of Management's Sustainable and Responsible Business conference track. She is the author of three books about the fashion business and retailing, and has also written book chapters and articles on retail buying, product development, and sustainability. She is a member of the organising committees for the Management and Environmental Sustainability conference and the International Colloquium on Design, Branding and Marketing (ICDBM).

Dr Daniella Ryding is a Lecturer in Fashion Marketing at the University of Manchester in the UK. An active researcher with over with over 40 published articles and several text book contributions, her main research interests focus on consumer behaviour within an international fashion retailing context. The author has more recently been engaged with the psychological cognitive and behavioural mechanisms impacting on consumer decsion-making, contributing to better understandings of memory and the ramifications for business marketing campaigns. Daniella also takes a proactive interest in sustainability and the circular economy, examining further the ecological and ethical principles which drive business strategy.

Dr Panayiota J. Alevizou is a Lecturer in Marketing at University of Sheffield, UK, where she teaches Marketing Theory and Practice, and Retail and Services Marketing. She is the Programme Director of International Business and Management at the University of Sheffield Management School and a member of the Centre for Research in Marketing and Society (CReiMS). She is particularly interested in exploring consumer behaviour, company communication, and labelling strategies by means of qualitative methods. Panayiota is a fellow of the Higher Education Academy and worked as a marketing consultant in Greece.

Dr Claudia E. Henninger is a Lecturer in Fashion Marketing Management at the School of Materials, the University of Manchester. She was awarded her PhD entitled 'Corporate Identity in the Contexts of the UK's Green Slow-Fashion Industry and Micro-Organisations' from the University of Sheffield in 2015. Claudia's research centres on corporate marketing, sustainability, and green consumer typologies in the context of the fashion industry. She has published in leading journals, contributed to edited books, and presented her work at various national and international conferences. Claudia is the Deputy Chair of the Academy of Marketing SIG Sustainability.

Dr. Annamma Joy is a professor of Marketing, Faculty of Management at the University of British Columbia, Okanagan campus. Her research interests are primarily in the area of consumer behaviour and branding with a special focus on luxury brands, fashion brand experiences, consumer behaviour in the People's Republic of China (PRC), sustainability in the fashion and wine industries, and aesthetic consumption. She has published several articles in consumer behaviour and marketing journals such as the *Journal of Consumer Research, Journal of Consumer Psychology, International Journal of Research in Marketing, Journal of Cross-cultural Psychology*, and *Journal of Economic Psychology, Consumption, Markets and Culture*. Dr. Joy has won several awards for her articles published in journals in addition to videos she helped produce.

Camilo Peña is a PhD student at the Faculty of Management—University of British Columbia (UBC), Okanagan Campus. His current work and research focuses on topics of sustainable consumer behaviours in the wine industry.

Dr Patsy Perry is a Lecturer in Fashion Marketing in the School of Materials at The University of Manchester. She gained her PhD in Corporate Social Responsibility in fashion supply chains from Heriot-Watt University in 2012, and has published a number of academic journal articles and book chapters on her research. She teaches on several undergraduate and postgraduate courses and supervises PhD students in the areas of sustainability and fashion marketing.

Joy Bucklow gained a first class honours degree in Contemporary Textiles from Lancaster University in 2013, and in 2016 started her third year PhD studies in the School of Materials, at the University of Manchester. Combined with her professional qualification as a Charted Management Accountant, she plans to use the skills and knowledge gained from her PhD on sustainability, consumerism and labelling, to start a textile design company using sustainable fibres.

Sara Li-Chou Han is a Research Associate at Manchester Metropolitan University. Her background lies in fashion design, styling, and social enterprise, and she is currently researching how circular economy fashion strategies can re-value post-consumer textiles and close 'values-action gaps' in supply chains.

Dr David Tyler is a Reader in Fashion Technology at Manchester Metropolitan University. With many years of experience in the garment industry and in Higher Education, he has developed research interests using UK and EU funding. His current projects include new product development, impact protection, apparel sustainability, and wearable technologies. He is involved with Resyntex: an EU-funded initiative to extend the circular economy to fashion products.

Ms Zhen Lai is a marketing consultant for the internet industry. She has received a merit in her MSc International Management and Marketing from the University of Sheffield in 2015. Silver's Master dissertation focused on sustainability in the fashion industry. Her dissertation was entitled 'An exploration of consumers' perspective towards eco-labelling in the UK's fashion industry', for which she received a distinction.

Ms Yanan Xu is a Marketing Assistant in the fashion industry. She received a distinction in her Masters Degree in Marketing and Management from Loughborough University in 2014, and her MSc. in International Fashion Retailing, awarded from the University of Manchester in 2016. Yanan Xu's MSc. thesis focused on sustainable luxury fashion and consumer behaviour. Her dissertation was entitled *Extending the Consumer Style Inventory (CSI) Framework to Understand Consumer Decision Making for Second-hand Luxury Clothing Consumption: UK Perspective.*

Ms Menglu Wang is a graduate from the University of Manchester. Her MSc. thesis examines sustainable fashion and its applications to consumer behaviour in the fashion industry by extending the Consumer Style Inventory (CSI) Framework to understand shopper motivations for vintage fashion in the UK market.

Archana is a Senior Account Manager at Intertek, where she manages product safety programs for key global accounts. She has worked in design, compliance, and product safety roles in the apparel industry. She has a MS in Fashion Studies from the University of Delaware where she delved into the world of corporate social responsibility. Archana grew up in India surrounded by a plethora of traditional textiles, native crafts, and interaction with artisans and weavers, which she pinpoints as the beginning of her career in the global apparel industry.

Carly Fox has previously studied pattern cutting, fashion and interior design as well as areas of psychology and education. Throughout her career she has gained design, production, sales and manufacturing experience in the UK, Europe, India and China working with both the high-street retail chains and within the luxury fashion market in areas of women's wear, men's wear and accessories. After a stint of being a fashion and lifestyle editor of a London music magazine she was invited to produce fashion shows and events working on projects such as London Fashion Week. Demand was such that she quickly moved into working with a select group of high net worth private clients styling all aspects of their lifestyle.

Angharad McLaren is a Lecturer in Textile Design, Sustainable Clothing Research Coordinator and former Research Fellow in Design for Clothing Longevity, at Nottingham Trent University, UK, with research interests in sustainable fashion and textiles, sustainable consumption, consumer behaviour and clothing longevity.

Dr Pallavi Singh is a Senior Lecturer in Marketing at Sheffield Business School, Sheffield Hallam University, Sheffield, UK. Before commencing her academic career, she was a Civil Servant in India. She obtained her PhD in Ethical Marketing from University of Sheffield Management School, Sheffield, UK; her MBA in Marketing also from University of Sheffield Management School (SUMS) UK; her Masters in Hindi Literature (Silver Medallist) and her Bachelors in Physics from the prestigious University of Allahabad in India. Her research interest includes environmental education in schools, and higher education institutions, sustainable consumption in families, socialization theory, green consumer behaviour, and child influence in family purchase decision-making. Her work has been presented at the Academy of Marketing Conference, World Environmental Education Congress and many more conferences across Asia and Europe. She is a reviewer with number of publications like the *Journal of Consumer Behaviour, South Asian Journal of Global Business Research*, and *Journal of Consumer Ethics*. She serves as consultant for social businesses, charity organisations, and not for profit organisations.

Dr Elaine Ritch is a Lecturer in Marketing and Programme Leader for the BA (Hons) International Marketing degree at Glasgow Caledonian University. She was awarded her PhD, entitled *Mothers' experience of sustainable fashion consumption: An existential phenomenological exploration within Edinburgh*, from Queen Margaret University in 2013. Elaine focuses her research on fashion consumption through a sustainability lens and has published in international journals and edited books, along with regularly presenting her work at international conferences.

Charlotte Rutter is a Senior Lecturer. With over a decade of lecturing in Fashion Management & Marketing (FMM) and as a co-founder of a successful fashion company, Charlotte has a wealth of experience to share through both an academic and professional lens. As Senior Lecturer at The University of Creative Arts (UCA), she has developed innovative and industry-relevant course content making the UCA FMM course one of the best in the country and leading to visiting posts at other universities including the University of the Arts London. Charlotte is passionate about developing research in the areas of FMM, sustainability, and ethics and consumer psychology, and has authored papers for publication and is a regular speaker at academic conferences. She has collaborated with Dr Kate Armstrong to design, write and deliver short courses and chapter content on specialised topic areas and is a Deputy Chair of the Fashion Marketing & Consumption SIG. Charlotte also works with companies in a consulting capacity to provide advisory and sounding board services through to full branding, marketing and business strategies.

Dr Marta Blazquez Cano is a Lecturer in Fashion Marketing at the School of Materials, University of Manchester. Marta holds a BA in

Advertising and PR and has developed a career in the advertising and marketing industry for more than 10 years. She was awarded a PhD in Marketing entitled 'Consumer experience in a multichannel retail environment: a cross-country study of the fashion sector. Marta's research interest includes omnichannel retail, experiential retail, channel integration, in-store technology, social media marketing, mobile marketing, consumer behaviour and sustainable fashion. She has published in leading journals, contributed to edited books and presented her work at various national and international conferences. Marta has been visiting researcher in the Oxford Institute of Research Management (OXIRM), University of Oxford, and has been invited lecturer on several occasions in China and Spain. She supervises a number of PhD and MSc students in the areas of fashion marketing and retailing.

Dr Kate Armstrong Current position: Assistant Dean: UG, Regents University London. She is a dynamic leader, innovator, manager and consultant with over 18 years of experience as an academic and branding consultant. PhD: qualitative, phenomenological, interpretive approach to explore consumer value systems and female consumption. Her research interests are diverse, but are centred around four broad research domains, including: (1) consumer psychology; (2) fashion; (3) creative and cultural Industries and (4) education. She has taught and researched in these areas in a number of Universities during her career. She is an experienced doctoral supervisor at both UG and PG level and has successfully supervised students to successful completion of their PhDs. She is regularly invited to present, chair and speak at industry and academic events and conferences. Her work is published in the *Journal of Marketing Management*, the *Journal of Customer Behaviour* and the *International Journal of Nonprofit and Voluntary Sector Marketing* and she is regularly invited to review papers in these and other, related journals. To consolidate her academic, commercial and research aspirations, she is founder and Chair the Fashion Marketing and Consumption SIG for the Academy of Marketing, of which she is the Chair. She is currently involved in several research projects that interrogate the intersection of fashion consumer psychology, consumption and engagement.

List of Figures

List of Tables

1

Introduction to Sustainability in Fashion

Claudia E. Henninger, Daniella Ryding,
Panayiota J. Alevizou and Helen Goworek

1.1 Idea for Sustainability in Fashion

> Anything that gets your blood racing is probably worth doing (Hunter S. Thompson)

For us as editors, sustainability in the fashion industry is a contemporary mega-trend that gets our *blood racing*. In the UK alone, the fashion

C.E. Henninger (✉) · D. Ryding
School of Materials, University of Manchester, Manchester, UK
e-mail: Claudia.Henninger@manchester.ac.uk;
Daniella.Ryding@manchester.ac.uk

P.J. Alevizou
Management School, University of Sheffield, Sheffield, UK
e-mail: P.J.Alevizou@sheffield.ac.uk

H. Goworek
Management School, University of Leicester, Leicester, UK
e-mail: hg77@leicester.ac.uk

C.E. Henninger et al. (eds.), *Sustainability in Fashion*,
DOI 10.1007/978-3-319-51253-2_1

industry contributes £26 billion directly to the British economy (BFC 2012, 2014), accounts for 2% of the world's Gross Domestic Product, and thus equates to an approximate value of £2.5 trillion (Fashion United 2016). These figures indicate that the global fashion industry plays a vital role in everyday life with one in every six people being employed within the fashion/apparel sector (Brown 2011).

The economic opportunities in the fashion industry have however come with a bleak backdrop, which has tarnished to some extent, the enthusiasm for those who take a keen interest in fashion. The Rana Plaza factory collapse (Parveen 2014), which witnessed more than 1,000 deaths and in excess of 2,000 fatal injuries, marks one of the greatest public outcries for more transparency within supply chains for security and ethical trading practices. Sustainability in recent times has thus become a priority for many fashion organisations, the overall industry having demonstrated one of the highest levels of negligence concerning exploitation of the workforce, social well-being, and drainage of the world's natural resources, when it comes to garment production. Integral to success and within the context of a circular economy, is first and foremost, an understanding of how to unlock vertical supply chains with a view to developing new business models, which contribute to improved sustainable value. Of equal importance is the need to fully understand how both government and businesses might work together to broaden the prospect of slowing down consumption, thereby convincing consumers to make more environmentally friendly choices as a way of enacting out a changing social value system. Yet, whilst sustainability in the fashion industry has received increased attention, the fashion and textiles context still remains underrepresented within the mainstream marketing and management literature (e.g. O'Cass and Lim 2001; Matthiesen and Phau 2005; Buresti and Rosenberger III 2006; Henninger 2015). The idea for our book *Sustainability in Fashion – A Cradle to Upcycle Approach* – emerged further to attendance at various multi-disciplinary conferences, many of which have started to dedicate research streams to issues of sustainability in the fashion industry within global contexts. Our book – *Sustainability in Fashion* – offers international application with a view to contextualising important developments within the fashion industry. The contributors use their diverse backgrounds and expertise to provide a contemporary approach in examining key theoretical concepts, constructs, and developments.

1.2 Sustainability and the Fashion Industry

Sustainability has previously been described as a *fuzzy concept* (Markusen 1999) that lacks a clear-cut definition. Thus, *sustainability* can be and is described in multifaceted ways and can incorporate an economic, social, and/or environmental angle. To reiterate this point further, *sustainability* is an intuitively understood concept that is interpreted in a very subjective manner and thus, person and/or context dependent (e.g. Gunder 2006; Henninger et al. 2016). This aspect is further reflected in this book, as all contributors discuss issues of *sustainability* within the fashion industry from very unique perspectives, with none of the authors necessarily defining the term in exactly the same way. This is further touched upon in the next section.

Sustainability in itself is not a new phenomenon, but rather has been investigated as early as the 1960s when consumers started to be more concerned about the impact their consumption patterns have on the natural environment (e.g. Peattie 1995; McCormick 2001; SustAinability 2011). The media reports about various *waves* of sustainability that have put a spotlight on the fashion industry – predominantly for negative reasons – such as labour right issues, anti-fur campaigns, rivers that turn red due to pollution, and clothing that ends up in landfill (e.g. EFF 2008; WRAP 2012; Matthews 2015). Although these negative examples seemingly overshadow the fashion industry, recent years have seen a dramatic change in the industry landscape. More and more retailers promote sustainable initiatives, which can take on a variety of shapes and actions. Examples of these initiatives are: Shwopping, which emerged as a new trend in 2012. Marks & Spencer is the key driver behind this initiative, creating it as part of their *Plan A* sustainability plan (M&S 2016); or H&M's 'Close the Loop' recycled clothing collection (Sowray 2015). At the same time, a majority of newly established businesses see sustainability less as an 'add-on', but rather incorporate aspects of sustainability – in form of environment, social, and/or economic components – at the core of their organisations. These changes may not come as a surprise, as companies continuously seek to react to consumer demands for more sustainable and environmentally friendly alternatives. Seeing as the fashion industry is the second most polluting industry globally (Egan 2011; BSR 2012; Henninger et al. 2016), we feel these changes cannot come soon enough.

1.3 Content of *Sustainability in Fashion*

Our book reiterates what authors have previously highlighted: sustainable fashion and sustainability in fashion are not fads that are going in and out of fashion, but rather necessities within the industry that are continuously increasing in importance. Extant research has predominantly focused on design issues of sustainable fashion from an arts and humanities perspective and currently lacking is an international fashion business perspective. Companies in the present sustainable era are compelled more than ever, to think and act strategically about changing market dynamics. Future survival on the companies' part thus relies on a full appreciation of how to make use of its internal resources and core competencies to successfully compete and innovate, within an evolving and significant circular economy. Our book addresses this gap in the literature and brings together contributions from a variety of academic backgrounds and experiences in the fashion industry, whilst furthermore providing a global perspective. All of our contributors have been carefully chosen for their expertise in the field of sustainability and fashion.

Chapter 2 – *The Epiphanic Sustainable Fast Fashion Epoch: A New Fashion Ethical Fashion Mandate* – is a UK contribution written by Dr Charlotte Rutter, Dr Kate Armstrong and Dr Marta Blazquez Cano. The chapter provides an engaging and somewhat daring introduction to our book by critically commenting on current issues of sustainability and ethics in the fashion industry. The authors provide an interesting take on *sustainability in fashion*, whilst at the same time raise key questions at the end of their chapter that can provide stimulating discussions and intriguing debates. One of the key questions raised is whether *all fashion brands should be sustainable and have ethical business practices.*

Chapters 3 and 4 both touch upon this question, by focusing on aspects concerning standards and eco-labels utilised in the fashion industry. Chapter 3 – *Sustainability and the Fashion Industry: Conceptualizing Nature and Traceability* – is a Canadian contribution written by Professor Annamma Joy and Mr Camilo Peña. This insightful contribution focuses on aspects of traceability, which would allow consumers to make informed choices about their purchases. The authors raise important concerns of trust in current certifications and traceability certifications and leave the reader with ideas for future research that could help shape the fashion industry further.

Chapter 4 – *The Influence of Eco-Labelling on Ethical Consumption of Organic Cotton* – is a UK contribution written by Ms Joy Bucklow, Dr Patsy Perry, and Dr Elaine Ritch. Their contribution follows on organically from Chapter 3, by providing the reader with an insight into consumers' perceptions of eco-labels, with specific focus on organic cotton. The authors provide a stimulating discussion on the status of organic cotton in the fashion industry and thus, put a renewed spotlight on an established research topic: eco-labels and certifications.

Chapter 5 – *An Exploration of Consumers' Perceptions Towards Sustainable Fashion – A qualitative study in the UK* – is a UK contribution written by Ms Zhen Lai, Dr Claudia E Henninger, and Dr Panayiota J Alevizou. By staying with the aspects of consumer perceptions, this chapter explores the wider associations consumers have with sustainable fashion. The authors illustrate that female and male participants have different perceptions of what constitutes sustainable fashion; whilst females may be tempted to buy into the 'short-term trends', males are seemingly more 'resistant'.

Chapter 6 – *Ethical Consumption Patterns and the Link to Purchasing Sustainable Fashion* – a UK contribution by Dr Claudia E Henninger and Dr Pallavi Singh takes the research in Chapter 5 further by quantitatively analysing patterns of ethical consumption and the link to sustainable fashion. The authors immerse themselves in the data to provide the reader with an insight into how ethical consumers can be profiled.

Chapter 7 – *Determining Effective Sustainable Fashion Communication Strategies* – a UK contribution by Ms Sara Li-Chou Han, Dr Claudia E Henninger, Dr Phoebe Apeagyei, and Dr David Tyler, moves away from consumer perceptions and focuses on an organisational perspective. The authors explore how sustainable businesses communicate and what knowledge they assume their consumers have. This insightful chapter opens a pathway for further research and clearly demonstrates the importance of communication, thereby linking back to Chapters 3 and 4.

Chapter 8 – *Fashion in a Circular Economy* – a Finnish contribution by Dr Kirsi Niinimäki, explores a fascinating topic: the circular economy. The conceptual chapter is written in an engaging way and provides food for thought by highlighting an alternative way to fashion production. The company perspective illustrates that changes in the industry are already apparent, yet there is still room for improvement.

Chapter 9 – *Investigating the Relationship Between Consumer Attitudes and Sustainable Fashion Product Development* – a UK contribution by Ms Angharad McLaren and Dr Helen Goworek is based on a Department for Environment, Food and Rural Affairs (DEFRA) project and provides a real life example of how consumers purchase, maintain, and dispose of garments. The mixed qualitative methods approach brings forward interesting findings that have implications for theory in terms of incorporating steps into the consumer decision-making and product development process to address sustainability in clothing. Practically McLaren and Goworek highlight that clothing companies can provide product sustainability guidelines for their product development teams and investigate their own customers' opinions of sustainable clothing.

Chapter 10 – *Social Sustainability in Apparel Supply Chains: Organizational Practices for Managing Sub-Contracted Homework* – a US contribution by Archana and Professor Marsha A Dickson moves the conversation to the apparel supply chain. The interesting contribution focuses on the Indian context and links to Chapters 3 and 4 by looking at certifications and standards used along the supply chain. The authors' methodology and implications for the fashion industry are presented in an engaging way that sparks ideas for further research.

Chapter 11 – *User Satisfaction and Dissatisfaction in the App Sharing Economy: An Investigation into Two-Sided Mobile Fashion Reselling and Swapping Markets* – is a Danish contribution by Dr Sarah Netter. The author utilises the SERVQUAL model and extends its content to fit a new research context. The results are fascinating and clearly illustrate a practical contribution to further enhance sustainability in the fashion industry.

Chapter 12 – *A Review of Secondhand Luxury and Vintage Clothing* – is a UK contribution by Dr Daniella Ryding, Ms Menglu Wu, Ms Carly Fox, and Ms Yanan Xu, which provides a conceptual examination of the significant rise in secondhand fashion retailing. The authors touch on the theme of sustainable consumption, exploring further the attitudinal and behavioural antecedents for secondhand luxury and vintage fashion; a sector which has experienced the most growth in secondhand clothing sales, and one which comprises of an evolving retail format which lends itself to the growing consumer popularity of purchasing and experiencing pre-loved and pre-worn garments.

In closing the loop of our introduction, the chapters presented in this edited work show a variety of interpretations of sustainability in the fashion industry. The chapters are not only written in an extremely engaging manner, but also encourage the reader to ask questions and undertake further research. The fashion industry is a key economic contributor and thus, provides an opportunity to be utilised as a research context. This edition is one of its kind and provides an international insight into the fashion industry. This book provides a glimpse of issues and concerns associated with the industry, which need to be further explored.

1.4 Dedications and Acknowledgements

This book is dedicated to our families and friends, who have supported our research. A special thank you goes to our wonderful contributors for making this book possible. Working on this edited book has been truly inspiring and we hope that our readers will agree with us in saying that the individual chapters are truly engaging and clearly highlight the authors' passion for sustainability and the fashion industry. The daring underlying tone of some chapters, as well as the key challenges that have been raised and discussed in our contributions provide room for discussions and debates.

The topical discussions and implications emerging from the contributions are valuable and relevant for anyone interested in sustainability in the fashion industry.

References

BFC (British Fashion Council). (2012). Annual report 2011–2012. BFC (online), retrieved: http://www.britishfashioncouncil.co.uk/uploads/media/290/31007.pdf, accessed: 26/01/2014.

BFC (British Fashion Council). (2014). Facts & figures AW14. BFC (online), retrieved: http://britishfashioncouncil.co.uk/news_detail.aspx?id=623, accessed: 26/05/2014.

Brown, S. (2011). Future factory: Sass Brown is coming to NTU. Future Factory (online), retrieved: http://futurefactory.weebly.com/live-event-streams.html, accessed: 20/03/2012.

BSR (Business of a Better World) (2012). Sustainable Fashion Design: Oxymoron No more?, BSR [online], retrieved: http://www.bsr.org/reports/BSR_Sustainable_Fashion_Design.pdf, accessed: 05/07/2013.

Buresti, F., & Rosenberger III, P. J. (2006). Brand personality differentiation in the Australian action-sports clothing market. *Marketing Bulletin, 17*(1): 1–16.

EFF (Ethical Fashion Forum). (2008). Fast fashion, cheap fashion. Ethical Fashion Forum (Online), retrieved: http://www.ethicalfashionforum.com/the-issues/fast-fashion-cheap-fashion, accessed: 17/06/2012.

Egan, D. (2011). Lily Cole says ethical fashion is an oxymoron. Is it?. The Guardian (online), retrieved: http://socialenterprise.guardian.co.uk/social-enterprise-network/2011/apr/05/sustainability-fashion-ethical, accessed: 05/07/2013.

Fashion United. (2016). Global fashion industry statistics – international apparel. Fashion United (online), retrieved: https://fashionunited.com/global-fashion-industry-statistics, accessed: 06/10/2016.

Gunder, M. (2006). Sustainability: Planning's saving grace or road to perdition? *Journal of Planning Education and Research, 26*: 208–221.

Henninger, C. E. (2015). Traceability the new eco-label in the slow-fashion industry? – Consumer perceptions and micro-organisations responses. *Sustainability*, *7*: 6011–6032.

Henninger, C. E., Alevizou, P. J., & Oates, C. J. (2016). What is sustainable fashion? *Journal of Fashion Marketing & Management*, *20*(4): 400–416.

M&S (Marks & Spencer). (2016). *Shopping. Ordinary clothes made extraordinary*. M&S (online), retrieved: http://www.marksandspencer.com/s/plan-a-shwopping, accessed: 07/10/2016.

Markusen, A. (1999). Fuzzy concepts, scanty evidence, policy distance: The case for rigour and policy relevance in critical regional studies. *Regional Studies*, *33*(9): 869–884.

Matthews, A. (2015). The environmental crisis in your closet. Newsweek (online), retrieved: http://europe.newsweek.com/environmental-crisis-your-closet-331530?rm=eu, accessed: 06/10/2016.

Matthiesen, I., & Phau, I. (2005). The 'HUGO BOSS' connection: Achieving global brand consistency across countries. *Journal of Brand Management*, *12*(5): 325–338.

McCormick, J. (2001). *Environmental Policy in the European Union*. Palgrave: Basingstoke, UK.

O'Cass, A., & Lim, K. (2001). The influence of brand associations on brand preference and purchase intention: An Asian perspective on brand associations. *Journal of International Consumer Marketing*, *14*(2/3): 41–71.

Parveen, S. (2014). Rana Plaza factory collapse survivors struggle one year on. BBC (online), retrieved: http://www.bbc.co.uk/news/world-asia-27107860, accessed: 06/08/2014.

Peattie, K. (1995). *Environmental Marketing Management: Meeting the Green Challenge*. Pitman Publishing: London, UK.

Sowray, B. (2015). *H&M launches 'Close the Loop', a collection made using your recycled clothes*. Telegraph (online), retrieved: http://www.telegraph.co.uk/fashion/brands/hm-closes-the-loop-with-collection-made-from-recycled-garments/, accessed: 07/10/2016.

SustAinability. (2011). Signed, sealed… delivered?, Behind certifications and beyond labels. SustAinability (online), retrieved: http://www.sustainability.com/library/signed-sealed-delivered-1#.UrrSpSiVfBw, accessed: 25/12/2013.

WRAP (Waste & Resources Action Programme). (2012). Valuing our clothes: The true cost of how we design, use and dispose of clothing in the UK. WRAP (online), retrieved: http://www.wrap.org.uk/sites/files/wrap/VoC%20FINAL%20online%202012%2007%2011.pdf, accessed: 15/07/2013.

Dr Claudia E. Henninger is a Lecturer in Fashion Marketing Management at the School of Materials, the University of Manchester. She was awarded her PhD entitled 'Corporate Identity in the Contexts of the UK's Green Slow-Fashion Industry and Micro-Organisations' from the University of Sheffield in 2015. Claudia's research centres on corporate marketing, sustainability, and green consumer typologies in the context of the fashion industry. She has published in leading journals, contributed to edited books, and presented her work at various national and international conferences. Claudia is the Deputy Chair of the Academy of Marketing SIG Sustainability.

Dr Daniella Ryding is a Lecturer in Fashion Marketing at Manchester University, UK. An active researcher with over 30 published articles and several text book contributions, her main research interests focus on consumer behaviour within an international fashion retailing context, and more recent research looks at neuromarketing. Daniella is also interested in sustainability; mainly the ecological and ethical principles which drive business strategy.

Dr Panayiota J. Alevizou is a Lecturer in Marketing at University of Sheffield, UK, where she teaches Marketing Theory and Practice, and Retail and Services Marketing. She is the Programme Director of International Business and Management at the University of Sheffield Management School and a member of the Centre for Research in Marketing and Society (CReiMS). She is particularly interested in exploring consumer behaviour, company communication, and labelling strategies by means of qualitative methods. Panayiota is a fellow of the Higher Education Academy and worked as a marketing consultant in Greece.

Dr Helen Goworek is MSc Marketing Programme Leader at University of Leicester, UK, and Chair of the British Academy of Management's Sustainable and Responsible Business conference track. She is the author of three books about the fashion business and retailing, and has also written book chapters and articles on retail buying, product development, and sustainability. She is a member of the organising committees for the Management and Environmental Sustainability conference and the International Colloquium on Design, Branding and Marketing (ICDBM).

2

The Epiphanic Sustainable Fast Fashion Epoch

A New Fashion Ethical Fashion Mandate

Charlotte Rutter, Kate Armstrong and Marta Blazquez Cano

2.1 Objectives

- To bring readers up to date with current academic understanding of the terms ethics, sustainability and these constructs in the context of fashion, specifically fast fashion
- To understand legal and governmental standards around ethical fashion
- To describe current poor and best practices of fast fashion brands

C. Rutter (✉)
University of Creative Arts, Epsom, UK
e-mail: crutter2@ucreative.ac.uk

K. Armstrong
Regents University London, London, UK
e-mail: kate.armstrong@regents.ac.uk

M. Blazquez Cano
University of Manchester, Manchester, UK
e-mail: Marta.BlazquezCano@manchester.ac.uk

C.E. Henninger et al. (eds.), *Sustainability in Fashion*,
DOI 10.1007/978-3-319-51253-2_2

- To provide case studies and application of The Ethical Fast Fashion Tipping Epoch
- To outline the future of ethical fashion futures
- To offer discussion points for academic, industry and student readers

2.2 Introduction

With this chapter, the authors aim to outline current standards and practices within the fashion industry in the context of sustainability, specifically, within fast fashion. Current academic and industry perspectives on the definitions of sustainable fashion will be reviewed along with an appraisal of existing legal and governmental standards, case studies and best practices from fashion brands.

2.2.1 Ethical Philosophy

Merriam-Webster (2016) defines ethics as:

> The discipline dealing with what is **good and bad** and with moral duty and obligation
>
> **2 a:** a set of moral principles or values **b:** a theory or system of **moral values** <the present-day materialistic ethic> **c** plural but singular or plural in construction: the **principles of conduct** governing an individual or a group <professional ethics> **d:** a guiding philosophy

Many different philosophical positions exist on what it means to be ethical and what morality means (Frankena 1973). Ethics are deeply rooted in philosophy and our personal ethics are socialised via our reference groups, peers, backgrounds and cultural influences. Broadly speaking, there are two schools of thought within ethics: (1) the utilitarian approach: ethics that relate to the consequences of an action and (2) the deontological approach: focuses on the manner in which the act is performed. That is, the end cannot justify the means and that all actions should be considered in the wider context of society.

In the fashion industry, we observe that we have moved from a widely accepted utilitarian approach to ethics, whereby fast fashion, speedy turnovers and overconsumption are typified within the high-street fashion stores. Change has been incremental and progressive over time, prompted by actions such as lobbying and disasters such as the Rana Plaza incident, Bangladesh, which have served as catalysts to stimulate change towards a more deontological fashion focus. We have not arrived at an ethical utopia yet, but our interest in and surveillance of the fashion industry from an ethical perspective has led us to this notion that we are amidst positive change. See Nantel and Weeks (1996) for more philosophical reflections on the ethics of business.

It has been noted that issues surrounding marketing ethics and social responsibility are inherently controversial and that there is a lack of agreement about the value of social responsible approaches on marketing activities (Carrigan and Attalla 2001). Different terms have been used to denominate that social responsible approach of businesses, such as corporate social responsibility (CSR), sustainable marketing, marketing ethics or environmental sustainability (Kotler and Armstrong 2010; Gupta and Godges 2012). On one side, CSR aims to assess and ensure that the business operations of a firm are ethical. Perry and Towers (2009) indicate that socially responsible firms should consider the impact of their actions on their stakeholders and make a balance between the needs of their stakeholders and their own need to make a profit. Conversely, ethics involves different areas and categories. Ethics in business has been defined as a set of ethical codes that establishes what is morally right and wrong in the business (Carrigan and Attalla 2001). These ethical frameworks allow corporations to follow these mandates, with aspirations that they will make a positive impact on business, individuals and the whole society (Mauro et al. 1999; Tota and Shehu 2012). Both ethics and social responsibility must respond to each other in the business' corporate culture and both require a complete corporate commitment (Kotler et al. 1996).

But is there a place for ethics and sustainable practices within the business of fashion?

2.2.2 Ethics and Sustainability in the Fashion Sector

The notion of ethics and sustainability in fashion is an abstruse phenomenon and appears as something of an oxymoron, particularly within the fast fashion sector, which exists solely to produce clothes that aim to satisfy fashion appetites that are never truly quenched.

Historically, sustainable fashion has been defined as:

> Fashionable clothes that incorporate fair trade principles with sweatshop-free labour conditions while not harming the environment or workers by using biodegradable and organic cotton. (Joergens 2006, p. 361)

The concept has more recently evolved to embrace a more flexible conceptualisation of the term:

> Clothing, which incorporates one or more aspects of social or environmental sustainability, such as Fair Trade manufacturing or fabric containing organic-grown raw material. (Gowerek et al. 2012, p. 938)

Fashion companies are urged by their stakeholders to reduce environmental impact on their activities and build a sustainable fashion business (Chan and Wong 2012; Gupta and Hodges 2012). Shen et al. (2012) emphasise a distinction between socially responsible business (SRB) and environmentally responsible business (ERB). The environmental impact includes the use of chemicals and pesticides in cotton plantations that pollute the ecosystem and can be dangerous for humans (ibid) and the disposal of textiles in landfill that damage the environment (Bianchi and Birtwistle 2012). To reduce this impact, the industry has responded with the introduction of small-scale ethical retailers and with the launch of sustainable ranges by large retailers (Goworek et al. 2012). Sustainable fashion can range from garments made from organic cotton to recycling textiles and convert them into clothing designs (Shen et al. 2012; Goworek et al. 2012).

More recently, there has been a growing interest in sustainable clothing production and consumption (Goworek et al. 2012). Different terms like 'eco-fashion', 'green fashion', 'fashion with a conscience' or 'ethical fashion' are proof of this increasing concern. There are some notable exceptions, such as H&M who show a strong commitment to ethics and sustainability within their conscious range and their annual sustainability report (H&M 2016).

Case Study: H&M

H&M is one of the fast fashion retailers more strongly committed with ethical and sustainable issues. They work in different areas including recycling and ethical production and they try to raise awareness about working conditions, animal welfare or sustainable materials (H&M 2015).

They produce part of their garments with organic cotton and have launched different *Conscious Collections* defined for them like being 'good for the people, the planet and your wallet' (H&M n.d.)

Recently they have organised the *World Recycle Week*, an initiative to collect up to 1,000 tons of unwanted garments in one week. The main objective of this action was to raise awareness about the importance of recycling and the cost of producing fashion garments in terms of environmental resources (H&M 2016).

However, the global view of sustainability within the fashion industry is not all so optimistic. Along with natural resources issues, there has been an increase of manufacturer's negligence concerning public health and security (Ryding et al. 2014). The last and more dramatic tragedy was the Rana Plaza factory in Bangladesh, which collapsed and killed more than 1,000 people and left over 2,500 injured (Ryding et al. 2014; Fashion Revolution 2016a). This issue and others are discussed in more detail in the *Fashion Legalities + Policies + Best Practices* section.

2.2.3 Consumer Consideration

Any discussion of ethical philosophy in a consumer context naturally leads to a focus on ethical consumption, which broadly includes a range of consumerist behaviours, such as animal welfare, ecology, sustainability or human rights that are driven by motivations and moral imperatives (Carrigan and Attalla 2001). Sustainability in a fashion context is linked to the concept of eco-fashion (Chan and Wong 2012), however, proceed with caution, as just because an individual is aware about sustainable fashion, does not always correlate with purchase behaviour (Joergens 2006). To extrapolate, just because sustainable fashion has permeated the fabric (pun intended) of society, does not automatically relate to an increase in eco-fashion sales.

Ancillary variables beyond eco-awareness include the importance of brand image in the role of sustainable fashion purchases relative to specific products (Ryding et al. 2014). For some consumers, ethical purchases will take place if there is no perceived real or imagined cost for the consumer in terms of added price or loss of quality (Carrigan and Attalla 2001; Gupta and Hodges 2012). Historically, consumers seem to be more concerned by animal abuse rather than unethical work practices and they will engage in ethical behaviour if it is something that could affect their health (Joergens 2006). To illustrate: reflection on the use of chemicals in the manufacturing process is a growing sustainable trend within the fashion industry, exemplified originally by brands such as Stella McCartney in the luxury sector and more recently, by Inditex, who owns (amongst others in their portfolio), fast fashion brand, Zara. It should be noted however that Joergen's (2006) research is over a decade old and observations of the fashion industry suggest that more consumers who would not necessarily classify themselves as 'ethical' have concerns around manufacturing processes, perhaps as they have been highlighted through the news and popular media and are no longer the domain of the ecologically aware minorities or 'eco-warriors'. This normalising of sustainable principles within the fashion industry in part forms the basis of our initial observation that we are in a 'tipping point' within the industry. To interrogate this supposition further, more research is required into this area: a good starting point would be around sustainable fashion typologies.

Previous research by Carrigan and Attalla (2001) into ethical segmentation is dated, but provides a comprehensive foundation that provides a historical viewpoint. They categorised four different types of ethical behaviour including (1) '*caring and ethical*', those who act on ethical considerations and are a minority; (2) '*confused and uncertain*' consumers who would like to shop ethically, but are confused about the contradictory messages around corporate ethical behaviour; (3) '*cynical and disinterested*' who have a lack of conviction about companies being truly ethical and will just buy ethically if there is no implication on value, brand choice and convenience and (4) '*oblivious*' consumers' ethical concerns are not considered in their purchase decisions (ibid). A plethora of ethical segments exist within the consumer psychological literature, but scant, recent research into fashion typologies exists and yet would add meaningful insight into the area.

In line with this, there appears to be a general lack of consumers' awareness around sustainability issues in fashion and about the difference that engaging in ethical behaviour could make (Shen et al. 2012). Several researchers maintain that some fashion brands need to provide more information in their advertising and promote the benefits of eco-fashion for consumers to make better ethical judgements (Carrigan and Attalla 2001; Chan and Wong 2012; Gupta and Hodges 2012; Shen et al. 2012). This emphasis on provenance and transparency is a relatively new call for action and more evidence within the fashion industry is permeating into the common fashion lexicon and communications. That is, it is becoming normalised to expect a fashion brand to making some effort into providing reports on sustainability or including an ecologically focussed collection or edit. The tipping point of normalising sustainable fashion is upon us.

2.2.4 Disseminating Sustainable Message

Social media has been a popular medium to communicate and popularise the notion of sustainable fashion practices. To illustrate, eco-friendly brand Reformation has launched 'RefScale', which allows its customers to discover the environmental impact of their clothes, accompanied by informative charts displaying individual garments' eco credentials (Howard 2016). Other lobbying movements such as,

Campaign for Clean Clothes and Labour Behind the Label are the manifestation of the consumer and industry desire for provenance, accountability and transparency within the industry. One of the most successful brands at championing the sustainable cause is, Fashion Revolution, which unifies its sentiment and consumer audiences through the adoption of a variety of hashtags including the compelling: #FashRev and #WhoMadeMyClothes. These encourage Instagrammers and Twitter users to engage with the global call to action through user generated content that showcases vivid and empowering images of consumers' own clothing labels, demanding brands to answer questions around their origin.

Case Study: Fashion Revolution

Fashion Revolution is a 'non-profit community interest company' (Fashion Anthropologist 2016), based in the UK. It was born on the 24th April 2013 when the Rana Plaza complex collapsed in Bangladesh and killed 1,134 people. Every year on the anniversary of the disaster, the Fashion Revolution Week takes place, with the main objective of raising awareness about the real cost of fashion (Parveen 2014).

The Fashion Revolution Week is organised in many different countries, 70 in 2015, and in many cities in each country. Different activities bring together activists, academics, experts, representatives from industry and students. Also different social media like Facebook and Twitter promote content all year long (Fashion Revolution 2016a).

One of the most relevant campaigns that Fashion Revolution is doing is #whomademyclothes. It motivates consumers to ask fashion retailers who have made the clothes they are wearing. People share a picture of the label of some clothing item in the webpage and include the hashtag #whomademyclothes creating a big online community of fashion conscious consumers (Fashion Revolution 2016b).

This notion of culpability puts the onus firmly back on the brands and manufacturers to be accountable for the origins of clothing, garments and the overall supply chain. Other influential ethical groups exist to investigate the poor practices in some overseas companies, such as the Ethical Fashion Forum (EFF).

Case Study: Ethical Fashion Forum

The EFF was born out of a British mindset amongst fashion designers and industry professionals who were concerned about the environment and the people behind the collections. Reports of sweatshop labour, exploitative conditions and environmental damage as a result of the fashion industry were widespread in the media. Limited awareness and information around sustainable sourcing presented challenging obstacles to the aspirations of these worried individuals. An ethical movement was in train, but this group was unsure how to take it forward. This group pushed forward and created the EFF in 2004 (formally established in 2005), in retaliation to the poor practices in fashion manufacturing and in support of the ethical and sustainable movement that was rippling throughout the industry (EFF n.d.a).

The goal of the EFF was to address some of the challenges they faced by resolving to take a unified approach, better communication and dissemination of information, pooled resources, and shared practices. An ethical fashion network would open markets for fair trade, organic and values led producers, and make it easier for fashion businesses to source and produce in a sustainable way (EFF n.d.b).

The EFF makes the claim that it is the industry body for sustainable fashion that represents 'over 10,000 plus members in more than 100 countries' (EFF n.d.b). It supports its members through the 'source' platform (set up in 2011): a global platform for sustainable fashion. 'SOURCE, is a ground breaking social enterprise set to transform livelihoods for 2.5 million people in the developing world and significantly reduce the environmental impact of the fashion industry' (EFF 2016).

This group firmly places the burden of origin and best practices on the brands themselves, not the lobbyists who highlighted the issues in the first place.

This concept of obligation is a signifier or our lament that we are at a tipping point within the fashion industry, whereby the weight of obligation from both a humane and chemical supply chain perspective, is firmly (or becoming more so), on fashion brands. We argue that this sentiment is becoming incrementally more expectant by the consumer and entrenched within fashion brands' business strategy (whether they really want to or not). This is the key driver behind our epiphany.

2.2.5 Fashion Legalities + Policies + Best Practices

This section outlines current legal guidelines and explores the future ethical guidelines that are currently being outlined and implemented. One of the more profound contributions to ethical fashion policy emerged out of the Rana Plaza disaster.

Case Study: Rana Plaza, Bangladesh

On the 24th of April 2013, 1,129 human beings died, over 2,500 were injured. The 2013 Rana Plaza accident was one of the biggest tragedies in history of the fashion industry and occurred due to a structural failure in the building. The search for the dead ended on 13 May 2013 with a death toll of 1,129. Approximately 2,500 injured people were rescued from the building alive. It is considered the deadliest garment-factory accident in history, as well as the deadliest accidental structural failure in modern human history (BBC 2013; Parveen 2014).

The building contained clothing factories, a bank, apartments and several shops. The shops and the bank on the lower floors immediately closed after cracks were discovered in the building. The building's owners apparently ignored warnings to avoid using the building after cracks had appeared the day before. Garment workers were ordered to return the following day, and the building collapsed during the morning rush-hour (BBC 2013; Parveen 2014).

Policies such as the Bangladesh Safety Accord were created in reaction to the Primark disaster and demonstrate that the tipping point is gathering momentum towards better practices and mandates. Accord was created to ensure that a tragedy of this magnitude would never occur again.

Through these disasters positive change has emerged. It is this optimism that this chapter chooses to focus on and our observations of its occurrence within the fashion sector served as the foundation upon which led to the ephiphanic epoch identification. As such, we make reference here to some best practices by fashion brands' internal sustainability policies, such as H&M, Zara and Gap to name but a few, chosen because they provide consumers with extensive information around the efforts, policies and practices that the brand are engaging with from a sustainable perspective.

Inditex for example, demonstrate agile and transparent performances, as they are beginning to implement changes to adhere to their own pledge to omit all toxic chemicals in their supply and manufacturing chain by 2020. Inditex's manufacturing processes have been described by Green Peace (2016) as 'exemplary'. Greenpeace launched their 'Detox Catwalk' project in 2011 to address the problem of the usage of toxic chemicals in fashion.

Sustainable manufacturing metrics, such as greenhouse emissions, environmental footprints, agile and lean developments, supply chain, and CSR strategies are fast becoming core communication slogans within fast fashion brands' strategies. Observations of the fashion industry from environmental groups, such as Greenpeace and their 'Detox Catwalk' report are referred to here as original articulations that modern, sustainably aware fashion brands do exist. Greenpeace have awarded fast fashion retailers such as Uniqlo, G-Star Raw, Espirit, H&M, Inditex (Zara), Levi Strauss & Co, M&S and many more positive examples of the sustainable direction of these fast fashion retailers and serve to further exemplify our insight that we are at a fast fashion tipping point epoch. These modern day sustainable endorsements are galvanising contemporary sustainable archetypes within the industry.

One of the plights of pioneers in this sector is to implement global rules and laws to protect the people and process across the world. Many companies may have an agreement in place with their factory applying and agreeing to UK law for example, but the factory may also abide by their country's rules and laws, which may not be aligned with the UK's progressively modern and human perspectives. This dichotomy between outsourcing and home production legalities mean that external factories may be legal in their own country, but not in ours. Assuring that the manufacturing process at each stage is legal and fair is a tricky and difficult one to manage. In response to this issue, brands like Inditex, through Zara, have made great progress and have the volition and resources to be trailblazers in this area (and feel an obligation to do so, as such a huge global brand).

The subject and topic is multilayered and so subjective that it is a potential minefield. All that companies can do is choose their ethical and sustainable stance that is on brand and right for the company, communicate their plan and commit to it. A move towards more transparent communications around manufacturing and the provenance of garments is occurring, exemplified by the 'Roadmap to Zero' project, which aims to tackle the issue of hazard chemicals in the global textile and footwear value-chain.

The Roadmap to zero is further evidence of the sustainable epoch the fashion industry has (and continues) to migrate towards.

2.2.6 Fast Fashion and Sustainability: The Tipping Point

Having established current understanding around ethical conversations across psychology, marketing and fashion disciplines. This section refers to the authors' observations, through their expertise as educators, authors and consultants in the areas of fashion marketing, that we are in a new era: The fast fashion sustainable epoch. Signified by a shift in attitudes and expectations towards sustainable fashion have become, or are becoming, normalised. By this we mean that fast fashion brands are beginning to show a shift towards changes in their manufacturing processes as exemplified by brands such as Inditex, Espirit and H&M at the forefront of this revolution. There is still some way to go, but the general thrust of this section and chapter is an optimistic one. The tipping point we describe is expectant, as we transition from a place of disapproving condemnation of fast fashion brands and their practices (albeit mostly warranted), towards promising aspirations in the wake of previous disasters.

To rationalise the fundamental tenets of our argument we take a historical perspective by looking back to the origins of ethical and sustainable clothing. Previously, the majority of sustainable and ethical clothing mainly originated from an activist minority voice and often from a place (or person) that was not fashion-driven but principle-driven creating a niche market segment and a small target consumer group. Garments did not have mass market appeal which created barriers, and therefore engagement to buy into, as the majority of the consumer base felt they were on the outside looking in (peripheral). Even if the majority/mass market were conscious and had their own ethics and sustainable principles the story and marketing behind these minority ethical clothing brands felt like you had to be fully engaged with the topic and life style which limited consumers participation; but similar to the fair-trade food life cycle this approach needed to happen within fashion to bring us where we are today – at the tipping point.

We have observed sustainable practices being implemented within businesses, such as the food industry. We borrow from the food industry to explain our epiphany, as it is between 5 and 10 years ahead of the fashion industry in terms of transparency and ethical awareness. To explain: it has endured devastating scandals from mad cow disease, through battery chickens, horsemeat and being blamed for the obesity and diabetes crisis. Through these scandals, new industry regulations were established, championed by key influencers like Jamie Oliver, who has been on his own culinary crusade. These market factors prompted high growth within the sector for organic, or welfare items. Companies ahead of the curve who bought labelling, provenance and transparency into their products and supply chain became market leaders and have benefitted from the lions' share of this growth. With tragedies like the Rana Plaza disaster and Primark child labour outrage, the fashion industry is experiencing its own public scandals, which amplifies the need for self-regulation, or for mandatory regulations to be imposed. We predict, with our tipping point epoch, that the fashion industry will follow a similar path to its food counterpart. The high-street and fast fashion brands that are ahead of the fashion ethical curve are evidenced by their choice to being transparent and honest about what they want to achieve, how they plan on achieving it, by when and reporting what went wrong along the way.

If we consider a fashion ethical spectrum through time, we can visualise how ethics in fashion has evolved from early lobbying, through to fair trade demands and how this has become exemplified through brand innovators (like Stella McCartney in the luxury market). We are beginning to observe the normalisation of sustainability within fast fashion brands manifested through their adoption of sustainable policies, performance indicators and mandates. It is this tipping point, the early stages of 'normalisation' of ethical fast fashion mind-sets that the authors have identified as a 'tipping point'. We observe the challenges that fashion retailers face have yet to face around manufacturing on a large scale, but also the opportunities that are attainable, as big manufactures like H&M, Zara and Mango pave the way in this new eco-epoch. Parent companies like Inditex are distancing themselves from the notion of fast fashion, preferring instead to be considered as a 'thoughtful' manufacturer of fashion. This sentiment offers further validation for the notion of a more optimistic future following the tipping point.

2.2.7 Summary: The Future of Sustainability in Fashion

We outline that just as we once thought of sustainable fashion as hippy, or for the minorities, we forecast that the future bodes well for fast fashion, as it makes great steps towards normalising working conditions and manufacturing techniques, so that the words ethical, sustainable and green become obsolete, as they are predictably accepted as industry standards.

Somewhat controversially, the authors' ancillary aim to the chapter is to emphasise how past lobbying efforts, in conjunction with tragic events within the fashion industry's manufacturing processes have provided the catalyst for a new era within fast fashion. We call this observation: *'the epiphanic sustainable fast fashion epoch'*. Before the reader derides and dismisses the authors' for having delusions of grandeur, please, let us explain. The epiphanic moment refers to the epiphany when the authors began to notice an emerging, optimistic trend towards sustainable practices, emerging from the fast fashion case studies under review. The 'epoch' denotes the era in which we find ourselves in: conscious, sustainable, fast fashion. This statement may appear as an oxymoron to most, as we are still in a fashion society where fast fashion is frowned upon as disposable, unethical, transient, with poor manufacturing practices. Admittedly, we find ourselves in the early commencement of this view of a movement towards more conscientious fast fashion providers and there is a long way to go before fast fashion is truly sustainable. Our point of differentiation from previous research is that we acknowledge the growing evidence of prodigious and more modest efforts within the fast fashion industry that should be recognised for their contributions. Just as we once thought of sustainable fashion as a hippy pastime, for the minorities, we forecast that the future bodes well for fast fashion, as it makes great steps towards normalising working conditions and manufacturing techniques, so that the words ethical, sustainable and green become obsolete, as they are predictably accepted as industry standards.

This view is not so utopian as it once was, as the industry is being assisted by Government legislation, consumer pressure, stakeholders and internal influences embodied by a new fashion workforce that are characterised by their ethical demands. Newcomers or fashion start-ups do not view these ethical positions as idealistic or novel as their predecessors might have. Rather, new fashion brands view them as ingrained standards entrenched into their attitudes and expectations, socialised by education and the time in which they were born into. These collaborative forces signify change and what we call, the epiphanic sustainable fast fashion epoch. A new ethical fashion mandate.

2.3 Discussion Questions

Discussion questions that have emerged as a result of the content put forward in this chapter are compiled here, so that readers may further engage with the subject matter. The questions/scenarios are not intended to be exhaustive, they simply serve as a catalyst for further expansion, debate and conversation amongst peers.

- What are ethics?
- What does it mean to be ethical?
- How do we learn about ethics?
- Give an example of 'being ethical'?
- Are ethics important in business?
- What does it mean to be sustainable?
- What is the difference between ethics and sustainability?
- Scenario: A friend of yours owns a sustainable fashion item; she/he never wears it and decides to dispose of it once they realise that it has no use in their wardrobe edit. What is your view on this behaviour?

- Fashion brands are attempting to move towards a 'circular economy' and 'closed loop' strategy as evidenced by the content put forward in the chapter. What is your view on this agile business tactic: is it a corporate ploy, or do you have confidence that the brands' conscience and actions are in good faith?
- Fish Leather and other resources/alternatives are now being used instead of animal leather – conduct your own research into these options and consider the impact on cost, sustainability and ethical attributes of these options as a viable prospect for fashion manufacturing.
- Should all fashion brands be sustainable and have ethical business practices?
- Create your spectrum of fashion ethics timeline to showcase the incremental changes within the industry from 'then to now'. Plot, observe and remark on what the key catalysts for change were in the fashion industry and when.

References

BBC. (2013). *Bangladesh factory collapse too passes 1,000.* BBC (online), retrieved: http://www.bbc.co.uk/news/world-asia-22476774.

Bianchi, C., & Birtwistle, G. (2012). Sell, give away, or donate: An exploratory study of fashion clothing disposal behaviour in two countries. *The International Review of Retail, Distribution and Consumer Research, 20*(3): 353–368.

Carrigan, M., & Attalla, A. (2001). The myth of the ethical consumer-do ethics matter in purchase behaviour? *Journal of Consumer Marketing, 18*(7): 560–578.

Chan, T. Y., & Wong, C. (2012). The consumption side of sustainable fashion supply chain. *Journal of Fashion Marketing and Management: An International Journal, 16*(2): 193–215.

EFF (Ethical Fashion Forum). (2016). *Source: The global platform for sustainable fashion.* EFF (online), retrieved: http://www.ethicalfashionforum.com/About-the-SOURCE-platform.

EFF (Ethical Fashion Forum). (n.d. a). *More information.* EFF (online), retrieved: https://www.ethicalfashionforum.com/the-issues/ethical-fashion.

EFF (Ethical Fashion Forum). (n.d. b). *About EFF.* EFF (online), retrieved: http://www.ethicalfashionforum.com/about-eff.

Fashion Anthropologist. (2016). *Fashion revolution: #whomadeyourclothes?*. Fashion Anthropologist (online), retrieved: http://fashionanthropologist.com/fashion-revolution-whomadeyourclothes/.

Fashion Revolution. (2016a). *Fashion revolution*. Fashion Revolution (online), retrieved: http://fashionrevolution.org/, accessed: 3/6/2016.

Fashion Revolution. (2016b). *Do something*. Fashion Revolution (online), retrieved: http://fashionrevolution.org/get-involved/ways-for-everyone-to-get-involved/.

Frankena, W. (1973). *Ethics*. Prentice-Hall: Englewood Cliffs, NJ.

Goworek, H., Fisher, T., Cooper, T., Woodward, S., & Hiller, A. (2012). The sustainable clothing market: An evaluation of potential strategies for UK retailers. *International Journal of Retail & Distribution Management, 40*(12): 935–955.

Green Peace. (2016). *Detox my fashion*. Green Peace (online), retrieved: http://www.greenpeace.org/international/en/campaigns/detox/fashion/.

Gupta, M., & Hodges, N. (2012). Corporate social responsibility in the apparel industry. *Journal of Fashion Marketing and Management: An International Journal, 16*(2): 216–233.

H&M. (2015). *Conscious actions*. H&M (online), retrieved: http://sustainability.hm.com/content/dam/hm/about/documents/en/CSR/2015%20Sustainability%20report/HM_SustainabilityReport_2015_final_FullReport_en.pdf.

H&M. (2016). *This is world recycle week*. H&M (online), retrieved: https://www.hm.com/us/life/culture/h-m-inside/2016/04/this-is-world-recycle-week

H&M. (n.d.). *H&M is committed to sustainability, and so are our people*. H&M (online), retrieved: https://career.hm.com/content/hmcareer/en_us/workin gathm/get-to-know-us/hm-conscious.html.

Howard, G. (2016). *How can fashion consumers stay engaged in the digital age?, Decode Fashion* (online), retrieved: http://blog.decodedfashion.com/stories/how-can-fashion-consumers-stay-engaged-in-the-digital-age, accessed 1/02/2017.

Joergens, C. (2006). Ethical fashion: Myth or future trend? *Journal of Fashion Marketing and Management: An International Journal, 10*(3): 360–371.

Kotler, P., Armstrong, G., Saunders, J., & Wong, V. (1996). *Principles of Marketing*. The European Edition. Prentice-Hall: Hemel Hempstead.

Kotler, P., & Armstrong, G. (2010). *Principles of marketing*. Pearson Education: Upper Saddle River, NJ.

Mauro, N., Natale, S. M., & Libertella, A. F. (1999). Personal values, business ethics and strategic development. *Cross Cultural Management: An International Journal, 6*(2): 22–28.

Merriam-Webster. (2016). Ethic. Merriam-Webster.com. Merriam-Webster, n.d. Web. 14 Oct. 2016.

Nantel, J., & Weeks, W. A. (1996). Marketing Ethics: Is there more to it than the utilitarian approach? *European Journal of Marketing, 30*(5): 9–19.

Parveen, S. (2014). *Rana Plaza factory collapse survivors struggle one year on.* BBC News (online). Available from: http://www.bbc.co.uk/news/world-asia-27107860.

Perry, P., & Towers, N. (2009). Determining the antecedents for a strategy of corporate social responsibility by small-and medium-sized enterprises in the UK fashion apparel industry. *Journal of Retailing and Consumer Services, 16*(5): 377–385.

Ryding, D., Navrozidou, A., & Carey, R. (2014). The impact of eco-fashion strategies on male shoppers' perceptions of brand image and loyalty. *International Journal of Business and Globalisation, 13*(2): 173–196.

Shen, B., Wang, Y., Chris, K. Y., & Momoko Shum, L. (2012). The impact of ethical fashion on consumer purchase behavior. *Journal of Fashion Marketing and Management: An International Journal, 16*(2): 234–245.

Tota, I., & Shehu, H. (2012). The Dilemma of business ethics. *Sciance and Direct Procedia Economics and Finance, 3*: 555–559.

Further Readings

Cao Huantian, C., Chang, R. M., Kallal, J., Manalo, G., McCord, J., Shaw, J., & Starne, H. (2014). Adaptable apparel: A sustainable design solution for excess apparel consumption problem. *Journal of Fashion Marketing and Management, 18*(1): 52–69.

Carey, L., & Cervellon, M. C. (2014). Ethical fashion dimensions: Pictorial and auditory depictions through three cultural perspectives. *Journal of Fashion Marketing and Management, 18*(4): 483–506.

Fletcher, K., & Emma Dewberry, E. (2002). Demi: A case study in design for sustainability. *International Journal of Sustainability in Higher Education, 3*(1): 38–47.

Fulton, K., & Seung-Eun Lee, S. E. (2013). Assessing sustainable initiatives of apparel retailers on the internet. *Journal of Fashion Marketing and Management: An International Journal, 17*(3): 353–366.

Henninger, C. (2015). Traceability the new eco-label in the slow-fashion industry? Consumer perceptions and micro-organisations responses. *Sustainability, 7*(5): 6011–6032.

Hill, J., & Lee, H. H. (2012). Young generation Y consumers' perceptions of sustainability in the apparel industry. *Journal of Fashion Marketing and Management: An International Journal, 16*(4): 477–491.

Jagel, T., Keeling, K., Reppel, A., & Thorsten, G. (2012). Individual values and motivational complexities in ethical clothing consumption: A means-end approach. *The Journal of Marketing Management, 28*(3–4): 373–396.

Low, W., & Davenport, E. (2005). Has the medium (roast) become the message? The ethics of marketing fair trade in the mainstream. *International Marketing Review, 22*(5): 494–511.

Manchiraju, S., & Sadachar, A. (2014). Personal values and ethical fashion consumption. *Journal of Fashion Marketing and Management, 18*(3): 357–374.

Muncy, J., & Vitell, S. (1992). Consumer ethics: An investigation of the ethical beliefs of the final consumer. *Journal of Business Research, 24*(4): 297–311.

Patsy, P., & Kyriakak, M. (2014). The decision-making process of luxury fashion retail buyers in Greece. *Journal of Fashion Marketing and Management, 18*(1): 85–106.

Charlotte Rutter is a Senior Lecturer. With over a decade of lecturing in Fashion Management & Marketing (FMM) and as a co-founder of a successful fashion company, Charlotte has a wealth of experience to share through both an academic and professional lens. As Senior Lecturer at The University of Creative Arts (UCA), she has developed innovative and industry-relevant course content making the UCA FMM course one of the best in the country and leading to visiting posts at other universities including the University of the Arts London. Charlotte is passionate about developing research in the areas of FMM, sustainability, and ethics and consumer psychology, and has authored papers for publication and is a regular speaker at academic conferences. She has collaborated with Dr Kate Armstrong to design, write and deliver short courses and chapter content on specialised topic areas and is a Deputy Chair of the Fashion Marketing & Consumption SIG. Charlotte also works with companies in a consulting capacity to provide advisory and sounding board services through to full branding, marketing and business strategies.

Dr Kate Armstrong Current position: Assistant Dean: UG, Regents University London. She is a dynamic leader, innovator, manager and consultant with over 18 years of experience as an academic and branding consultant. PhD: qualitative, phenomenological, interpretive approach to explore consumer value systems and female consumption. Her research interests are diverse, but are centred around four broad research domains, including: (1) consumer psychology; (2) fashion; (3) creative and cultural Industries and (4) education. She has taught and researched in these areas in a number of Universities during her career. She is an experienced doctoral supervisor at both UG and PG level and has successfully supervised students to successful completion of their PhDs. She is regularly invited to present, chair and speak at industry and academic events and conferences. Her work is published in the *Journal of Marketing Management*, the *Journal of Customer Behaviour* and the *International Journal of Nonprofit and Voluntary Sector Marketing* and she is regularly invited to review papers in these and other, related journals. To consolidate her academic, commercial and research aspirations, she is founder and Chair the Fashion Marketing and Consumption SIG for the Academy of Marketing, of which she is the Chair. She is currently involved in several research projects that interrogate the intersection of fashion consumer psychology, consumption and engagement.

Dr Marta Blazquez Cano is a Lecturer in Fashion Marketing at the School of Materials, University of Manchester. Marta holds a BA in Advertising and PR and has developed a career in the advertising and marketing industry for more than 10 years. She was awarded a PhD in Marketing entitled 'Consumer experience in a multichannel retail environment: a cross-country study of the fashion sector. Marta's research interest includes omnichannel retail, experiential retail, channel integration, in-store technology, social media marketing, mobile marketing, consumer behaviour and sustainable fashion. She has published in leading journals, contributed to edited books and presented her work at various national and international conferences. Marta has been visiting researcher in the Oxford Institute of Research Management (OXIRM), University of Oxford, and has been invited lecturer on several occasions in China and Spain. She supervises a number of PhD and MSc students in the areas of fashion marketing and retailing.

3

Sustainability and the Fashion Industry: Conceptualizing Nature and Traceability

Annamma Joy and Camilo Peña

3.1 Introduction

A first step in discussing sustainability in fashion is to recognize an inherent truth: Fashion is a polluting and resource-intensive industry, even as its future success depends on reducing its environmental and social imprint across the entire life cycle of garment production. That means reducing the impact associated with cultivating and producing textile fibres, and establishing a foundation of good practices at all levels. It also means moving beyond focusing on only a few fibre types—typically cotton and polyester, or a blend thereof—and creating a portfolio of alternate fibres with low-resource intensity and potentially rich cultural traditions.

The manufacture of both cotton and polyester fibres is detrimental to the environment, albeit in different ways. Cotton has the greatest negative environmental impact (Butow 2014), given its ubiquity in

A. Joy (✉) · C. Peña
The University of British Columbia, Kelowna, BC, Canada
e-mail: annamma.joy@ubc.ca; camiloandres.pena@gmail.com

C.E. Henninger et al. (eds.), *Sustainability in Fashion*,
DOI 10.1007/978-3-319-51253-2_3

apparel manufacture. According to the World Wildlife Fund (2016): "It can take more than 20,000 litres of water to produce 1 kg of cotton; equivalent to a single T-shirt and pair of jeans". Non-organic cotton production relies on environmentally harmful pesticides; "2.4% of the world's crop land is planted with cotton and yet it accounts for 24% and 11% of the global sales of insecticide and pesticides respectively" according to World Wildlife Fund quoted above. But while polyester production uses significantly less water and no pesticides, it requires more than three times the energy of cotton production (Cherrett et al. 2005). Worse yet, given the lack of sustainability inherent in the production of both fibres, worldwide demand for both is increasing (Carmichael 2015).

Nylon and wool are detrimental to the environment as well; nylon is derived from petroleum, and wool requires extensive land use, leading to over-grazing and generating substantial wastewater during the multiple washes used to clean wool fibres (Defra 2010). Most environmental impacts, common to all the fibres listed above, occur during the production and consumption stage (Chapman 2010).

3.2 The Case for Sustainability

Sustainability, as defined by the Brundtland World Commission on Environment and Development (United Nations 1987) is development that meets the needs of the present without compromising those of the future. The consensus of the scientific community states that if development continues with business as usual, earth's key resources will be depleted faster than any possible rate of replenishment (Martin and Schouten 2011), with unsustainable growth setting in motion potentially devastating economic, social, and environmental concerns. We argue that the concept of producing unlimited goods—a worldview with roots in the advent of industrial capitalism, with a concomitant notion that availability of fossil fuel and other non-renewable resources is limitless—is inherently problematic. Trawick and Hornborg (2015) suggest that production methods in many developing nations take into account that resources are limited, which allows for collaborative use of such scarce resources as water. To achieve sustainability, industries in developed nations must take the same approach, which necessitates embracing decreased consumption. We believe that the time is past due to revisit the notion of the limited good.

In the management literature, Gladwin et al. (1995) consider the predominance of a technocentric paradigm in business markets, in contrast to its ecocentric counterpart. Balancing both perspectives results in what the authors term a sustaincentric worldview. We use their framework to evaluate fast and slow fashion and define the primary elements of a sustaincentric perspective within the fashion industry. In technocentrism, humans have the right to exploit nature—they are in essence superior to nature, as viewed through an anthropocentric hierarchy with humans at the pinnacle. In this view, nature is instrumental and monetarily quantifiable—a commodity for the asking, with an implied assumption that economic growth and technological innovation preclude considerations of future generations and resources. In the technocentric worldview, as the authors argue, the economy is a closed system isolated from nature, where exchange value circulates only between industries and households. Human wants are unlimited; the corresponding ideal of a good life dominates. Consequently, individuals act to maximize their own utility, as predicated by the optimal economic framework of laissez–faire capitalism. In the ethos of ethnocentrism, more growth is not just good, but is actually the best of all possible worlds.

Technocentrism is open to criticism, in that it ignores the interdependence of human and natural capital. An emphasis on global efficiency suppresses attention to an appropriate ecological scale and the fair distribution of resources, property rights, and social constructs such as fair labour practices. Reliance on the efficient operations of markets ignores marginalized segments of society including women, children, and future generations. Technocentrism promotes dualistic thinking in placing the natural world and human nature in opposition, thus limiting or even severing the connections between these two realms that are central to sustainable thinking.

Because technocentrism is anthropocentric, it elevates men over women (Warren 1994) given that women are, through their potential for creating life and their perceived role as nurturers, stereotypically associated with nature, as well as the reverse (i.e. the phrase "mother nature"). In the view of many (e.g. Gladwin et al. 1995) technocentrism supports a growth dependent on markets, and thereby perpetuates inequality, privileging a wealthy minority at the expense of the larger community. To a large extent, the decline in renewable resources, increased pollution, and inequality are well-documented as the inevitable results of technocentrism (Gladwin et al. 1995; Martin and Schouten 2011).

In response to technocentrism, the ecocentric worldview emerged (Bailey and Wilson 2009). In this view, human capital and natural capital are complementary: Humans dependent on ecological abundance (Gladwin et al. 1995, p. 887). Thus, humans co-exist with nature rather than rule it, and changes in human action have ripple effects on nature, and the reverse. Holistic rather than dualistic thinking is paramount to this paradigm, with ethical priority accorded to the whole rather than the individual. The "good life" therefore calls for voluntary simplicity and a reduction in the consumption of material goods, with inequality ameliorated through redistribution. The task of preserving natural capital is paramount.

Ecocentrism by its nature downplays the intellectual capacity of humans, in that it does not directly address poverty and human rights, given its emphasis on ecology over economics and social factors. Ecocentrism, the above authors note, falls short on offering practical solutions in a world increasingly ravaged by human activity, and fails to integrate cultural and natural goals. As a more effective alternative, the authors argue in favour of sustaincentrism. In common with ecocentrism, sustaincentrism embraces the interdependence of nature and humans, the importance of satisfying non-material needs in non-material ways, and reducing preoccupation with materialism. However, in sustaincentrism, ecological and social externalities are internalized, with ecology, economics, and ethics inextricably intertwined. Sustaincentrism focuses on the interrelatedness of events and actions, and advocates that all human values depend on a healthy, ecological, economic, and social context, combining ecocentrism with pragmatic economic and social considerations.

In this view, earth must be preserved through respectful stewardship in current contexts. While humans are part of the biosphere, human intellect is recognized. Ethics, according to the above authors "are broadly homocentric, grounded in the good of both human and non-human nature. Sustaincentric ethics actively embrace the full conceptualization of political, civil, social, economic and cultural human rights" (ibid., p. 891). The temporal frame covers both intra-generational and inter-generational responsibilities: equity and foresight.

Extraction and use of natural resources must be limited due to the vulnerability of nature to support such actions; at the very least, such actions should be below the levels at which the deterioration of natural systems can occur. Technologies can be developed, but must be used ethically. Ecology and economy are not in opposition, but safeguards must be in place such that exploitation will be minimized. Poverty is eliminated through fair labour practices and expanding social services. Growth without end, unfolding within a closed system, is deemed untenable.

While sustainability concerns were not crucial to the fashion industry in the past, trends are changing, as key players promote more ecologically forward-thinking fashion production processes and consumption (Henninger et al. 2016). One movement in particular, formed by many key stakeholders, is slow fashion.

3.3 Slow Versus Fast Fashion

Slow fashion, in common with slow food, stands in opposition to industrialization and homogeneity, or "McDonaldization" (Ritzer 2011). In the ideology of slow fashion, artisanship and long-term utility trump fast fashion's catering to short-term gratification, with consumers experiencing constant demand for new products (Barnes and Lea-Greenwood 2006). An article of fast fashion is the essence of planned obsolescence, designed to fray after a set number of wearings (often as few as 10): Fast fashion's raison d'etre is volume over quality. Producing clothing quickly and cheaply inevitably devalues human labour and ecologically responsible production materials and methods. To devotees of fast fashion, the environmental and social costs embodied by such clothing, as they are in fast food, are immaterial.

Clark (2008) views slow fashion as "sustainable fashion solutions, based on the repositioning of strategies of design, production, consumption, use, and reuse, which are emerging alongside the global fashion system, and are posing a potential challenge to it. The slow approach offers more sustainable and ethical ways of being fashionable that have implications for design, production, consumption, and use" (ibid., p. 428). Moreover, an ideology of attentiveness and mindfulness of the various stakeholders involved in fashion production (Fletcher 2008) encourages identifying fashion's underlying values and economic priorities (Fletcher 2010).

The slow fashion movement proposes to retake the values of quality offering fewer but more durable items. Slow fashion companies offer two fashion collections per year; in contrast, fast fashion businesses produce as many as 20 (Henninger et al. 2016). Such rapid turnover encourages impulse purchases and frequent visits to retail stores to check on an ever-changing selection, as what was purchased only a few weeks earlier is now passé. The "fast" in fast fashion refers not only to the speed of production but also to the speed with which consumers desire continuous novelty. While seemingly infinite varieties of products are on offer, economies of scale and industrial production limit what can actually be produced. Thus, cotton and polyester dominate, even as a sustainable fashion industry requires greater fibre variety, such as organic cotton, hemp, bamboo, and lyocell. Polyester is dependent on oil as its source; moving away from petroleum may be essential in fostering sustainable production.

Fast fashion elicits contradictory consumer behaviours in the context of sustainability. Consumers who diligently select food products based on ethical, health, and environmental concerns may have no such concerns for apparel products (Joy et al. 2012). Why consumers would be more concerned with the provenance of what they eat versus what they wear is a conundrum, a display of cognitive dissonance. While media may downplay awareness of social and environmental issues in apparel production (Morgan and Birtwistle 2009), it is nonetheless consumers themselves who lack an interest in questioning and critiquing apparel supply chains. When it comes to clothing purchases, consumers, at a visceral level, appear to feel that the less they know about how their new clothes were manufactured the better.

For change to occur, as Fletcher (2014, p. XVI) notes, "a more holistic approach is essential—the cumulative values, discernments, habits of mind, industrial practices, business models, economic logic, deep societal forces and aggregated industrial practices that make up the fashion and textile sector". Understanding sustainability requires a systems approach because it depends on production steps working in concert rather than on any one step viewed in isolation. The overarching framework consists of materials, processes, people, design, and speed for promoting sustainability. As Fletcher (2014, p. XVII) argues, "Sustainability in fashion and textiles fosters ecological integrity, social quality and human flourishing through products, action, relationships and practices of use".

The fashion industry as a whole must create consumer desire for limited consumption of high-quality slow fashion as opposed to frequent consumption of low-quality fast fashion. The business model must change, while recognizing that small-scale fibre production must be processed at multiple locations near markets, which can increase its footprint. Much as the lure of certain wines is linked to their specific place of production, so fashion can stoke interest in place-specific fibres, designs, and dyes.

Traceability and the notion of nature are key to fostering a more responsible and ethical consumption of apparel products. Furthermore, a connection between apparel products and nature will foster more scrutiny of environmental issues in apparel production. We believe that by not only building awareness of fast fashion's ecological and social harmfulness but also promoting the benefits of slow fashion and sustainability—in part via traceability initiatives—consumers' fashion and apparel purchase behaviour will more likely be influenced by ethical considerations, in a sea change from previous consumer fashion purchase behaviour (Joergens 2006).

3.4 Consumer Awareness and a New Market for Ethical Products

As with other environmental and social movements, the quest for cleaner and fairer fashion supply chains needs leaders. Some may come from marginalized market segments, such as those dissatisfied with current market offerings and seeking more choice. One trigger for mobilization is the development of a collective identity (Scaraboto and Fischer 2013). We argue that by channelling images of nature through transparency in the supply chain, and connecting those images with the final product (i.e. fashion apparel), critical consumers can forge a collective identity, a bloc concerned with sustainability, which can eventually affect the market.

In community-supported agriculture, for example, consumers and entrepreneurs have created a countervailing market response to the co-optation of countercultural movements into dominant and mainstream forms (Thompson and Coskuner-Bali 2007), presenting a planned mobilization towards market change, in accordance with Scaraboto and Fischer's (2013) analysis. Such responses can change a market segment significantly, leading to the production and promotion of offerings distinct from those provided by mainstream markets.

Dolbec and Fischer (2015) analyse the impact of consumers engaged in market dynamics without a specific coordinated plan, in the specific context of the fashion industry. In such cases, change can be profound, and also accidental. As a means of inciting change within fashion, consumers who make their desire for sustainable garments known may well have the power to push the industry to meet their needs. If the consumer market is there, the product line will follow.

3.5 The Role of Traceability

Traceability arose in the mid-1980s as a means to reassure consumers about the safety of food products, as increasing fears of contamination led consumers to seek information on how their food was grown or raised (Penton Media 2011). Until the mid-1980s, traceability was used primarily for logistical purposes, providing a means of managing inventory and production (Bonnin and Ngo 2009). Following a series of crises in the European food industry, increased transparency regarding the steps involved along the supply chain from producers to consumers was clearly needed. The development of traceability programs eventually took hold in the USA and Canada, between 2003 and 2004, after the mad cow disease case in Washington state (Pouliot and Sumner 2008). Food producers needed traceability to protect the reputation of their brands, and to guarantee their products' origins (ibid), by tracing products within a specific facility or along a supply chain (Bellon-Maurel et al. 2014).

Traceability is viewed as a necessity in the food industry, with top chefs along with other food representatives pioneering the use of traceability (Penton Media 2011). The local farm-to-table food movement has further pushed traceability to the forefront. Many industries have incorporated traceability as a key asset in achieving superior quality (Suber 2012). Organizations that adopt traceability can make their supply chains more efficient and adaptable (Galliano and Orozco 2013).

3.6 Traceability Equals Transparency

While traceability in the context of food products is primarily a means of confirming food safety and adherence to health concerns and dietary restrictions, with an emphasis on animal welfare concerns, in the apparel industry traceability results in transparency, in that it informs customers of the environmental impact of clothing and production, and of the labour conditions involved in production and manufacturing. Tracing all apparel products and certifying transparency in the supply chain could be beneficial in both boosting the demand for responsibly made products, and in making products manufactured under questionable conditions less appealing.

For consumers with specific ethical concerns in mind, traceability systems are needed to ensure a product is in line with their values (Robert-Demontrond 2009). For this market niche, supply chains must be transparent and open to both certification and third-party assessments to reduce the practice of "green-washing" (presenting a product as "green" (sustainable) without any reliable verification). It can be difficult to verify certain ethical claims from supply chains. For certain objective and measurable indicators such as energy and water usage, supply chains might easily report and assess their own performances, but for more subjective and difficult-to-measure indicators, such as working conditions, safety policies, and animal welfare, third-party monitoring and evaluation are crucial.

For measurable and quantifiable indicators, life cycle assessment (LCA), a method for evaluating the environmental performance of products and services, can be implemented along the supply chain. Such evaluation can be complex, requiring significant time and resources. LCA dates back to the 1970s, when pollution control, energy efficiency, and others gained public currency; its public appeal continues to spread (Guinée et al. 2011).

From an ethical standpoint, corporations at least theoretically have an obligation to inform consumers about the environmental impact of their products, following consumers' own concerns for the morality of their agency (Del Savio and Schmietow 2013). Over time, some companies have adopted a moral approach, as traceability evolved from health crisis prevention to an assurance of quality, certified, and sustainable choices. Current discourses of "natural", "organic", and "local" products have pushed traceability's implementation into smaller supply chains, with regulated definitions and certifications backing up such claims.

Tracing apparel items back to their raw materials and manufacturing processes can be daunting. In some cases, trust becomes central to the relationship between suppliers and apparel manufacturers, which then translates to eco-labels that inform consumers about the certified processes implemented in supply chains (Henninger 2015). However, not all eco-labels face thorough scrutiny. Both in the literature and in our own interviews with apparel industry stakeholders, flaws are readily apparent. If third parties involved in certification receive a percentage from the sales of certified products, the assessment for certified procedures may relax or simply not happen at all. Manufacturing entities along the supply chain whose processes have been deemed acceptable may sub-contract to other, smaller entities, whose sourcing or manufacturing processes may be entirely unknown. Such complications and deceptions have led some consumers and stakeholders to doubt certifying agencies and eco-labels. The entire supply chain, from fibre production through product creation, must be transparent for certification to be truly effective.

Traceability and certification often involve higher costs for consumers, if a producer shifts the costs of traceability initiatives to a product's final price. Poghosyan et al. (2004) argue that traceability should command a price premium when public welfare benefits or competitive advantages result. Tsakiridou et al. (2011) suggest that traceability is an added value, and therefore worthy of a price premium. Spanish beef consumers, as an example, disagree. They see providing food safety as a minimum responsibility for producers, and are unwilling to pay a premium for a guarantee of safety (Angulo et al. 2005). Thus, guarantees can be seen as either an added benefit, or as one that should routinely be available as a matter of corporate responsibility.

When we track a product to its different processes and actors, we confront the realities of outsourcing to low-wage countries, and of a given product's hidden costs, such as labourers trapped in deplorable working conditions, and polluted air, water, and soil. These realities, especially in food and apparel, are heavily connected to the concept of nature. Since agricultural crops are these products' origins, there is always a starting point on the land. Nature is the first supplier.

3.7 Nature

Nature can be studied from many perspectives and understood as a combination of material and discursive elements. Neither an external objective nor a purely socially constructed entity, nature is a fluid and contested effect of assembling material and discursive elements (Canniford and Shankar 2013).

In studies of the subjective and symbolic perspectives of nature, we see that individuals rely on nature for identity creation purposes as part of a specific agenda and in opposition to an alternate discourse (Luedicke et al. 2010). Collective meanings and ideals can shape a group's identity (ibid.). As Belk (1988) shows, the extension of self can operate at an individual and a collective level, contributing to consumers' identities. As de Burgh-Woodman and King (2013) argue, the concept of the human/nature connection is tied to a symbolically sustainable discourse, which often does not extend beyond a material/practical statement. This human-nature connection as a construct in Western cultural discourse can be traced back to Greek mythology in its turbulent relationship with natural elements, as represented by each Greek deity. The relationship with nature and the human/nature connection have evolved over time; today's related discourses are necessarily linked to and often driven by the development of environmentalism.

Along with the writings of the naturalists, activists, and environmental philosophers Aldo Leopard, John Muir, and Henry David Thoreau, Rachel Carson's "Silent Spring" (1962) stands out as one of the most influential figures in environmentalism (Griswold 2012). Some suggest her work gave birth to the modern environmental movement (Michaud 2010). Carson opposed the Christian belief that nature existed to serve man and argued that technological innovations such as pesticides, through which humans seek to control nature, would disrupt earth's natural ecosystem (Carson 1962; Michaud 2010). The notion of accepting our collective societal role as stewards of this fragile ecosystem is criticized in the environmental ethics literature for having anthropocentric, speciesist, and sexist connotations (Welchman 2012).

The environmental movement has spread into different areas from its original opposition to pesticides in particular and pollution in general to include opposition to genetically modified organisms (GMOs). Vandana Shiva, an Indian environmental activist, embraces this opposition, stating that "GMO" stands for "God, Move Over", although not without criticism from the media (e.g. Entine 2015; Specter 2014) and academic writers (e.g. Gilbert 2013; Herring 2006). Shiva argues that pre-colonial North America, in having unity in feminine and masculine principles, engendered stronger ecological values than those brought to the New World by European culture (McGurty 2011). Without feminine values, Shiva argues, men would separate from women and nature, and ecological disaster would occur; the eco-feminist women tree huggers (who form handholding circles around trees to prevent deforestation) from the Chipko Movement in northern India embody this necessary feminine principle required for preventing ecological catastrophe (ibid.).

Perhaps in a reflection of the distrust endemic to many environmental discourses (as seen, e.g. in corporate green-washing), the term "tree hugger" is officially identified in the Merriam-Webster Dictionary as "someone who is regarded as foolish or annoying because of being too concerned about protecting trees, animals, and other parts of the natural world from pollution and other threats".

Moreover, the formerly straightforward environmental model of sustainable agricultural production embodied by organic food has become a set of standards adapted to the demands of large corporate farming (Thompson and Coskuner-Balli 2007).

How can environmental discourses align with fashion to offer a veridic and inspiring call to change? How can they differentiate from vague green-washing claims that have created more antagonists against than supporters for sustainability? We propose a return to a simple, romantic nature, where consumers can detach from everyday life and be immersed in a separate space.

3.8 Romantic Discourses of Nature

Canniford and Shankar (2013) consider sublime, sacred, and primitive discourses to be unified into the romantic ideology of an external nature serving as the quintessential romantic concept, where the pure self can be freed of the limitations of family, gender, and other social roles (Illouz 1997). Participation in romantic experiences of nature gives individuals sources of stability, joy, and ecstasy, and possibly even provide meaning to life (Belk et al. 1989). Individuals routinely try to commune with nature when they undergo romantic experiences; Native Americans are considered to have perfected the dynamics of living in harmony with nature (Arnould and Price 1993). Many advertising efforts have built a level of expectation around the sacred pilgrimage towards parts of the world still untouched by humankind (Belk et al. 1989).

In communion with nature, we rely on nature (e.g. having an awareness of time based solely on tracking the sun and moon (Arnould and Price 1993)). This reliance can be seen in other contexts, such as when nature is an external force that can be neither controlled nor tamed; thus human activities are left to the mercy of nature, a state that aligns with the primitive discourse of nature, whose sublime and sacred constructs oppose the modern, industrial, and stressful way of living (Canniford and Shankar 2013). Re-enacting past practices that might seem rustic and countercultural becomes a means of evoking a nostalgic and heroic time when life was simpler (Belk and Costa 1998); in such contexts, nature is revered and a "quasireligious naturalism" is evidenced, aligned with the sacred discourse of nature (ibid. 234).

3.9 Tracing Nature

Having discussed the relevance of traceability to the fashion industry and the notion of nature as a key element in identity construction, we turn to assembling a discourse that fosters sustainably produced apparel via traceability and protects nature (the external environment) from harm.

A first step is to embed nature into the fashion discourse through a holistic view in which each item of apparel cannot be divorced from its origins in nature and manufacture. Once a garment is experienced both as one component and as part of nature, perceptions towards this item change markedly, much as might happen with food; when we build awareness of the animals and processes involved in creating a hamburger patty, we see it from a different angle.

The transparency engendered by traceability creates awareness of the exploitation involved in apparel production—not only of such tragedies as the 2013 Rana Plaza collapse in Dhaka, Bangladesh, the single deadliest clothing factory accident in history but also of the day-to-day nightmare of low-wage labour (Joy 2013). In response to searing images from Rana Plaza, consumers, politicians, NGOs, academics, and other stakeholders scrutinized how such factories are run, aiming their outrage in particular at apparel brands that sourced from this specific factory, such as Walmart, Benetton, Joe Fresh, Mango, and Primark, among others. Such events open consumers' eyes to the costs, borne by others, of cheaply made clothing, and have pushed companies and their supply chains to be more transparent.

We cannot stall until a new mass tragedy occurs in another part of the supply chain to increase awareness, particularly since every step of the supply chain has the potential for setting in motion lethal events, such as pollution, whose impact is gradual and does not necessarily generate headlines (i.e. wearing masks on city streets to protect one's ability to breathe incrementally becomes a normalized activity). Once traceability

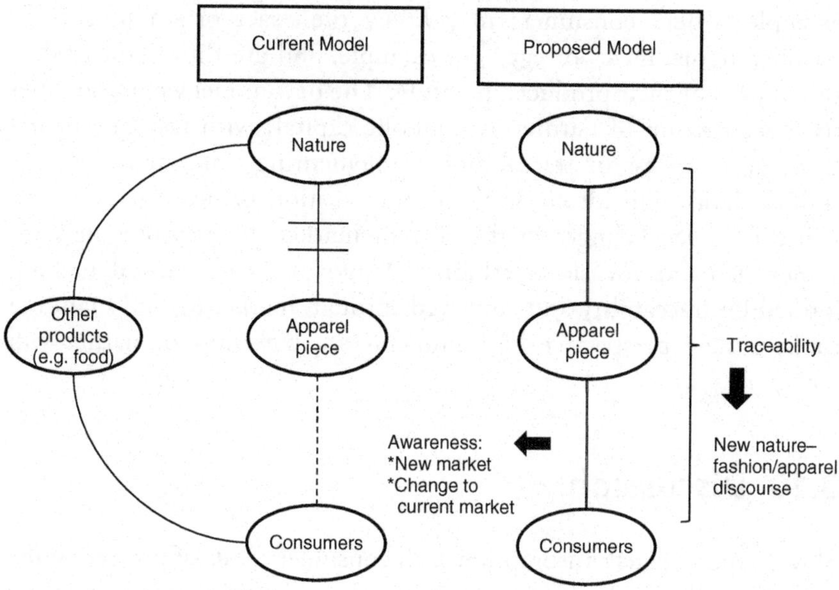

Fig. 3.1 Current vs. proposed fashion apparel model

of an entire supply chain has been ensured, transparency can be apparent and processes certified. This information may now be passed on to brands that can construct a story on how each garment has been made, whether it is organic and features natural dyes, for example; and on the value of consumers making choices that support sustainability. Deepening the story might include discourses on protecting the environment and communion with nature, allowing an individual to see the article of clothing, the plant source of fibres, the artisans involved in manufacture, and nature itself within a holistic view in which each element is connected to the whole. Once an article of clothing is no longer experienced in a vacuum, with its environmental and social impact visible for all to see, consumers become aware of their role in that impact.

Figure 3.1 summarizes the model presented in this chapter. The current fashion apparel discourse is disconnected from nature; consumers do not see an article of apparel as part of nature but rather as a product of industrial processes, unlike in the world of organic food, for example, where consumers may know the exact origin of specific produce items, meat, or eggs, for example, and are thus connected to the sources of their products in nature. The new model we propose ties the construction of nature (as symbolic capital) with fashion apparel through a process of traceability. Implementing transparency in the supply chains will ideally facilitate the creation of new markets, and will drive deep changes in the current market, by encouraging consumer demand for slow fashion. Thanks to these new dynamics, ignited by traceability and conveyed through marketing and branding tools, a new perspective of fashion as an extension of nature will emerge.

3.10 Discussion

Slow fashion aligns consumption with consumer ideals of protecting the natural world. Consumers who perceive their identities as incorporating both an appreciation for of-the-moment fashion and a commitment to the environment will likely find this symbolic value both meaningful and indicative of new approaches to consumption. To embrace that goal, slow fashion must focus on a sustaincentric paradigm; only through responsible processes can high-quality and ethical products be produced. Once the fashion industry commits to sustainability, traceability is the sole effective method for certifying the industry's adherence to the ideals of slow fashion.

Tracing becomes imperative once certification is accepted commercially as essential. Consumers want reassurance that the labels and certifications they see on apparel products are genuine, which can only happen when every raw material, supplier, transportation mode, and process is tracked from the source. Because any apparel company will have an innate conflict of interest in marketing the green qualities of a given garment—describing a garment as sustainable instantly justifies a higher price—externalizing tracing services can eliminate such conflict by maintaining transparency. After fashion companies have implemented tracing processes, certification should be done by third parties untainted by any possible appearance of professional *quid pro quo*.

In showing the practices used throughout a supply chain and showcasing nature as the first supplier of all apparel items, the fashion world can heighten consumers' connection to nature. Once consumers become more aware of the processes involved in apparel production, this connection with nature may ignite a new perspective on clothing, one that actively wants sustainably produced fibres and manufacturing processes, and that sees slow fashion, despite the higher cost, as far more desirable —indeed, as imperative—in comparison with fast fashion. As the disinterest in environmental issues implicit in the production and consumption of fast fashion becomes ever more widely recognized, consumers will inevitably be faced with whether they are motivated in their consumption patterns primarily by short-term gratification, or by their commitment to long-term sustainability values. While these values are in and of themselves symbolic, their impact on the actual environment is undeniably both real and immediate.

The slow fashion ideal of quality and longevity will become appealing once each garment embodies nature from the consumers' perspective. Once we see more than the piece of apparel—once we see in our mind's eye the entire process of producing a garment—the value of longevity and quality becomes an associated necessity of the newly built relationship between the consumer and the product. This new built image will necessarily be constructed from a deep understanding of the product story; consumers interested in the sources of their products have sophisticated questions and demands. Superficial commitments and shallow slogans were never enough. Once a holistic sense of nature binds consumers to the earth and to each other—once clothing becomes more than a representation of personal style and self-presentation via movement, texture, design, colour, and the like, and in addition becomes an expression of personal dedication to sustainability—true, verifiable commitment will be not simply desired but also required.

For companies to have a profit motivation to implement sustainable practices, traceability, and to connect their products with nature, demand must exist: new, larger markets must come into being. As a first approach to engaging such markets, codifying the link between nature's discourse and the fashion apparel industry, as argued above, has the ability to be effective. The new market creation process is, in its essence, a clash between brand images, as market creation involves social legitimation, and an innovation that actually discourages frequent consumption may be viewed as contradicting social norms, values, and institutions (Giesler 2012). For many consumers, frequent shopping is a pastime that provides pleasure, with each new purchase providing a temporary sensation of excitement and promise. Why not indulge, when indulging feels good? Slow fashion, in contrast, encourages a modicum of self-restraint, of purchasing for long-term gain rather than only short-term pleasure. What happens when consumers are presented with a different approach to consumption when doppelgänger brand images ("a family of disparaging images and stories about a brand . . . circulated in popular culture . . . " (Thompson et al. 2006, p. 50)) introduce brand meanings that might influence consumers' beliefs and behaviours (ibid.)? Such images already define lower-end apparel companies as connected to factories featuring dangerous and even lethal working conditions.

3.11 Future Research

Our research presents a clear categorization of the discourses on nature and traceability applicable to sustainable fashion, and will benefit companies implementing transparent traceability standards. It is by necessity limited, given the lack of empirical evidence (excluding secondary data derived from previous empirical research). Future research in the timely areas of consumer and producer perceptions of nature and traceability, and their interrelationship with sustainability, will be necessary to empirically validate our findings.

An interesting avenue for future inquiry concerns the origins of the cognitive dissonance that enables consumers to follow a sustainable ideology when purchasing food, or engaging in recycling practices, but to shelve their ideology when choosing apparel. Food nurtures; if it also harms, its very definition is at stake, concerns which are less relevant in apparel products (Joy et al. 2012). Does this fact explain consumers' contradictory approaches to their purchases? Or is this contradiction derived from consumer distance from the sources and processes involved in creating fashion? Moreover, consumers may not trust traceability certifications and eco-labels, viewing them with suspicion as advertising rather than truthful statement.

Price is certainly an issue when facing a choice between sustainably produced slow fashion and low-cost fast fashion. While organic food has higher prices than the alternatives, the price differential is nonetheless not hugely significant; because consumers purchase food repeatedly, the higher cost is accrued over time. The pricing for eco-conscious clothing, however, is significant compared to fast fashion, and the high price is far harder to ignore, unless cost is of no import. Fastfashion garments will undoubtedly be of lower quality with a shorter life span, but fastfashion adherents seek gratification in the moment. What processes can effectively wean consumers from focusing only on short-term gratification? How can consumers develop such strong emotional need for sustainable clothing that price is no longer a deterrent? As we argue, connection to the natural world can ameliorate consumer distance from the natural and human cost of their clothing, but what marketing campaigns will be most effective in conveying this connection? How can corporations accustomed to keeping costs low to encourage higher sales accept a new approach, of accepting higher production and manufacturing costs for the greater good? Such questions are worthy of further exploration.

The battle between brand images and ideals in the fashion industry is increasingly gathering steam, as recognition of global climate change and human injustice takes centre stage in consumers' awareness. The resulting structures and discourses will change markets and relationships between consumers and producers in ways we can imagine, but not yet fully foresee. We can safely assume, however, that the implications of these changes will be far-reaching, deeply affecting how consumers reach purchase decisions and construct identities of the self within the context of an imperilled natural world.

References

Angulo, A. M., Gil, J. M., & Tamburo, L. (2005). Food Safety and Consumers' Willingness to Pay for Labelled Beef in Spain. *Journal of Food Products Marketing, 11*(3): 89–105.

Arnould, E. J., & Price, L. L. (1993). River Magic: Extraordinary Experience and the extended Service Encounter. *Journal of Consumer Research, 20*(1): 24–45.

Bailey, I., & Wilson, G. A. (2009). Theorising Transitional Pathways in Response to Climate Change: Technocentrism, Ecocentrism, and the Carbon Economy. *Environment and Planning A, 41*(10): 2324–2341.

Barnes, L., & Lea-Greenwood, G. (2006). Fast Fashioning the Supply Chain: Shaping the Research Agenda. *Journal of Fashion Marketing and Management, 10*(3): 259–271.

Belk, R. W. (1988). Possessions and the Extended Self. *Journal of Consumer Research, 15*(2): 139–168.

Belk, R. W., & Costa, J. A. (1998). The Mountain Man Myth: A Contemporary Consuming Fantasy. *Journal of Consumer Research, 25*(3): 218–240.

Belk, R. W., Wallendorf, M., & Sherry, Jr., J. F. (1989). The Sacred and the Profane in Consumer Behavior: Theodicy on the Odyssey. *Journal of Consumer Research, 16*(1): 1–38.

Bellon-Maurel, V., Short, M. D., Roux, P., Schulz, M., & Peters, G. M. (2014). Streamlining Life Cycle Inventory Data Generation in Agriculture using Traceability Data and Information and Communication Technologies—Part I: Concepts and Technical Basis. *Journal of Cleaner Production, 69*: 60–66.

Bonnin, C. A., & Ngo, M.-A. (2009). Enjeux juridiques de la traçabilité alimentaire. *Gestion 2000, 26*(3): 93–108.

Butow, J. (2014). Sustainability Issues and Strategies in the Outdoor Apparel Brand Industry. Master of Environmental Studies Capastone Projects, Department of Earth and Environmental Science (online), retrieved from: http://repository.upenn.edu/mes_capstones/60, [accessed on 29/08/2016].

Canniford, R., & Shankar, A. (2013). Purifying Practices: How Consumers Assemble Romantic Experiences of Mature. *Journal of Consumer Research, 39*(5): 1051–1069.

Carmichael, A. (2015). Man-Made Fibers Continue To Grow. Textile World (online), retrieved from: http://www.textileworld.com/textile-world/fiber-world/2015/02/man-made-fibers-continue-to-grow/, [accessed on: 23/09/2016].

Carson, R. (1962). *Silent Spring*. Houghton Mifflin: New York.

Chapman, A. (2010). Mistra Future Fashion—Review of Life Cycle Assessments of Clothing. MISTRA (online), retrieved from: http://www.oakdenehollins.co.uk/media/232/2010_mistra_review_of_life_cycle_assessments_of_clothing.pdf, [accessed on: 23/09/2016].

Cherrett, N., Barrett, J., Clemett, A., Chadwick, M., & Chadwick, M. J. (2005). Ecological Footprint and Water Analysis of Cotton, Hemp and Polyester. Stockholm Environment Institute (online), retrieved from: https://www.sei-international.org/mediamanager/documents/Publications/SEI-Report-EcologicalFootprintAndWaterAnalysisOfCottonHempAndPolyester-2005.pdf, [accessed on: 23/09/2016].

Clark, H. (2008). Slow + Fashion —An Oxymoron —or a Promise for the Future...? *Fashion Theory—Journal of Dress Body and Culture, 12*(4): 427–446.

De Burgh-Woodman, H., & King, D. (2013). Sustainability and the Human/Nature Connection: a Critical Discourse Analysis of Being "Symbolically" Sustainable. *Consumption Markets & Culture, 16*(2): 145–168.

Defra. (2010). The Role and Business Case for Existing and Emerging Fibres in Sustainable Clothing. Department for Environment Food and Rural Affairs (online), retrieved from: http://randd.defra.gov.uk/Default.aspx?Menu=Menu&Module=More&Location=None&Completed=2&ProjectID=16095, [accessed on: 23/09/2016].

Del Savio, L., & Schmietow, B. (2013). Environmental Footprint of Foods: The Duty to Inform. *Journal of Agricultural and Environmental Ethics, 26*: 787–796.

Dolbec, P.-Y., & Fischer, E. (2015). Refashioning a Field? Connected Consumers and Institutional Dynamics in Markets. *Journal of Consumer Research, 41*(6): 1447–1468.

Entine, J. (2015, January). "Eco-Warrior" Vandana Shiva, at $40,000 a Speech, Rejoins Hawaii Anti-GMO Crusade, But Truth Is the Victim. The Huffington Post (online), retrieved from http://www.huffingtonpost.com/jon-entine/eco warrior-vandana-shiva-_b_6528032.html, [accessed on 01/08/2016].

Fletcher, K. (2008). *Sustainable Fashion & Textiles: Design Journeys*. Earthscan: Oxford.

Fletcher, K. (2010). Slow Fashion: An Invitation for Systems Change. *Fashion Practice, 2*(2): 259–266.

Fletcher, K. (2014). *Sustainable Fashion and Textiles: Design Journeys*, 2nd edn. Routledge: New York.

Galliano, D., & Orozco, L. (2013). New Technologies and Firm Organization: The Case of Electronic Traceability Systems in French Agribusiness. *Industry & Innovation, 20*(1): 22–47.

Giesler, M. (2012). How Doppelgänger Brand Images Influence the Market Creation Process: Longitudinal Insights from the Rise of Botox Cosmetic. *Journal of Marketing, 76*(6): 55–68.

Gilbert, N. (2013). A Hard Look at GM Crops. *Nature, 497*(7447): 24–26.

Gladwin, T. N., Kennelly, J. J., & Krause, T.-S. (1995). Shifting Paradigms for Sustainable Development: Implications for Management Theory and Research. *The Academy of Management Review, 20*(4): 874–907.

Griswold, E. (2012, September). How "Silent Spring" Ignited the Environmental Movement. The New York Times (online), retrieved from: http://www.nytimes.com/2012/09/23/magazine/how-silent-spring-ignited-the-environmental-movement.html, [accessed on 01/08/2016]

Guinée, J. B., Heijungs, R., Huppes, G., Zamagni, A., Masoni, P., Buonamici, R., Ekvall, T., & Rydberg, T. (2011). Life Cycle Assessment: Past, Present, and Future. *Environmental Science & Technology, 45*(1): 90–96.

Henninger, C. E. (2015). Traceability the New Eco-label in the Slow-fashion Industry?—Consumer Perceptions and Micro-organisations Responses. *Sustainability, 7*: 6011–6032.

Henninger, C., Alevizou, P. J., Oates, C. J., & Cheng, R. (2016). Communicating Sustainability: The Case of Slow-Fashion Micro-organizations, in A. Genus (ed.) *Sustainable Consumption: Design, Innovation and Practice*, Chapter 6: 83–96. Springer International: Cham, Switzerland.

Herring, R. J. (2006). Why did "Operation Cremate Monsanto" Fail?: Science and Class in India's Great Terminator-Technology Hoax. *Critical Asian Studies, 38*(4): 467–493.

Illouz, E. (1997). *Consuming the Romantic Utopia: Love and the Cultural Contradictions of Capitalism*. University of California Press: Berkeley, CA.

Joergens, C. (2006). Ethical Fashion: Myth or Future Trend? *Journal of Fashion Marketing and Management, 10*(3): 360–371.

Joy, A. (2013). Fast Fashion, Luxury Brands and Sustainability. www.worldfi nincialreview.com/p=738 (July 13) (editor's choice)

Joy, A., Sherry, Jr., J. F., Venkatesh, A., Wang, J., & Chan, R. (2012). Fast Fashion, Sustainability, and the Ethical Appeal of Luxury Brands. *Fashion Theory: The Journal of Dress, Body & Culture, 16*(3): 273–296.

Luedicke, M. K., Thompson, C. J., & Giesler, M. (2010). Consumer Identity Work as Moral Protagonism: How Myth and Ideology Animate a Brand-Mediated Moral Conflict. *Journal of Consumer Research, 36*(6): 1016–1032.

Martin, D., & Schouten, J. (2011). *Sustainable Marketing*. Pearson Prentice Hall: New Jersey, USA.

McGurty, E. M. (2011). Environmentalism and identity-politics, in A. Elliot (ed.) *Routledge Handbook of Identity Studies*, Chapter 17: 291–306. Routledge: New York.

Michaud, J. (2010, April). Eighty-Five from the Archive: Rachel Carson. The New Yorker (online), retrieved from: http://www.newyorker.com/books/double-take/eighty-five-from-the-archive-rachel-carson, [accessed on: 01/08/2016].

Morgan, L. R., & Birtwistle, G. (2009). An Investigation of Young Fashion Consumers ' Disposal Habits. *International Journal of Consumer Studies, 33*: 190–198.

Penton Media. (2011, November 2). Traceability: Tracking from Farm to Fork. *Natural Foods Merchandiser*, 8–10.

Poghosyan, A., Gonzalez-Diaz, F., & Bolotova, Y. (2004). Traceability and Assurance Protocols in the Global Food System. *International Food & Agribusiness Management Review*, *7*(3): 118–126.

Pouliot, S., & Sumner, D. A. (2008). Traceability, Liability, and Incentives for Food Safety and Quality. *American Journal of Agricultural Economics*, *90*(1): 15–27.

Ritzer, G. (2011). *The McDonaldization of Society 6*. Pine Forge Press: Thousand Oaks, CA.

Robert-Demontrond, P. (2009). Le Label Kasher: perspectives sur la dynamique commerciale d'un système de traçabilité de produits sain(t)s. *Décisions Marketing, Janvier-Ma*, *53*: 19–29.

Scaraboto, D., & Fischer, E. (2013). Frustrated Fatshionistas: An Institutional Theory Perspective on Consumer Quests for Greater Choice in Mainstream Markets. *Journal of Consumer Research*, *39*(6): 1234–1257.

Specter, M. (2014, August). Seeds of Doubt. The New Yorker (online), retrieved from: http://www.newyorker.com/magazine/2014/08/25/seeds-of-doubt, [accessed on: 01/08/2016].

Suber, T. (2012). Using Traceability to Protect Supply Chain Integrity. *Dairy Foods*, *113*(6): 76.

Thompson, C. J., & Coskuner-Balli, G. (2007). Countervailing Market Responses to Corporate Co-optation and the Ideological Recruitment of Consumption Communities. *Journal of Consumer Research*, *34*(2): 135–152.

Thompson, C. J., Rindfleisch, A., & Arsel, Z. (2006). Emotional Branding and the Strategic Value of the Doppelgänger Brand Image. *Journal of Marketing*, *70*(1): 50–64.

Trawick, P., & Hornborg, A. (2015). Revisiting the Image of the Limited Good. *Current Anthropology*, *56*(1): 1–27.

Tsakiridou, E., Mattas, K., Tsakiridou, H., & Tsiamparli, E. (2011). Purchasing Fresh Produce on the Basis of Food Safety, Origin, and Traceability Labels. *Journal of Food Products Marketing*, *17*(2/3): 211–226.

United Nations. (1987). *Report of the World Commission on Environment and Development: Our Common Future*. UN Documents: Oslo, Norway.

Warren, K. J. (Ed.) (1994). *Ecological feminism: Environmental philosophies*. Routledge: London, UK.

Welchman, J. (2012). A Defence of Environmental Stewardship. *Environmental Values, 21*(3): 297–316.

World Wildlife Fund. (2016). Cotton: Awater Wasting Crop. World Wide Fund For Nature (online), retrieved from: http://wwf.panda.org/about_our_earth/about_freshwater/freshwater_problems/thirsty_crops/cotton/, [accessed on: 22/09/2016].

Dr. Annamma Joy is a professor of Marketing, Faculty of Management at the University of British Columbia, Okanagan campus. Her research interests are primarily in the area of consumer behaviour and branding with a special focus on luxury brands, fashion brand experiences, consumer behaviour in the People's Republic of China (PRC), sustainability in the fashion and wine industries, and aesthetic consumption. She has published several articles in consumer behaviour and marketing journals such as the *Journal of Consumer Research, Journal of Consumer Psychology, International Journal of Research in Marketing, Journal of Cross-cultural Psychology*, and *Journal of Economic Psychology, Consumption, Markets and Culture*. Dr. Joy has won several awards for her articles published in journals in addition to videos she helped produce.

Camilo Peña is a PhD student at the Faculty of Management—University of British Columbia (UBC), Okanagan Campus. His current work and research focuses on topics of sustainable consumer behaviours in the wine industry.

4

The Influence of Eco-Labelling on Ethical Consumption of Organic Cotton

Joy Bucklow, Patsy Perry and Elaine Ritch

4.1 Introduction

Apparel is the largest sector in the global fibre industry, and is highly technical, fast changing and demanding in design, fashion, colour, aesthetics and performance (Farrington et al. 2005). The dominant textiles in today's UK fashion market are cotton (natural) and polyester (synthetic), as they have a similarly affordable price, offer the desired qualities of versatility and durability and can be used for a wide range of applications (Turley et al. 2010). Cotton is one of the world's most popular and polluting fibres (Riello 2013), and hence sustainability is a key issue in

J. Bucklow (✉) · P. Perry
School of Materials, The University of Manchester, Manchester, UK
e-mail: joy.bucklow@gmail.com; Patsy.Perry@manchester.ac.uk

E. Ritch
School for Business & Society, Glasgow Caledonian University, Glasgow, Scotland
e-mail: Elaine.Ritch@gcu.ac.uk

C.E. Henninger et al. (eds.), *Sustainability in Fashion*,
DOI 10.1007/978-3-319-51253-2_4

cotton farming (Babu et al. 2013; Grose 2009). To prevent crop failure, pesticides and synthetic fertilisers are used in cotton farming. However, these have been blamed for birth defects in humans, killing fish, birds and livestock, eradicating beneficial insects, depleting soil and yields, increasing production costs and reducing profits (Gopalakrishnan and Nithiyakumar 2008).

Organic cotton production is defined as using organically certified or untreated seed and farming methods that are free from synthetic chemical inputs (Myers and Stolton 1999). In the case of organic food, research suggests that consumers' belief in the added health attributes is a greater motivation to purchase organic than wider concern for the environment (Cowe and Williams 2000). Capitalising on this, food brands and UK supermarkets have increased their organic selection in recent years. Greater interest in healthy eating and healthy lifestyles (Kraft and Goodell 1993) provides optimism for organic cotton consumption. And this interest in organic food could encourage fashion and textile retailers to expand their organic ranges; however, little is known of how consumers interpret the concept of organic cotton within the context of fashion, particularly as motivation for organic food is health-driven, whilst this is less obvious for organic textiles. Although research has shown that chemicals applied during production to cotton plants can be absorbed by the skin during contact (Lee and Sevier 2008), consumer awareness of this is low (Westervelt 2015). Coupled with perceptions of cotton as a natural product (Hiller Connell 2010; Ritch 2015) and assumptions that chemical residue can be managed within the laundry process (Ritch 2015), the concept of organic is therefore neutralised. Consumers may conclude that organic fibres are unnecessary for fashion, especially given their price premium. Furthermore, the information provided that the multiplicity of eco-labels can create confusion and mistrust by consumers when buying fashion and textile products: there are currently 459 eco-labels in 197 countries and 25 industry sectors (Ecolabel Index 2015). Finally, the attitude-behaviour gap (Boulstridge and Carrigan 2000) suggests that consumers' environmental concerns do not always translate into ethical purchasing behaviour, for a number of reasons.

Research suggests that fashion consumers firstly consider style and price criteria in the fashion purchase decision-making process (Joergens 2006; Goworek et al. 2012). Whilst there is much research on consumer perceptions of ethical garment labels such as Fair Trade or "sweatshop free" (Shaw et al. 2006, 2007; Jones and Williams 2012), there is less research focusing on the use of organic cotton in the fashion market, despite its increasing popularity (Textile Exchange 2016).

4.2 Organic Cotton Production

Cotton farming methods are diverse and have environmental impacts that are not necessarily compatible with the principles of sustainability, in terms of energy use, materials use (seed, fertilisers etc.), water use, biodiversity, CO_2 emissions, effluents and water run-offs (Wakelyn and Chaudhry 2009). Accessibility and availability of inputs such as energy, materials, water, land, labour and finance affect the choice of cotton farming method and thus impact on sustainability (Williamson et al. 2005). Such inputs are dependent on geographical location, availability of natural resources, local climate, access to technology, farmer expertise, pest problems and soil conditions (Grose 2009). Several methods of growing cotton have been developed to address these issues, which are: conventional, organic, biological (bio) and genetically modified (GM) (Forster et al. 2013). Further alternatives include transitional cotton, grown in the transitional time period between conventional and organic cotton (Wakelyn and Chaudhry 2009), and Bio IPM systems, a form of conventional cotton which recognises and manages biological systems in the field, and reduces pesticides by removing the need to substitute one chemical for another (Grose 2009). Due to the multitude of factors (Grose 2009) within each of these methods, there can be good and bad practices, sustainable and unsustainable practices, and continuous evolvement.

Characteristics of organic farming include biodiversity, integration, natural plant nutrition, sustainability, natural pest management (Kuepper and Gegner 2004), biological cycles and activity (United States Department of Agriculture [USDA] National Organic Program [NOP] 2015), minimal off-farm inputs and ecological harmony (Wakelyn and Chaudhry 2009). Organic farming requires a whole systems approach which considers soil fertility and natural pest control, whilst maximising productivity (Tu et al. 2006). Organic cotton production addresses concerns for the environment and also workers involved in production, so may include a social element whereby farmers are paid an increased price, similar to Fair Trade (Fletcher 2008).

From a market perspective, organic cotton continues its popularity (Textile Exchange 2016), but remains a niche rather than mainstream market (Illge and Preuss 2012). Overall, there is a global under-supply of organic cotton, which accounts for less than 1% of all cotton produced (C&A 2015; Textile Exchange 2016). The top global buyers of organic cotton, such as C&A, H&M, Inditex and Nike (Textile Exchange 2016), may therefore blend organic and non-organic cotton in their products (Textiles Intelligence 2012).

The main reason for the success of organic cotton has been due to the negative environmental impact of pesticides used in conventional cotton, which in its traditional form ignored the causes of any pest infestations and relied instead on scheduled pesticide applications (Beyond Pesticides 2007). These methods may have led to adverse long-term or irreversible agricultural consequences, as the increasing cycle of insect population resulted in an increased number of chemical sprays (Wakelyn and Chaudhry 2009). Statistics support the argument of eliminating pesticides from cotton production. For example, the World Health Organisation (WHO) estimates one million pesticide poisonings annually, resulting in 20,000 deaths (Rustin 2014). However, the counterargument for pesticide use is that crop failure would negatively affect land and water resources, labour and livelihoods (Anderson et al. 2008). Furthermore, organic production can be more expensive than conventional cotton production (Wakelyn and Chaudhry 2009) due to increased record keeping (Grose 2009), high certifications costs (Bruce and Laroiya 2007), the potential risk of lower yields and the risk of reduced lint quality (colour grade and leaf rating), increased cost of hand weeding and possibility of lower grades (Swezey et al. 2007). Whilst adoption of new technologies could improve the production process, the expensive cost (e.g. irrigation systems) may take longer to recoup for the organic farmer (Wakelyn and Chaudhry 2009).

With regard to pesticide use, it would be inaccurate to suggest chemical sprays are widely misused or overused in conventional cotton production today, due to the wide availability of crop protection products, heavy regulation in developed countries and to some extent in developing countries, improved cost control, Better Management Practice (BMP), Integrated Pest Management (IPM) systems and Water Usage Efficiency (WUE) practices (Wakelyn and Chaudhry 2009). Furthermore, agricultural chemicals are developed to be less persistent in the environment, less toxic to humans, and "narrow spectrum", so that they precisely target the plant or problem pest rather than all insects (Grose 2009). Many of the environmentally responsible methods used in organic cotton production are also employed in conventional cotton practices, such as cover crops, trap crops, strip cropping, wind breaks, biological control of insects (pheromone trapping and mating disruption) (Cotton Australia 2013; Wakelyn and Chaudhry 2009). The argument between conventional and organic cotton has therefore evolved over the past two decades, as in this time, cotton has undergone a radical change in morphology following the introduction of GM seed, which has profoundly transformed cotton farming. Transformation to GM seed involves injecting a naturally occurring bacterium (*Agrobacterium tumefaciens*) into the cotton plant's genome to change its genetic structure (Orford et al. 2007), making it more resistant to specific pests, such as the bollworm. GM cotton represents over 70% of all cotton fibre produced (GMO Compass 2014), as shown in Fig. 4.1, whilst conventionally grown cotton is estimated at 28% of global cotton fibre production, with the remaining balance split equally between bio and organic production (Textile Exchange 2016).

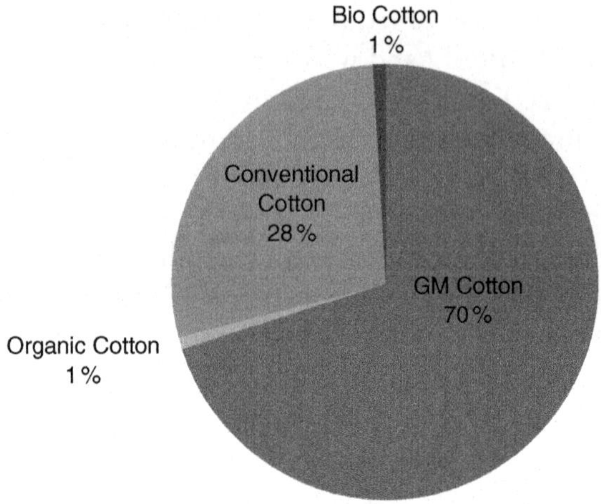

Fig. 4.1 Estimated global cotton production 2014 (GMO Compass 2014; Textile Exchange 2016)

4.3 The Development of Ethical Consumption

Ethical consumption refers to the "conscious and deliberate choice" to choose products and services that have not been produced through exploitative practices (Crane and Matten 2003, 341). This spans various concerns, from "oppressive regimes, human-rights, labour-relations, land-rights, the environment, irresponsible marketing, Fair Trade, nuclear power, armaments, animal-testing, factory-farming and political donation" (Newholm and Shaw 2007, 255). Growing concern for climate change has encouraged consumers to consider the ecological sustainability of the products they purchase (Tsarenko et al. 2013); concurrently, the global textile and fashion industry has also faced accusations of worker exploitation, such as low wages and poor working conditions (Smestad 2009). Sustainability is a topical concept that acknowledges resources are finite and seeks to ensure that future economic and societal development "meets the needs of the present without compromising the ability of future generations to meet their own needs" (WCED 1987). This is particularly important as industrialisation and population growth have resulted in environmental degradation and increasing inequality worldwide (World Commission on Environment and Development [WCED] 1987). Organisations are required to be profitable, to remain in business and provide employment; however, this should be aligned with respect for the environment and workers.

Ethical consumption research studies largely began in the 1990s (Vitell 2003) by seeking to identify what inspires the practice of ethical consumption (e.g. Freestone and McGoldrick 2008). Some researchers have sought to establish ethical consumers' characteristics and lifestyle traits (Paço and Raposo 2010); however, others acknowledged the application of ethics to consumption is more complex (Carrington et al. 2010; Bray et al. 2011) and examined why certain choices are made (Szmigin et al. 2009). Various studies have endeavoured to further segment and delineate green and environmental consumers (Ellen et al. 1991; Moisander 2007; Roberts 1996; Roberts and Bacon 1997). This leads to the notion of a conscious consumer (an increased mindfulness in purchasing decisions), which Edwards (2005) suggested is a more holistic and systematic approach where all aspects of the product are considered, including production, life cycle, disposal and social concerns (including the impact upon communities as well as workers' rights).

Although conscious consumers are starting to demand producers and retailers to be proactive in their sustainability policies and processes and provide healthy non-toxic products (Goworek 2011), some consumption markets make sustainability easier to practice, due to mainstream availability of alternative options (Joy et al. 2012). For example, the expansion of sustainably produced food in mainstream supermarkets (McDonald et al. 2009), coupled with marketing from the food industry to advise consumers of behaviours and practices that pertain to sustainable food purchase, use and disposal behaviours, has both supported and encouraged consumers who want to practice sustainable behaviours in the context of grocery shopping. Within the fashion and textile market, there is less availability (Hiller Connell 2010) and less signposting of alternative options (Moulds 2015).

Adding to the complexity, conscious consumers may apply a hierarchy of attributes when seeking ethical alternative products, as other social and economic forces impact on their behaviour (e.g. family, convenience, price), so that compromises may be reached in decision-making processes (Szmigin et al. 2009). Some of their decisions may be based on self-interested factors, such as possible health benefits of organic foods (Cowe and Williams 2000). However, consumers' ethical concerns do not always translate into purchasing behaviour.

4.4 The Attitude-Behaviour Gap in Ethical Consumption

A common thread throughout the ethical consumption literature is that behaviours are inconsistent, due to the aforementioned issues of market choice and availability (Auger and Devinney 2007). Ethical purchase intentions do not always translate into purchase behaviour (Davies et al. 2012), due to other influencing variables (Thøgersen 2000), and growing environmental concerns do not always translate into action (Bratt et al. 2011). Although attitudes may influence intention, they do not always convert into behaviour (Tzilivakis et al. 2012). This was evidenced in Grunert et al's (2014) sustainable food labelling study (including Fair Trade, Rainforest Alliance, Carbon Footprint and Animal Welfare), which suggested that although high levels of concern were conveyed at a general level, low levels of concern were demonstrated in actual purchase behaviour. Similarly, Ritch (2015) found that UK consumers were confused as to how sustainability applied to fashion and were sceptical of organic cotton.

The "attitude-behaviour gap" in ethical consumption refers to the disparity between the number of consumers who profess to be motivated by moral values and the actual sales of sustainably produced products (Carrington et al. 2010). It was first identified by Boulstridge and Carrigan (2000) and subsequently noted in recent research (Davies et al. 2012; Bray et al. 2011; Szmigin et al. 2009; Auger and Devinney 2007; Shaw et al. 2007). Although well documented, the

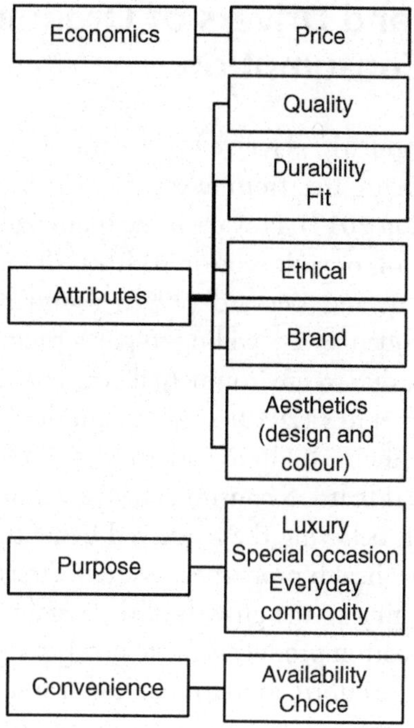

Fig. 4.2 Product factors and attributes involved in consumer purchase decision for fashion (Adapted from Davies et al. 2012; Ha-Brookshire and Norum 2011; Armstrong et al. 2015; Jones and Williams 2012)

attitude-behaviour gap remains poorly understood. In some consumption contexts, limitations of availability within the marketplace could be responsible, especially for fashion and textiles, where consumption is motivated by style, appearance and price (Ritch 2015; Goworek et al. 2012; Niinimäki 2010; Joergens 2006). Figure 4.2 below shows the wide range of product factors and attributes involved in the consumer purchase decision for fashion items. The type of product affects attitudes towards ethical attributes, and specific product attributes such as brand, design, purpose, durability and colour all affect willingness to pay for fashion items (Ha-Brookshire and Norum 2011; Armstrong et al. 2015; Jones and Williams 2012; Casadesus-Masanell et al. 2009).

4.5 Barriers and Drivers of Organic Cotton Consumption

Organic cotton is popularly perceived to be the most ecological form of cotton production, being free from allergenic, carcinogenic or toxic chemicals (Soil Association 2015). However, the main barrier for consumers is the price premium of organic cotton (Hustvedt and Bernard 2008). Nonetheless, Hustvedt and Bernard (2008) found that their sample of US undergraduate students were willing to pay a premium for socks made from organic cotton, due to environmental concern rather than any consumer benefits. Gam et al's (2010) study of mothers purchasing organic cotton clothing for their children had similar findings. Hustvedt and Dickson (2009) found that US consumers were willing to pay a premium for an organic t-shirt, believing the perceived benefits were both personal (in terms of additional health properties for the wearer) and environmental (in terms of contributing to the growth of the organic industry).

Although organic cotton producers make no claims for additional health benefits, neither is there information to enable consumers to understand the product attributes organic cotton has over conventional cotton. Casadesus-Masanell et al (2009, 207) noted that "an organic cotton garment is indistinguishable to the sight and touch from a garment made of conventionally grown cotton". Exploratory research on consumer perceptions of organic cotton (Ritch 2015; Hiller Connell 2010) identified confusion surrounding the meaning of organic cotton. Being a plant, cotton was perceived as a natural product (as opposed to man-made); therefore, organic status was viewed sceptically as a means to charge a premium price for an unnecessary attribute. This suggests that consumer knowledge levels of fashion production, including the processes involved in the production of fibres, materials and garments, are low. Without knowledge and understanding of the issues that organic production addresses, consumers are unlikely to be motivated to buy organic cotton, for either personal or wider ideological benefits. Additionally, styles are limited, further hindering organic clothing sales (Hiller Connell 2010), since most fashion consumers buy on the basis of style and price (Joergens 2006; Goworek et al. 2012). No obvious benefit to the consumer has been evidenced for organic textiles in relation to the growing method used, and in fact it is a common misconception that only certified organic cotton is pesticide and residue-free (Kuepper and Gegner 2004), as no difference has been found between organic and conventional cotton in this regard (Wakelyn and Chaudhry 2009). Furthermore, there has been a lack of factual statements to back up the claims made when advertising organic cotton, with some adverts using misleading or incorrect information (Wakelyn and Chaudhry 2009). Finally, there is no legal requirement to label cotton as organic, bio, GM or conventional. Therefore, the existence of environmentally positive determinants may not always be apparent or clear to consumers wishing to make a conscious choice in their product selection (Buckley 2013).

To be successful in the mainstream fashion marketplace, eco-friendly textiles should be attractive, fit for purpose and affordable (Sherburne 2009), as the vast majority of consumers make purchasing decisions on appearance, functionality, fashionability, quality, performance and price (Goworek et al. 2012; Hiller Connell 2010; Joergens 2006). It follows that consumers would not sacrifice basic functional features, such as colour uniformity, light and wash fastness, or shrinkage, for the sake of ethical or environmental benefits. To meet consumer demand for good aesthetic and durability properties, organic textiles should meet the same quality parameters that consumers expect from conventional textiles (Wakelyn and Chaudhry 2009).

4.6 The Process of Eco-Labelling

Textile eco-labels cover many areas, such as agriculture, fibre content and processing. Many of these eco-labels are integrated and follow the principles of other eco-labels. The main umbrella textile eco-labels to which other labels appear to adhere to are: European Union (EU), Textile Exchange (TE), United States Department of Agriculture (USDA), International Federation of Organic Agriculture Movements (IFOAM) and Global Organic Textile Standard (GOTS).

Eco-labels can be national (such as the UK's Soil Association) or multinational (such as GOTS). Consumer reliability on product-specific labels, such as Supima® for cotton, is comparable with harmonised multi-national labels (Van Amstel et al. 2007), such as GOTS. Despite this, harmonised labels (which are often multi-national) dominate international trade by positively affecting consumer perceptions of the differentiation in price and quality of a product (Mälkönen 2005). Eco-labels can be verified by an independent third party standard setting body such as GOTS, or a voluntary/self-declared one (i.e. without outside monitoring) such as a retailer's own label, for example, M&S's Plan a policy for textile recycling. As long as the market accepts the standard, then the use of eco-labels can increase market share and create product differentiation. However, voluntary or self-declared labels may also invite fraudulence and greenwashing, due to their lack of independent verification and audit. Therefore, veracity is required throughout the supply chain, including producers, distributors, government and certification bodies (Scheer et al. 2008), to promote products produced under desirable environmental conditions, and these messages need to be communicated fairly and clearly to consumers (Moore and Wentz 2009). Some argue the need for eco-laws to be in place, as there are currently no consequences for the label producers, and consumers cannot tell ineffectual mimic labels apart from the original accurate labels (Buckley 2013). Another possibility is government certified eco-labelling for products that are proven to exert less of a strain on the natural environment (Muldoon 2006). Multiple labels within one product category can be advantageous, particularly if the consumer has full knowledge of the eco-labelled product. Youssef and Abderrazak (2009) found that the introduction of a second alternate eco-label in the market promotes the environmental qualities of the first label. For example, GOTS and Fair Trade are both used in bed-linen and may appear together on the same product. However, when consumers are uncertain of the labelling requirement, a multitude of eco-labels decreases the information value of the label and raises consumer confusion (Harbaugh et al. 2011). With new technologies such as modern production techniques and analytical laboratories, alongside the rapid dissemination of information, the production of eco-labels can be more transparent, cost-effective and accurate (Moore and Wentz 2009), which could reduce consumer confusion. Many labelling guidelines (such as the Federal Trade Commission and ISO) do not permit the use of the term "sustainable", unless it can be referenced to a set of verifiable and independently set criteria (Wakelyn and Chaudhry 2009; Moore and Wentz 2009), since otherwise, the term cannot be objectively defined (Wakelyn and Chaudhry 2009).

As the processing of cotton can have a significant environmental impact, this factor is a criterion in many eco-label initiatives (e.g. GOTS, Oeko-Tex Standard 100 and the EU Ecolabel). However, the complex realities of cotton production and processing are difficult to convey in a label, particularly where narrow definitions and over-simplified statements are used (Grose 2009). The certifying agency must be accredited and recognised by buyers, and the system must be independent and transparent. Self-certification, in the case of large growers, and involvement of local government agencies in certification, particularly in developing countries, could lower certification costs for organic producers. The fee for certification must be low enough that it does not add significantly to the cost of production, otherwise it can become a disincentive to grow organic cotton (Wakelyn and Chaudhry 2009). The specific cost in labelling is the certification cost, which due to economies of scale and production complexities means only a limited number of attributes can be marketed (Bruce and Laroiya 2007). It is important that organic certification takes place throughout the whole cotton chain to have any credibility in the consumer decision-making process, which includes certification at the growing stage and again at the processing stage (Wakelyn and Chaudhry 2009). The Organic Trade Association adopted voluntary organic standards for fibre processing requirements for post-harvest handling, processing, recordkeeping and labelling, as has the Textile Exchange. Under GOTS, the whole supply chain is certified, from field to final product, this providing assurance for consumers with respect to environmental, social and animal welfare standards (Reinhold 2014).

4.7 The Influence of Eco-Labelling on Ethical Consumption

Product information is made available to consumers via many sources, including labels on the garment itself. Eco-labels are a voluntary form of environmental labelling and focus on ecological and environmental aspects of the product, providing a means of differentiation in the minds of consumers. Other forms of environmental labelling include government-mandated labels (such as the mandatory European Energy label) and self-declarations by the retailer or brand, for example, stating use of recycled content or non-use of certain chemicals (D'Souza 2004). Eco-labels identify overall environmental preference of a product within a product category based on life cycle considerations (Global Ecolabelling Network 2015), or an environmental goal, cause or objective, allowing consumers to make a considered choice. Eco-labelling initiatives can improve a retailer's competitive position, increase market share, help to enter and develop new markets, and strengthen commercial reputation (Brennan and Croft 2013; D'Souza 2004).

Across various product categories, research suggests that eco-labels play an important role in influencing consumers' purchase intentions (Delmas and Grant 2014; Grankvist and Biel 2007; Rahbar and Wahid 2010; D'Souza et al. 2011; Brennan and Croft 2013). However, Thøgersen (2000) suggested that they can only influence consumers who have a pro-environmental attitude, and the extent to which they could influence purchase intentions is based on several prerequisites such as knowledge, confidence and perception of the corporate environmental reputation of an eco-label (D'Souza et al. 2011; Rahbar and Wahid 2010). The level of information provided about the sustainability of textiles and the multiplicity of eco-labels can create consumer confusion and mistrust (Brécard 2014; Youssef and Abderrazak 2009). Therefore, eco-label design should prioritise clarity and simplicity to promote alternative options in the minds of consumers (Taufique 2014).

The type of product and its attributes are a determining factor in consumer preference for an ethical purchase. Davies et al. (2012) found the ethical attributes of luxury products were perceived to be less significant than for commodity products. Utilitarian benefits refer to the functionality and efficiency of the product, which can elevate consumers' perceptions of product quality, safety or performance (Bodur et al. 2014). However, some studies examining ethical attributes (Luchs et al. 2010; LeBoeuf and Simmons 2010) found that some products with ethical attributes may actually decrease preferences, suggesting that some green products can be perceived as inferior when compared to a comparable regular product (Lin and Chang 2012).

According to classic consumer behaviour theory, attitudes can be an important explanation as to why people perform certain behaviours (Ajzen and Fishbein 1980; Fishbein and Ajzen 1975). Behaviour can be predicted by the attitude of the consumer, which is linked to knowledge and personal experience (Spruyt et al. 2007). This was confirmed in Ochoa's (2009) association study where higher organic food purchases were associated with greater knowledge about organic clothing. Attitudes towards eco-labelled products can be positive or negative (Grankvist and Biel 2007), which accordingly affect the translation into purchase behaviour.

4.8 The Status of Organic Cotton in the UK Fashion Market

Increasing regulatory pressure and media focus on the fashion industry provide an opportunity for key fashion retailers and brands to become leaders in sustainability, so that other brands will follow. However, it could also be contended that smaller niche brands are leading the way in sustainable processes and business, for example, Braintree, People Tree and Beaumont Organic in the UK market, and therefore the bigger brands must follow (Textiles Intelligence 2014). Ilge and Preuss' (2012) case study compared the sustainable cotton sourcing and marketing practices of H&M and a small fashion retailer, concluding that small companies may well pave the way for larger brands to follow, therefore taking the role of early adopters, whilst larger retailers are better placed to achieve greater market penetration.

Some retailers focus exclusively on organic cotton, whilst others such as Marks & Spencer, H&M and Patagonia use different types of sustainable cotton, including recycled or reclaimed, Fair Trade and BCI cotton. In terms of large fashion retailers, C&A is the largest global user (by volume) of organic cotton (Textile Exchange 2016), and has been using certified organic cotton to either the Organic Content Standard (OCS) or GOTS since 2004. Organic cotton is marketed under C&A's Bio Cotton brand, which covers men's, ladies, children's and baby products. To promote organic to the mainstream and increase market penetration, C&A do not pass the extra cost of the raw material on to their consumers, but instead retail it at the same price as conventional products (C&A n.d.). To promote the quality and performance of the Bio Cotton range, an in-store and online marketing communication campaign in 2014 highlighted the durability of the garments in terms of resistance to fading and shrinkage (C&A n.d.)

After C&A, H&M is the second largest global user of organic cotton by volume (Textile Exchange 2016). It aims to provide fashion and quality at the best price in a sustainable way, to overcome the negative aspects associated with ethical fashion. It began blending organic cotton into cotton garments in 2004 and moved to 100% organic cotton from 2007, which is certified independently to the OCS or GOTS. Organic cotton products are retailed under its Conscious Collection brand and made available online as well as in-store to maximise availability for consumers. H&M asserts that the quality and versatility of the fabric are comparable to non-organic cotton, thus assuring consumers that basic functional features need not be sacrificed for organic credentials (H&M n.d.).

Pioneers who linked fashion with environmentalism and initiated the eco-fashion movement (Thomas 2008) include Esprit (with their Ecollection in 1991) and high-performance outdoor clothing retailer Patagonia, which began using organic cotton in 1996 and became the world's largest user by volume during the late 1990s (Ilge and Preuss 2012). Well-known for its pioneering environmentalism, Patagonia is known for high-quality products with a focus on functionality and durability over fashion (Casadesus-Masanell et al. 2009) and organic cotton is independently certified to the USDA's National Organic Program (Patagonia n.d.). Unlike H&M, which introduced organic cotton into its collections gradually, Patagonia immediately replaced all conventional cotton with 100% organic cotton. Patagonia explained the environmental benefits of the switch to consumers and assured them that product quality would not suffer, but did not hide the fact that this entailed a significant price increase (Casadesus-Masanell et al. 2009). However, Casadesus-Masanell et al. (2009) concluded that Patagonia's consumers were willing to pay substantial price premiums for eco-friendly products, but given their higher incomes and better education than the average US consumer, this may not be the case in all levels of the marketplace.

4.9 Conclusion

The organic movement has been successful in drawing consumers' attention to the issue of pesticides and chemicals used in cotton. Over time, however, the argument has moved on from the niche area of organic to wider concepts of sustainability, and eco-labels have adapted to incorporate many more environmental messages. Within the fashion market, consumers may face many dilemmas in product purchase decisions, which involve quality, style, price, private benefits and wider concerns. Since organic cotton offers no discernible product or health benefit to non-organic cotton, there is a challenge in marketing it to mainstream consumers. A further challenge, which also applies to ethical or eco-friendly clothing in general, lies in its negative associations of higher prices, aesthetic disadvantages, lack of choice and an unfashionable image. Greater initiatives from both small and large fashion retailers aim to overcome the negative stereotypes of ethical and eco-friendly clothing by providing stylish and fashionable designs, quality and durability, without price premiums. However, since fashion is also an emotional, cultural and visual journey, the perceived trade-off between sustainability and aesthetics or sustainability and price could present a lesser challenge than previously thought.

References

Ajzen, I., & Fishbein, M. (1980). *Understanding Attitudes and Predicting Social Behaviour*. Prentice Hall: London.

Anderson, K., Valenzuela, E., & Jackson, L. A. (2008). Recent and prospective adoption of genetically modified cotton: A global computable general equilibrium analysis of economic impacts. *Economic Development and Cultural Change*, *56*(2): 265–296.

Armstrong, C. M., Niinimäki, K., Kujala, S., Karell, E., & Lang, C. (2015). Sustainable product-service systems for clothing: Exploring consumer perceptions of consumption alternatives in Finland. *Journal of Cleaner Production, 97*: 1–10.

Auger, P., & Devinney, T. M. (2007). Do what consumers say matter? The misalignment of preferences with unconstrained ethical intentions. *Journal of Business Ethics, 76*(4): 361–383.

Babu, K. M., Selvadass, M., & Somashekar, R. (2013). Characterization of the conventional and organic cotton fibres. *Journal of the Textile Institute, 104*(10): 1101–1112.

Beyond Pesticides. (2007). What is integrated pest management? Retrieved from http://www.beyondpesticides.org/resources/safety-source-on-pesticide-providers/what-is-integrated-pest-management [accessed 17/10/16].

Bodur, H. O., Gao, T., & Grohmann, B. (2014). The ethical attribute stigma: Understanding when ethical attributes improve consumer responses to product evaluations. *Journal of Business Ethics, 122*: 167–177.

Boulstridge, E., & Carrigan, M. (2000). Do consumers really care about corporate responsibility? Highlighting the attitude-behaviour gap. *Journal of Communication Management, 4*(4): 355–363.

Bratt, C., Hallstedt, S., Broman, G., Robèrt, K.-H., & Oldmark, J. (2011). Assessment of eco-labelling criteria development from a strategic sustainability perspective. *Journal of Cleaner Production, 19*(14): 1631–1638.

Bray, J., Johns, N., & Kilburn, D. (2011). An exploratory study into the factors impeding ethical consumption. *Journal of Business Ethics, 98*: 597–608.

Brécard, D. (2014). Consumer confusion over the profusion of eco-labels: Lessons from a double differentiation model. *Resource and Energy Economics, 37*: 64–84.

Brennan, R., & Croft, R. (2013). Eco labels in Germany. *Journal of Consumer Behaviour, 12*(4): 341–359.

Bruce, C., & Laroiya, A. (2007). The production of eco-labels. *Environmental and Resource Economics, 36*: 275–293.

Buckley, R. (2013). Sustainability: Three reasons for eco label failure. *Nature*, 500: 151.

C&A. (2015). Making organic cotton mainstream. Retrieved from http://www.c-and-a.com/uk/en/corporate/company/newsroom/featured-stories/2015/making-organic-cotton-mainstream/ [accessed 17/10/16].

C&A. (n.d.). Bio Cotton – taking organic mainstream. Retrieved from http://www.c-and-a.com/uk/en/corporate/company/sustainability-old/products/bio-cotton/ [accessed 17/10/16].

Carrington, M. J., Neville, B. A., & Whitwell, G. J. (2010). Why ethical consumers don't walk their talk: Towards a framework for understanding the gap between the ethical purchase intentions and actual buying behaviour of ethically minded consumers. *Journal of Business Ethics, 97*(1): 139–158.

Casadesus-Masanell, R., Crooke, M., Reinhardt, F., & Vasishth, V. (2009). Households' willingness to pay for "green" goods: Evidence from Patagonia's Introduction of organic cotton sportswear. *Journal of Economics & Management Strategy, 18*(1): 203–233.

Cotton Australia. (2013). BMP cotton best management practices. Retrieved from http://www.bmpcotton.com.au/ [accessed 17/10/16].

Cowe, R., & Williams, S. (2000). *Who are the Ethical Consumers?* The Co-operative Bank: London.

Crane, A., & Matten, D. (2003). *Business Ethics*. Oxford University Press: New York.

D'Souza, C. (2004). Ecolabel programmes: A stakeholder (consumer) perspective. *Corporate Communications: An International Journal, 9*(3): 179–188.

D'Souza, C., Taghian, M., & Lamb, P. (2011). An empirical study on the influence of environmental labels on consumers. *Corporate Communications: An International Journal, 11*(2): 162–173.

Davies, I. A., Lee, Z., & Ahonkhai, I. (2012). Do consumers care about ethical-luxury? *Journal of Business Ethics, 106*(1): 37–51.

Delmas, M. A., & Grant, L. E. (2014). Eco-labeling strategies and price-premium: The wine industry puzzle. *Business & Society, 53*(1): 6–44.

Ecolabel Index. (2015). All ecolabels. Retrieved from http://www.ecolabelindex.com/ecolabels/ [accessed 17/10/16]

Edwards, A. (2005). *The Sustainability Revolution: Portrait of a Paradigm Shift*. New Publishers Canada: British Columbia.

Ellen, P. S., Wiener, J. L., & Cobb-walgren, C. (1991). The role of Perceived Consumer Effectiveness in Motivating Environmnetally Conscious Behaviours. *American Marketing Association, 10*(2), 102–117.

Farrington, D. W., Lunt, J., Davies, S., & Blackburn, R. S. (2005). Poly(lactic acid) fibers, in R. S. Blackburn (Ed.) *Biodegradable and Sustainable Fibres*, Chapter 6: 191–220, Woodhead Publishing: Cambridge.

Fishbein, M., & Ajzen, I. (1975). *Beliefs, Attitude, Intention and Behaviour: An Introduction to Theory and Research*. Addison-Wesley: London.

Fletcher, K. (2008). *Sustainable Fashion and Textiles*. Routledge: London.

Forster, D., Andres, C., Verma, R., Zundel, C., Messmer, M. M., & Mäder, P. (2013). Yield and economic performance of organic and conventional cotton-based farming systems – results from a field trial in India. *PloS One*, 8(12), 1–15.

Freestone, O. M., & McGoldrick, P. J. (2008). Motivations of the ethical consumer. *Journal of Business Ethics, 79*: 445–467.

Gam, H. J., Cao, H., Farr, C., & Kang, M. (2010). Quest for the eco-apparel market: A study of mothers' willingness to purchase organic cotton clothing for their children. *International Journal of Consumer Studies, 34*: 648–656.

Global Ecolabelling Network [GEN]. (2015). Global ecolabelling network [GEN] – home. Retrieved from http://www.globalecolabelling.net/ [accessed 17/10/16].

GMO Compass. (2014). Genetically modified cotton: Global area under cultivation. Retrieved from http://www.gmo-compass.org/eng/agri_biotechnology/gmo_planting/343.genetically_modified_cotton_global_area_under_cultiva tion.html [accessed 17/10/16].

Gopalakrishnan, D., & Nithiyakumar, M. (2008). Organic cotton: An overview. *Asian Textile Journal, 17*(1): 35–42.

Goworek, H. (2011). Social and environmental sustainability in the clothing industry: a case study of a fair trade retailer. *Social Responsibility Journal, 7*(1), 74–86.

Goworek, H., Fisher, T., Cooper, T., Woodward, S., & Hiller, A. (2012). The sustainable clothing market: An evaluation of potential strategies for UK retailers. *International Journal of Retail & Distribution Management, 40*(12): 935–955.

Grankvist, G., & Biel, A. (2007). Predictors of purchase of eco-labelled food products: A panel study. *Food Quality and Preference, 18*, 701–708.

Grose, L. (2009). Sustainable cotton production, in R. S. Blackburn (Ed.) *Sustainable Textiles: Life Cycle and Environmental Impact*, Chapter 2: 33–62, Woodhead Publishing: Cambridge.

Grunert, K. G., Hieke, S., & Wills, J. (2014). Sustainability labels on food products: Consumer motivation, understanding and use. *Food Policy, 44*: 177–189.

H&M. (n.d.) http://about.hm.com/en/About/sustainability/commitments/con scious-fashion/more-sustainable-materials/cotton.html [accessed 17/10/16].

Ha-Brookshire, J. E., & Norum, P. S. (2011). Willingness to pay for socially responsible products: Case of cotton apparel. *Journal of Consumer Marketing, 28*: 344–353.

Harbaugh, R., Maxwell, J. W., & Roussillon, B. (2011). Label confusion: The Groucho effect of uncertain standards. *Management Science, 57*(9): 1512–1527.

Hiller Connell, K. Y. (2010). Internal and external barriers to eco-conscious apparel acquisition. *International Journal of Consumer Studies, 34*(3): 279–286.

Hustvedt, G., & Bernard, J. C. (2008). Consumer willingness to pay for sustainable apparel: The influence of labelling for fibre origin and production methods. *International Journal of Consumer Studies, 32*(5): 491–498.

Hustvedt, G., & Dickson, M. A. (2009). Consumer likelihood of purchasing organic cotton apparel: Influence of attitudes and self-identity. *Journal of Fashion Marketing and Management, 13*(1): 49–65.

Illge, L., & Preuss, L. (2012). Strategies for sustainable cotton: Comparing niche with mainstream markets. *Corporate Social Responsibility and Environmental Management, 19*: 102–113.

Joergens, C. (2006). Ethical fashion: Myth or future trend?. *Journal of Fashion Marketing and Management, 10*(3): 360–371.

Jones, A. R. W., & Williams, G. (2012). Perceptions of fair trade labelling and certification. *Journal of Fashion Marketing and Management, 16*(2): 246–265.

Joy, A., Sherry Jr., J. F., Venkatesh, A., Wang, F., & Chan, R. (2012). Fast fashion, sustainability and the ethical appeal of luxury brands. *Fashion Theory, 18*(3): 273–296.

Kraft, F. B., & Goodell, P. W. (1993). Identifying the health conscious consumer. *Journal of Health Care Marketing, 12*(3): 18–26.

Kuepper, G., & Gegner, L. (2004). Organic crop production overview. ATTRA. Retrieved from https://attra.ncat.org/attra-pub/summaries/summary.php?pub=66 [accessed 17/10/16].

LeBoeuf, R. A., & Simmons, J. P. (2010). Branding alters attitude functions and reduces the advantage of function-matching persuasive appeals. *Journal of Marketing Research, 47*(2): 348–360.

Lee, M., & Sevier, L. (2008). The A-Z of eco fashion. Retrieved from http://www.theecologist.org/green_green_living/clothing/269326/the_a_z_of_eco_fashion.html [accessed 17/10/16].

Lin, Y.-C., & Chang, C. A. (2012). Double standard: The role of environmental consciousness in green product usage. *Journal of Marketing, 76*(5): 125–134.

Luchs, M. G., Naylor, R. W., Irwin, J. R., & Raghunathan, R. (2010). The sustainability liability: Potential negative effects of ethicality on product preference. *Journal of Marketing, 74*(5): 18–31.
Mälkönen, V. (2005). Harmonization versus mutual recognition of national eco-labels. *Discussion papers /Faculty of Social Sciences, Department of Economics, University of Helsinki; 612.*
McDonald, S., Oates, C., Thyne, M., Alevizou, P., & McMorland, L.-A. (2009). Comparing sustainable consumption patterns across product sectors. *International Journal of Consumer Studies, 33*(2): 137–145.
Moisander, J. (2007). Motivational complexity of green consumerism. *International Journal of Consumer Studies, 31*: 404–409. http://doi.org/10.1111/j.1470-6431.2007.00586.x.
Moore, S. B., & Wentz, M. (2009). Eco-labeling for textiles and apparel, in R. S. Blackburn (Ed.) *Sustainable Textiles: Life Cycle and Environmental Impact*, Chapter 10: 214–230, Woodhead Publishing: Cambridge.
Moulds, J. (2015). Can big brands catch up on sustainable fashion? Retrieved from https://www.theguardian.com/sustainable-business/sustainable-fashion-blog/2015/mar/24/composting-clothes-sustainable-materials-biodegradable [accessed 17/10/16].
Muldoon, A. (2006). Where the green is: Examining the paradox of environmentally conscious consumption. *Electronic Green Journal, 1*(23), 1–18.
Myers, D., & Stolton, S. (Eds.) (1999). *Organic Cotton: From Field to Final Product.* ITDG Publishing: London.
Newholm, T., & Shaw, D. (2007). Studying the ethical consumer: A review of the research. *Journal of Consumer Behaviour, 6*: 253–270.
Niinimäki, K. (2010). Eco-clothing, consumer identity and ideology. *Sustainable Development, 18*(3): 150–162. doi: 10.1002/sd.455.
Ochoa, L. M. C. (2009). Will "eco-fashion" take off? A survey of potential customers of organic cotton clothes in London. *AD-minister.*
Orford, S., Delaney, S., & Timmis, J. (2007). The genetic modification of cotton. *Cotton: Science and Technology, 1*: 103–129.
Paço, A. M. F., & Raposo, M. L. B. (2010). Green consumer market segmentation: Empirical findings from Portugal. *International Journal of Consumer Studies, 34*(4): 429–436.
Patagonia. (n.d.). Organic cotton. Retrieved from: http://www.patagonia.com/organic-cotton.html [accessed 17/10/2016].

Rahbar, E., & Wahid, N. A. (2010). Ethno-cultural differences and consumer understanding of eco-labels: An empirical study in Malaysia. *Journal of Sustainable Development, 3*(3): 255–262.

Reinhold, E. (2014) Why the time is right to go organic. Retrieved from http://source.ethicalfashionforum.com/article/why-the-time-is-right-to-go-organic [accessed 17/10/16].

Riello, G. (2013). *Cotton: The Fabric that Made the Modern World*. Cambridge University Press: New York.

Ritch, E. L. (2015). Consumers interpreting sustainability: Moving beyond food to fashion. *International Journal of Retail and Distribution Management, 43*(12): 1162–1181.

Roberts, J. (1996). Green consumer in the 1990s: Profile and Implications for advertising. *Journal of Business Research, 36*(3): 217–231.

Roberts, J. A., & Bacon, D. R. (1997). Exploring the subtle relationships between environmental concern and ecologically conscious consumer behavior. *Journal of Business Research, 40*(1): 79–89. http://doi.org/10.1016/S0148-2963(96)00280-9.

Rustin, S. (2014). Cotton trade: Where does your T-shirt grow?. Retrieved from http://www.theguardian.com/environment/2014/aug/09/cotton-growers-benin-organic-pesticides [accessed 17/10/16].

Scheer, D., Rubik, F., & Gold, S. (2008). Enabling developing countries to Seize eco-label opportunities.

Shaw, D., Hogg, G., Wilson, E., Shiu, E., & Hassan, L. (2006). Fashion victim: The impact of fair trade concerns on clothing choice. *Journal of Strategic Marketing, 4*(14): 427–440.

Shaw, D., Shiu, E., Hassan, L., Bekin, C., & Hogg, G. (2007). Intending to be ethical: An examination of consumer choice in sweatshop avoidance. *Advances in Consumer Research, 34*: 31–38.

Sherburne, A. (2009). *Achieving sustainable textiles: A designer's perspective*, in R. S. Blackburn (Ed.) *Sustainable Textiles: Life Cyle and Environmental Impact*, Chapter 1: 3–32, Woodhead Publishing: Cambridge.

Smestad, L. (2009). The sweatshop, child labor, and exploitation issues in the garment industry. *Fashion Practice, 1*(2): 147–162.

Soil Association. (2015). Soil association: Organic cotton. Retrieved from http://www.soilassociation.org/whatisorganic/organictextiles/organiccotton [accessed 17/10/16].

Spruyt, A., Hermans, D., De Houwer, J., Vandekerckhove, J., & Eelen, P. (2007). On the predictive validity of indirect attitude measures: Prediction of consumer choice behavior on the basis of affective priming in the picture-picture naming task. *Journal of Experimental Social Psychology, 43*(4): 599–610.

Swezey, S. L., Goldman, P., Bryer, J., & Nieto, D. (2007). Six-year comparison between organic, IPM and conventional cotton production systems in the Northern San Joaquin Valley, California. *Renewable Agriculture and Food Systems, 22*(1): 30–40.

Szmigin, I., Carrigan, M., & McEachern, M. G. (2009). The conscious consumer: Taking a flexible approach to ethical behaviour. *International Journal of Consumer Studies, 33*(2): 224–231.

Taufique, K. M. R., Siwar, C., Talib, B., Sarah, F. H., & Chamhuri, N. (2014). Synthesis of constructs for modeling consumers' understanding and perception of eco-labels. *Sustainability, 6*: 2176–2200.

Textile Exchange. (2016). *Organic Cotton Market Report 2016.*

Textiles Intelligence. (2012). *Global Apparel Markets.*

Textiles Intelligence. (2014). Global apparel markets.

Thøgersen, J. (2000). Psychological determinants of paying attention to eco-labels in purchase decisions: Model development and multinational validation. *Journal of Consumer Policy, 23*: 285–313.

Thomas, S. (2008). From "green blur" to ecofashion: Fashioning an eco-lexicon. *Fashion Theory – Journal of Dress, Body and Culture, 12*(4): 525–540. http://doi.org/10.2752/175174108X346977.

Tsarenko, Y., Ferraro, C., Sands, S., & McLeod, C. (2013). Environmentally conscious consumption: The role of retailers and peers as external influences. *Journal of Retailing and Consumer Services, 20*(3): 302–310.

Tu, C., Ristaino, J. B., & Hu, S. (2006). Soil microbial biomass and activity in organic tomato farming systems: Effects of organic inputs and straw mulching. *Soil Biology and Biochemistry, 38*(2): 247–255.

Turley, D., Horne, M., Blackburn, R. E. S., Laybourn, S., Copeland, J., & Harwood, J. (2010). *The Role and Business Case for Existing and Emerging Fibres in Sustainable Clothing.* DEFRA: London.

Tzilivakis, J., Green, A., Warner, D., McGeevor, K., & Lewis, K. (2012). A framework for practical and effective eco-labelling of food products. *Sustainability Accounting, Management and Policy Journal, 3*(1): 50–73.

United States Department of Agriculture [USDA] National Organic Program [NOP]. (2015). Organic regulations |agricultural marketing service.

Van Amstel, M., De Brauw, C., Driessen, P., & Glasbergen, P. (2007). The reliability of product-specific eco-labels as an agrobiodiversity management instrument. *Biodiversity and Conservation, 16*: 4109–4129.

Vitell, S. J. (2003). Consumer ethics research: Review, synthesis and suggestions for the future. *Journal of Business Ethics, 43*(1): 33–47.

Wakelyn, P. J., & Chaudhry, M. R. (2009). *Organic Cotton: Production Practices and Post-Harvest Considerations. Sustainable Textiles,* Chapter 11: 231–301, Woodhead Publishing: Cambridge.

Westervelt, A. (2015). Sweat it out: Could your sportswear be toxic? Retrieved from https://www.theguardian.com/lifeandstyle/2015/jun/02/toxics-apparel-nike-adidas-reach [accessed 17/10/16].

Williamson, S., Ferrigno, S., & Vodouhe, S. D. (2005). Needs-based decision-making for cotton problems in Africa: A response to Hillocks. *International Journal of Pest Management, 51*(4): 219–224. doi: 10.1080/09670870500384033.

World Commission on Environment and Development [WCED]. (1987). *WCED Our Common Future (The Brundtland Report).*

Youssef, A. B., & Abderrazak, C. (2009). Multiplicity of eco-labels, competition and the environment. *Journal of Agricultural & Food Industrial Organization, 7*(2): 1–22. doi: 10.2202/1542-0485.1271.

Joy Bucklow gained a first class honours degree in Contemporary Textiles from Lancaster University in 2013, and in 2016 started her third year PhD studies in the School of Materials, at the University of Manchester. Combined with her professional qualification as a Charted Management Accountant, she plans to use the skills and knowledge gained from her PhD on sustainability, consumerism and labelling, to start a textile design company using sustainable fibres.

Dr Patsy Perry is a Lecturer in Fashion Marketing in the School of Materials at The University of Manchester. She gained her PhD in Corporate Social Responsibility in fashion supply chains from Heriot-Watt University in 2012, and has published a number of academic journal articles and book chapters on her research. She teaches on several undergraduate and postgraduate courses and supervises PhD students in the areas of sustainability and fashion marketing.

Dr Elaine Ritch is a Lecturer in Marketing and Programme Leader for the BA (Hons) International Marketing degree at Glasgow Caledonian University. She was awarded her PhD, entitled *Mothers' experience of sustainable fashion consumption: An existential phenomenological exploration within Edinburgh*, from Queen Margaret University in 2013. Elaine focuses her research on fashion consumption through a sustainability lens and has published in international journals and edited books, along with regularly presenting her work at international conferences.

5

An Exploration of Consumers' Perceptions Towards Sustainable Fashion – A Qualitative Study in the UK

Zhen Lai, Claudia E. Henninger and Panayiota J. Alevizou

5.1 Introduction

The emergence of sustainability in fashion is not a recent occurrence, but rather has seen various waves of environmental, social, and economic concern (e.g. Belz and Peattie 2009), such as anti-fur campaigns in the 1980s and protests against unethical working conditions in the 1990s/2000s (Brown 2011; Gam 2011). What has previously been described as a passing 'fad' is now taken seriously by the British government and an increasing number of fashion organisations across the industry (BBC 2013).

Z. Lai (✉) · P.J. Alevizou
University of Sheffield, Sheffield, UK
e-mail: SilverLai@foxmail.com; P.J.Alevizou@sheffield.ac.uk

C.E. Henninger
School of Materials, The University of Manchester, Manchester, UK
e-mail: Claudia.Henninger@manchester.ac.uk

C.E. Henninger et al. (eds.), *Sustainability in Fashion*,
DOI 10.1007/978-3-319-51253-2_5

The past decades have seen an emergence of 'sustainable fashion' terminologies, such as eco-, green-, slow-, and ethical-fashion, which are used interchangeably (Carey and Cervellon 2014). In its most basic form, sustainable fashion, as part of the slow-fashion industry, is often described as the antipode to fast-fashion, which is mass-produced, cheap, changes within a fortnight, and often associated with a 'throw away' attitude (Watson and Yan 2013). Slow-fashion on the other hand, seeks to slow down the pace of the current fashion life cycle by producing a maximum of four fashion lines annually, focus on quality rather than quantity, and are not mass-produced (Joergens 2006; Joy et al. 2012). Initially, sustainable fashion had a negative connotation, which only more recently changed. With both high-street and high-end retailers introducing more sustainable garments such as 'the Conscious Line' (H&M), 'Plan A' (M&S), and Stella McCartney's newest creations, consumers are seemingly becoming receptive of purchasing 'fashion with a conscience' (Liggett 2010). Although past research in the field of sustainable fashion has predominantly focused on consumers' awareness of sustainable fashion, their attitudes towards these types of garments, and their impact on consumer purchasing behaviour (Goworek et al. 2013; Shen et al. 2013), the majority of extant research – especially on awareness and perception – is quantitative in nature, lacking to report new insights into consumers associations with sustainable fashion. This research contributes to knowledge by exploring consumers' perceptions of sustainable fashion through a qualitative research methodology, by further focusing on aspects of gender and age. This research addresses two questions:

1. How do the research participants perceive sustainable fashion?
2. What influences consumers to purchase sustainable fashion?

5.2 Literature Review

5.2.1 Sustainable Fashion

Although sustainable fashion is not a new phenomenon the actual concept lacks a clear-cut definition (Shen et al. 2013). For the purpose of this chapter sustainable fashion coincides with the definition of sustainable development in that it incorporates environmental (e.g. less harming production techniques, such as upcycling or recycling), social (e.g. safe working conditions and working environment), and economic elements (e.g. financial viability of the business model) (Belz and Peattie 2009). Garments classified as 'sustainable fashion' can best be described as those 'goods and services that respond to basic needs and bring a better quality of life, while minimizing the use of natural resources, toxic materials and emissions of waste and pollutants over the life-cycle, so as not to jeopardize the needs of future generations' (IISD 2015).

Within the fashion industry the aspect of sustainability becomes increasingly important with cutting-edge designers from high-street to luxury brands implementing changes across their supply chain thereby focusing on the well-being of workers, more environmentally friendly resources, and renewable and/or recycled materials (Weller 2012). Fletcher (2008) highlights that there are four guiding principles that need to be considered to classify fashion lines as 'sustainable'. First, any items produced must be child labour free across the entirety of the supply chain. Second, materials utilised within the production process should be less harming to the natural environment, recycled, upcycled, and/or more durable. Thus, it portrays the opposite to the 'throw away' fashion attitude often associated with fast fashion. Examples of such materials are organic cotton, which is grown by using less pesticides and toxic fertilisers, bamboo, as a fast growing, renewable, natural resource, or making use of previously owned garments (e.g. Joy et al. 2012; Henninger 2015). Overall the design process should be centred on a lifetime extension and less on fast moving consumer trends, thereby developing a classic style that does not go in and out of fashion quickly. Third, the production process must be in an ethical and socially responsible manner, paying workers fair wages and, ideally, create jobs in the country of origin by producing locally. Sustainable fashion has a local focus thereby not only supporting the local community and creating jobs, but also reducing transportation millage and costs. Last, the creation of long-term relationships across the supply chain is vital within the process of producing sustainably, which allows the negotiation of fair prices and wages and developing a strong network that fosters the creation of sustainable fashion (Yip 2010).

5.2.2 Outlook of the Fashion Industry

Although sustainability in fashion is increasing in importance, the fashion industry as a whole is one of the biggest polluters globally (BSR 2012). Thus, the phrase 'sustainable fashion' could be seen as an oxymoron, as the garment industry is designed to satisfy an artificially created 'fashion appetite' (Sharma and Hall 2010, p. 2) that produces over 30 kg of textile waste per person annually in the UK (WRAP 2012). This bleak outlook however is set against a new horizon as efforts are made to change this situation and develop a supply chain that is socially, economically, and environmentally responsible (Bennie et al. 2010). The Textile Exchange (2015) indicates that the top ten global fashion retailers now use 25% more organic cotton within their 2013 fashion lines, which implies a 10% increase in the organic cotton market in 2014. Moreover, fashion designers, such as Monkee Genes, Verlaine & Rimbaud Paris, or American Apparel, incorporate sustainable aspects into their brand identity. Nevertheless, the sustainable fashion market remains underdeveloped, with a relative low market share, which can be explained as sustainable fashion is still seen as less fashionable than its high-street equivalents (Weller 2012).

5.2.3 Sustainable Fashion Consumption in the UK

In the UK the Government actively promotes and supports sustainable fashion initiative, such as the Sustainable Clothing Roadmap and Action Plan (SCRAP), which aims to 'improv[e] the sustainability of clothing across its lifecycle, from the crops [. . .] grown to make the fabrics, to the design and manufacture of the garment, retail, use and end-of-life' (DEFRA 2011). The fashion industry is deeply engrained with the UK's history, thus it is not surprising that it is part of the sustainable fashion avant-garde (BFC 2015). Over the past decade the UK fashion industry has seen a change in its landscape, with consumers increasingly demanding garments that are more sustainable (Wigley et al. 2012). That said, extent research has found contradicting results: whilst consumers are interested in more sustainably produced garments, the majority of these consumers will still seek out cheap fashion alternatives (Joergens 2006; Pookulangara and Shepard 2013). Moreover, Pookulangara et al. (2011) suggest that 'green consumer behaviour' has thus far not translated into the fashion industry. Although other industry sectors, such as food or energy may have seen a move towards more ethical and sustainable choices, fashion consumers are seemingly unwilling to pay higher prices, sacrifice their choice of products, and/or actively look where to purchase these garments (Carrigan and Attala 2001; Chan and Wong 2012). To explain, although the general population is inclined to purchase products that are described as 'green', 'eco', 'sustainable', and 'organic' they are still not seen as being as important as aspects of quality and price (EC 2009). The latter has a major influence on the consumer's buying decision, especially when it comes to clothing (Carrigan and Attalla 2001). A viscous circle emerges, in that consumers may be aware that overconsumption has negative environmental consequences, yet the fashion appetite is continuously fostered by producing, promoting, and selling new collections with short turnaround times of only two weeks (Joy et al. 2012).

Even though consumers generally seem to have a positive connotation and perceptions towards sustainability, they acknowledge that they cannot base their consumption decisions solely on this aspect, as consumers feel they do not know a lot about sustainability in the apparel industry (Hiller Connell 2010). For instance Gam and Banning (2011) explored consumers' self-expressed definitions of sustainability in the apparel industry. They found that consumers predominantly focused on environmental aspects, such as the use of organic materials, as well as recycling products, and greening the overall production process. Extant research emphasises the lack of consumer knowledge of the impact of garment purchases and indicates that consumers request more information on the effects of their consumption to make more educated decisions (Hiller Connell 2010). A *need-to-know* consumer attitude emerges that pressures businesses to produce more information, which clearly highlights the values and practices of their organisation (Feitelberg 2010). Research suggests that consumer attitudes and intentions are affected by prior knowledge about the apparel industry and its values and practices (Bhaduri and Ha-Brookshire 2011). Yet, although consumers want to have more information on what organisations do and how they manufacture garments, they do not necessarily trust information provided by these organisations and are rather suspicious of what their (organisations') actual intentions are (Bhaduri and Ha-Brookshire 2011), which further highlights the challenges of communications.

Clothing purchase has also been linked to aspects of aesthetic preferences, fit (Gam 2011a), symbolism, enjoyment (Oh 2002), a boost of the sense of self-worth, and improve of self-presentation (Goldsmith et al. 1991). Garments act as a vessel of self-expression and create an identity (Winge 2008), which usually involves a strong emotional consumer experience (Niinimäki 2015). These additional evaluative criteria make the inclusion of sustainability in apparel purchasing decisions especially complicated (Gam 2011a) and calls for more research into consumers' perceptions of sustainable fashion garments. This research contributes to knowledge by investigating the contradicting results in the literature further through conducting in-depth interviews. This research focuses on consumers' perceptions and consequently their willingness to purchase sustainable fashion by gaining an understanding of their motivations and potentially improving the currently existing attitude-behaviour gap.

5.3 Methodology

This research is exploratory in nature and utilises a qualitative design to explore consumer perceptions of sustainable fashion. Semi-structured, in-depth interviews were conducted with 16 participants to gain an understanding of their feelings, experiences, and opinions of what they believe eco-fashion is. The terms sustainable-, eco-, and green-fashion are used interchangeably within this research, thereby following a general trend in the literature. Interview questions were based on the literature review and predominantly focused on understanding how interviewees interpret 'sustainable fashion', what associations they have with the term, and what their considerations are when shopping for garments.

Each interview was conducted on a face-to-face basis, which further allowed the researchers to observe body language and facial expressions. To gain a balanced view of sustainable fashion both male and female participants were chosen, utilising a combination of snowball and convenience sampling. The interview duration averaged 35 minutes. Table 5.1 provides an overview of the individuals, who participated in this research.

The rich qualitative data sets were iteratively coded and re-coded over several months following Easterby-Smith et al.'s (2008) seven step guide of familiarisation, reflection, conceptualisation, cataloguing, re-coding, linking, and re-evaluation. Following this loose coding guide allowed for patterns and themes to emerge organically. The researchers coded each of the interviews individually, before comparing and contrasting the themes that emerged. Discrepancies were carefully discussed and reviewed. The data was shown to the research participants for validation.

Limitations of this research are: first, the sample size of only 16 participants is relatively low. However, this study is exploratory in nature and thus, tried to identify whether there is a need to further research consumer perceptions of sustainable fashion. Although past research has identified that demographics may play an important role within the decision-making process of purchasing sustainable fashion, the results are not conclusive. Second, qualitative research does not allow generalisation of findings. However, qualitative research enables the researchers to produce key insights in the topic studied, which can provide the basis for further investigations.

Table 5.1 Summary of data collection

Interview (Is)	Gender	Age	Interview (Is)	Gender	Age
1	M	60	9	M	21
2	M	25	10	F	40
3	F	42	11	M	22
4	M	22	12	F	26
5	M	20	13	F	22
6	F	59	14	F	23
7	F	24	15	F	32
8	F	22	16	M	33

5.4 Findings and Discussion

5.4.1 Perceptions and Attitudes Towards the Sustainable Fashion Movement

The opinion about sustainable fashion was twofold: On the one hand, participants agreed that the industry in itself needs to change and become more environmentally and socially responsible, yet, on the other hand, consumers seemed to have a low level of awareness of the movement and believe it is dated. A majority of interviewees highlighted that they already saw a slight change in availability of clothing, such as the H&M conscious line and organically certified T-shirts. However, it seems that consumers have reservations towards these garments, as H&M is not necessarily seen as a representative of *'sustainable brands'* (Is15 F). Data indicate that consumers seem to have a limited view on what sustainable fashion implies and are unconvinced of actions taken by fashion retailers that produce more sustainable garments. Interviewee 4 (M) mentions *'I welcome that many products or companies are more sustainable. More and more brands follow this trend. That could be a big thing'.* This concurs with a previous point made by the same interviewee, who also implies that sustainable fashion is a trend that is currently emerging. Whilst positively perceived, data suggest that sustainability is a 'trend' that is short-lived and has not yet peaked. It becomes apparent that those companies that utilise, for example, organic cotton, bamboo, and/or recycled materials leave a positive impression on consumers, which makes consumers more inclined to purchase garments from these brands (Is9 M; Is10 F). Interviewee 10 (F) insists that she will think about purchasing sustainable fashion, if it was easily accessible, but implies that this is not always the case. Participants state that retailers need to make it easier for consumers to identify sustainably produced garments. *'I think it needs to be easy, only because I feel like at the moment... if there is ethically and locally produced clothing it should all be in one shop, or it could be if it is a High Street shop it has a giant banner and says sustainable... ethically produced, local whatever... But having said that, like I said before... I don't think that there are enough places to... actually find... those shops; it is not that easy'*

(Is15 F). Moreover, Interviewee 14 (F) believes that *'they need to elaborate on what they are doing as many people did not know that they use sustainable materials for their products'*. This implies that the communication process between retailers and consumers may be underdeveloped with consumers wanting to receive more information on their garments in terms of production (e.g. country of origin, working conditions) and materials (e.g. organic, reused, reclaimed).

In summary, findings from this research concur with previous studies in that consumers are generally speaking attracted and inclined to purchase sustainable fashion (D'Souza 2004), yet this may not necessarily led to an active purchasing behaviour (Carrigan and Attalla 2001). Data moreover suggest that sustainability in fashion seems to be perceived as a short-term trend that is not currently developed to this maximum potential. Overall, consumers seem less aware of critical underpinnings associated with the slow-fashion movement. This can be attributed to issues such as accessibility to products and information, awareness of effects the fashion industry has on the social and natural environment, and/or the implications fashion consumption has on the product life cycle. Findings suggest that there is a need to further raise awareness of what sustainable fashion means to organisations, which can be transferred to the consumers, who will be able to understand why production techniques have changed and how to easily identify garments that are part of the slow-fashion movement.

5.4.2 Associations of Sustainable Fashion

To understand consumers' perceptions of sustainable fashion it was vital to gain information on how they describe items that are classified as 'sustainable'. The words most commonly associated with sustainable garments are *'natural'* (Is4 M, Is16 M), *'simple'* (Is7 F), and *'locally made'* (Is15 F). These aspects fit with how sustainable fashion is described in the literature (e.g. Fletcher 2008). Interviewee 5 (M) further highlights that sustainable fashion for him is only a fad, which *'maybe will develop into a new fashion style'*, but currently lacks a mainstream feel. From the interview it becomes apparent that he neither sees a future for sustainable garments nor a demand for these types of garments. He highlights that there are not many companies in the marketplace that would follow the trend of producing sustainable fashion, which implies that the demand for these garments would be limited – '*people don't ask for it, companies don't produce it*' (Is5 M). A reason for this short-term perspective may be that *'it's a frustrating process . . . I don't think there are enough places to, to actually find them, but when they do exist it is easy to recognize "oh yeah" that is locally made, but finding those shops . . . it's not that easy . . . it's frustrating*' (Is16 M).

Describing sustainable fashion as a 'fad' implies that these male consumers do not recognise the underlying issues that are associated with slow-fashion. Similarly, they seem to have difficulties locating sustainable fashion items in their daily shopping routines. This implies that there may be a lack of availability in the market, or a lack of communication that highlights where these garments can be purchased. Data indicate that there is also a lack of consumer education, in that especially male consumers seem to be unaware of what sustainable fashion is and how it can be defined. Although 'we are dealing with increasingly sophisticated consumers' (Carrigan and Attalla 2001, p. 571), who are demanding more sustainable garments (Wigley et al. 2012), 'this does not necessarily translate into wise or ethical buying practice' (Carrigan and Attalla 2001, p. 571) as the supply chain, thus far, has not fully adapted to the changes in the marketplace and may lack the ability to cater for the consumer needs and wants. This concurs with a report conducted by Mintel (2009) that indicates that the ethical and sustainable clothing market remains underdeveloped (EFF 2012). In summary, our research suggests that incorporating sustainable decisions when purchasing garments seems to be a somewhat frustrating and challenging process (Gam 2011a), due to the lack of knowledge, awareness, and education. Consumers see sustainable fashion as a 'fad' or just another buzzword, which highlights the need to further educate consumers about the background of sustainable fashion.

Male participants highlighted that key shopping criteria for them are quality and aesthetics. Interviewees suggested that sustainable fashion has a more natural feel, which can be slightly rough to the touch, and is predominantly lower in quality compared to fast fashion counterparts. To explain, Interviewee 7 (M) commented on the actual fabrics and materials used and insisted that *'eco-clothing looks like more natural, but a little rough, not so smart in general'* (Is7 M) further stressing the importance of design and fashion technology. Interviewee 9 (M) voiced his concern in regards to the quality of the clothing and the suitability for his occupation: *'like the T-shirts, from the quality you could tell it's eco. It is not a long stay item. It is a very strange style and the material too natural for me'*. Similar concerns were raised by Interviewee 16 (M), who states that when they are making a purchasing decision *'it will always come down to quality, because I don't like re-buying clothes...so if... it's fair trade and if that also means it will last and it is good quality and all those things, but they are not always hand in hand'*. To conclude, an issue that emerges from the interviews with male consumers is the fact that sustainable garments may not necessarily be associated with high quality, but rather with being unfashionable and expensive.

Contrarily, female participants seem to have a more positive connotation towards sustainable fashion garments indicating that they have *'unique elements'* (Is15 F). Female consumers seem more inclusive of market, social, and environmental issues in their understanding of sustainable fashion. Alongside aspects of local production and supporting workers in the country of origin, female consumers also indicate that ethical labelling and environmentally friendly materials are part of sustainable fashion. Data suggest that female consumers clearly distinguish between sustainable fashion, high-street fashion, and high-end fashion. They indicate that sustainable fashion differs from high-street and high-end fashion in that the styles are basic in nature and not necessarily fashionable. For instance, Interviewee 6(F) associates sustainable fashion with fair trade and states that *'fair trade clothes tend to be simple in design and functional, rather than high-end fashion. This is a look that I prefer... the high-end'* highlighting that design and high-end clothing remain priorities in her decision-making. This indirectly concurs with what has previously been highlighted in that sustainable fashion should be 'timeless' and less affected by change (e.g. Fletcher 2008; Henninger 2015).

An interesting finding thus far from both female and male participants is that sustainable fashion is seen as less fashionable than fast fashion counterparts. No specific reasons were given as to why this may be the case other than that the materials used make these garments less trend influenced. Having said that overall it seems that female participants are more inclined to choose sustainable fashion as they appreciate the style and see unique features in the collections – whether these are fashionable or not has not explicitly been mentioned. On the other hand, male interviewees are seen to be more sceptic and strongly believe that sustainable fashion and quality do not always go hand in hand. A question that emerges is whether consumers receive enough information and education from suppliers and retailers about features of sustainable fashion and how these compare to high-street and high-end products. Our study also highlighted the importance of the 'image of the sustainable fashion industry' and stressed that consumers may have more negative associations than positive. We found that the concept of sustainable fashion is abstract in the mind of consumers and is associated with an *emerging* trend that *may or may not stay*. Consumers seem to take a *hypothetical scenario* approach when discussing sustainable fashion indicating that the issues and problems facing the fashion industry are relatively alien and distant. Finally, our research clearly highlights a distinctive approach to sustainable fashion from female and male consumers calling for more research into gender perceptions.

5.4.3 Influencers Affecting Consumers' Purchasing Decisions

To understand how the knowledge of sustainable fashion and the 'sustainable fashion movement' influence consumers' purchasing decisions, it is vital to explore their clothing purchasing behaviour in more general terms. Participants were asked to highlight how they decide on which garments to purchase. The majority of interviewees immediately mentioned price as a key influencer (Is5 M; Is10 F; Is13 F). Interviewee 8 (F) states *'it always feels like it (sustainable fashion) costs a lot more money, which I don't have... so you know... the first thing I'm gonna spend money on is going to be food not ethically produced clothing'.* However, *'if it was not much higher price I will go for eco-fashion, if it looks nice I will take it'* (Is1 M). It is noteworthy to highlight that a majority of participants have neither actively looked for sustainable fashion nor purchased any sustainable garments purposefully. Nevertheless, they assume that these garments *'tend to be more expensive than products without eco-information'* (Is11 M) that can be purchased on the high-street, as food products that are labelled as 'organic' cost more than those that have no certifications. Several participants claim (Is11 M; Is16 M) that higher prices discourage consumers from making a sustainable purchase decision, especially when it comes to fashion items. Male participants felt quite strongly about the price difference and insist that *'truly being ecological should not affect the price of a product'* (Is2 M). Contrary, female participants state that price premiums are not only justified, but necessary. *'The price may be higher if the retailer has had to pay the suppliers more to give them a realistic price, but I think that this is acceptable'* (Is6 F). Having said that, Interviewee 10 puts this further into perspective stating that higher prices are only justified for certain products, but not all. For example, jackets that are ideally long-lasting should be of higher quality and durable, thus a price premium is acceptable for this product, yet an everyday T-shirt should not show a difference in price simply because it uses environmentally friendly raw materials or falls into an 'ethical' category (Is10 F). The analysis indicates that consumers are willing to purchase sustainable garments, if they are of the same quality and at the same cost. This research concurs with previous studies (e.g. Carrigan and Attalla 2001; D'Souza 2004) suggesting that consumers are price sensitive and believe it is the retailers/suppliers responsibility to produce fashion in a more sustainable manner, thereby not putting additional costs onto the end-user. A question that emerges is how increased costs from producing sustainable garments should be absorbed, if the end-consumer is unwilling to do their part by purchasing everyday garments at a slightly higher cost. Interestingly, this research found that male consumers are more passionate about this specific issue, as opposed to female participants, who are willing to pay more – for certain products. Female consumers seemed to be more fashion oriented, which could present an opportunity for slow fashion, in that retailers could target male consumers more specifically.

Further influencers that have an impact on purchasing decisions are availability of products, the convenience of shopping for this product, and personal preference. Interviewee 6 (F) highlights that she usually goes to a couple of shops when purchasing clothes, but does not like the idea of having to go out of her way to get what she is looking for. *'If it's not available, well it's not. I wouldn't run to six other shops just to get a sustainable T-shirt, if another one fits just fine'* (Is6 F). Interviewee 15 (F) concurs with this comment and further elaborates that the sustainable alternatives need to be right next to their counterparts, otherwise it would just be *'such a hassle to get them and look for them, and just trouble you don't really need'*. Data suggest that the female participants may look for sustainable fashion alternatives, yet these need to be obviously placed in the shop and readily available. Contrary, Interviewee 5 (M) insists that for him it does not matter whether sustainable articles are available or not, as he only purchases garments of brands that he is familiar with and likes. With sustainable garments being described as less fashionable they do not present an alternative to exclusive, unique, and high-end styles preferred by Interviewee 5. Interviewee 11 (M) concurs: *'it does not have much of impact, I will probably only buy the clothes if I like them and they are not too expensive'*. This implies that personal preferences outweigh aspects of sustainability for the male participants. No further considerations are given to eco-friendly or organic materials, if these are not used within clothing lines they already intent to purchase. This finding concurs with extant research that suggests consumers are not interested in eco- or sustainable products, if they are not utilised already by their favourite brand (Carrigan and Attalla 2001). Thus, it could be implied that shopping routines and purchase intentions may not always be influenced by the availability of sustainable fashion products.

Further influencers that were mentioned by participants are quality, opinion of reference groups, value, style, colour, fashionability, durability, and brand names. The majority of these attributes were not associated with sustainable fashion.

In summary, although this research found similar results than past studies, data clearly indicate that male and female consumers differ in terms of their willingness to pay for sustainable fashion. This aspect has previously not been explored and needs to be followed up with a larger research sample. Moreover, this research found that even if products are available, especially male participants in this research might not necessarily purchase these alternatives, which could be linked to a previous observation that sees sustainability as a short-term trend that is not fully developed.

5.4.4 Sustainable Fashion – Who Is Responsible?

A question that emerged from the findings is that of responsibility and ownership of a more sustainable lifestyle in terms of an alternative fashion wardrobe. The general consensus provided by the interview data is that consumers ideally like to have the option of purchasing sustainable clothes, but whether or not these options are bought depends on who offers these garments. The majority of interviewees agreed that sustainability should not be singled out as an issue, but automatically be incorporated across the supply chain and within the garment production process. In other words, environmental, social, and economic responsibility and sustainability should not be unique selling propositions and exceptional, but rather the norm within the fashion industry. Interviewee 7 (F) highlights that *'if you know... if everyone would do it, products would have... they would sell for the same price and then it's not a big thing anymore, it's like a no brainer. You pick the eco one'.* However, before this can be a reality it is vital for consumers to be able to trust brands and their claims. Factory accidents in the news, false promises and claims in advertising, as well as initial teething problems in the food industry are highlighted as aspects that shake consumers' confidence in sustainable fashion (Is15 F; Is16 M).

Interviewees insisted that it is the responsibility of the UK government and large fashion retailers to foster the sustainable fashion movement and make sure it will be a success. Various participants (Is7 F; Is2 M) feel they do not have a big influence on whether sustainable fashion spreads, as they do not have the power to change anything. *'Yeah, well I guess I can demand to... get more sustainable choices, but if that's gonna be a reality? Maybe, I would hope... but, I guess it's just too appealing to throw stuff out and companies do what makes the most money, right?'* (Is15 F). Interviewee 2 (M) further insists that companies should just put some of their profits aside and reinvest these in a more sustainable supply chain, which would benefit everyone. On the other hand, a majority of participants highlighted that sustainable fashion should not be part of a 'blame game', but rather be seen as everyone's responsibility whereby small steps have to be taken by everyone (Is11 M; Is13 F).

The issue of trust is not a new phenomenon to be observed in conjunction with sustainable products (Carrigan and Attalla 2001; Koszewska 2011). However, what is new is the fact that consumers seem to be more familiar with the term sustainability and sustainable fashion and start acknowledging that changes need to happen, whilst at the same time request for more education. Although this may be a slow process, findings show signs of change within the industry and in terms of consumption behaviour as sustainable products, if available, are seen as real alternatives.

5.5 Conclusion

This chapter focused on two research questions: (1) How is sustainable fashion perceived, (2) What influences consumers to purchase sustainable fashion? In answering the first question it becomes apparent that sustainable fashion is perceived as a luxury commodity that lacks quality. Male and female participants have different views of the concept and clearly express their opinions. Whilst females see sustainable fashion as unique, fashionable items, the males' view is almost the polar opposite. The results indicated a clear male-female divide. Contrarily, question two had unanimous results in that quality, price, aesthetics, and availability are seen as key influencers in the decision-making process of purchasing fashion items. Consumers indicated that aspects such as price, quality, availability, and convenience are seen as trade-offs that hinder them to purchase sustainable fashion. Findings suggest that a lack of communication from the industry side further contributes to consumers lacking key information that would enable them to make an informed choice to purchase sustainable fashion. Sustainable fashion still seems to be branded differently to fast-fashion and is often associated with a lack of aesthetics and a more natural look. Consumers overall still seem to be confused on what sustainable fashion is and why it emerged. Industry players, including fast-fashion brands with a sustainable garment line, need to provide more information on their garments and make this easily accessible to consumers. A clear story of sustainable fashion needs to emerge throughout the industry, which would help consumers to understand aspects of sustainable fashion, which currently seems to be fuzzy and full of misinterpretations. A key contribution of this chapter is that it clearly highlights that there is a difference between male and female attitudes and perceptions towards sustainable fashion. The exploratory nature of this research enabled to gain an insight into how these participants describe sustainable fashion. Future research could focus on gender and age and investigate a larger sample to validate these preliminary findings.

References

BBC. (2013). *Peers urge support for sustainable fashion.* 20 March 2013, BBC [online], retrieved from: http://www.bbc.co.uk/democracylive/house-of-lords-21850300 [accessed on: 05/07/2013].

Belz, F., & Peattie, K. (2009). *Sustainability Marketing A Global Perspective*, 1st ed., Wiley: Glasgow.

Bennie, F., Gazibara, I., & Murray, V. (2010). *Fashion futures 2025, LEVI STRAUSS & CO.*, Forum for the Future [online], retrieved from: https://www.forumforthefuture.org/sites/default/files/project/downloads/fashionfuturespresentationpdf.pdf [accessed on: 05/01/2015].

BFC (British Fashion Council). (2015). *The value of the UK fashion industry*, BFC [online], retrieved from: http://www.britishfashioncouncil.com/uploads/media/62/16356.pdf [accessed: 20/01/2016].

Bhaduri, G., & Ha-Brookshire, J. E. (2011). Do transparent business practices pay? Exploration of transparency and consumer purchase intention. *Clothing and Textiles Research Journal*, 29(2): 135–149.

Brown, S. (2011). *Future factory: Sass Brown is coming to NTU.* Future Factory *[online]*, retrieved from: http://futurefactory.weebly.com/live-event-streams.html [accessed: 20/03/2012].

BSR (Business of a Better World). (2012). *Sustainable fashion design: Oxymoron no more?*, BSR [online], retrieved from: http://www.bsr.org/reports/BSR_Sustainable_Fashion_Design.pdf [accessed on: 05/07/2013]

Carey, L., & Cervellon, M. C. (2014). Ethical fashion dimensions: Pictorial and auditory depictions through three cultural perspectives. *Journal of Fashion Marketing and Management*, 18(4): 483–506. doi:10.1108/JFMM-11-2012-0067.

Carrigan, M., & Attalla, A. (2001). The myth of the ethical consumer – Do ethics matter in purchase behaviour? *Journal of Consumer Marketing*, 18(7): 560–578. doi: 10.1108/07363760110410263.

Chan, T. Y., & Wong, C. W. Y. (2012). The consumption side of sustainable fashion supply chain: Understanding fashion consumer eco-fashion consumption decision. *Journal of Fashion Marketing and Management*, 16(2): 193–215.

DEFRA (Department of Environment Food and Rural Affairs). (2011). *Sustainable clothing roadmap: Progress report 2011*. DEFRA [online], retrieved from: https://www.gov.uk/government/uploads/system/uploads/attachment_data/file/69299/pb13461-clothing-actionplan-110518.pdf [accessed: 05/07/2013].

D'Souza, C. (2004). Ecolabel programmes: A stakeholder (consumer) perspective. *Corporate Communications: An International Journal*, 9(3): 179–188. doi: 10.1108/13563280410551105.

Easterby-Smith, M., Thorpe, R., & Jackson, P. (2008). *Management Research*, 3rd edn, SAGE Publications: London, UK.

EC (European Commission). (2009). *European's attitudes towards the issue of sustainable consumption and production*. EC [online], retrieved from: http://ec.europa.eu/public_opinion/flash/fl_256_en.pdf [accessed: 20/01/2016].

EFF (Ethical Fashion Forum). (2012). *The market for ethical and sustainable fashion products*. EFF [online], retrieved from: http://source.ethicalfashionforum.com/assets-uploaded/documents/Market_for_sustainable_fashion_Briefing.pdf [accessed: 20/01/2016].

Feitelberg, R. (2010). Fashion's new order: Transparency. *Womens Wear Daily*, 199: 16.

Fletcher, K. (2008). *Sustainable Fashion and Textiles: Design Journeys*. London: Earthscan.

Gam, H. J. (2011a). Are fashion-conscious consumers more likely to adopt eco-friendly clothing? *Journal of Fashion Marketing and Management*, 15(2): 178–193.

Gam, H. J., & Banning, J., 2011. Addressing sustainable apparel design challenges with problem-based learning. *Clothing and Textiles Research Journal 29*(3): 202–215.

Goldsmith, R., Heitmeyer, J., & Freiden, J. (1991). Social values and fashion leadership. *Clothing and Textile Research Journal*, 10(1): 37–45.

Goworek, H., Hiller, A., Fischer, T., Cooper, T., & Woodward, S. (2013). Consumers' attitudes towards sustainable fashion: Clothing usage and disposal. *Sustainability in Fashion and Textiles*, 17: 376–392. doi: http://dx.doi.org/10.9774/GLEAF.978-1-909493-61-2_25.

Henninger, C. E. (2015). Traceability the new eco-label in the slow-fashion industry? – Consumer perceptions and micro-organizations responses. *Sustainability*, 7(5): 6011–6032. doi: 10.3390/su7056011.

Hiller Connell, K. Y. (2010). Internal and external barriers to eco-conscious apparel acquisition. *International Journal of Consumer Studies, 34*(1): 279–286.

IISD (International Institute for Sustainable Development). (2015). *Definitions & concepts*. IISD [online], retrieved from: http://www.iisd.org/susprod/principles.htm [accessed on: 15/01/2016].

Joergens, C. (2006). Ethical fashion: Myth or future trend? *Journal of Fashion Marketing and Management*, 10(3): 360–371. doi: 10.1108/13612020610679321.

Joy, A., Sherry, J. F., Venkatesh, A., Wand, J., & Chan, R. (2012). Fast fashion, sustainability, and the ethical appeal of luxury brands. *Fashion Theory, 16*(3): 273–296. doi: 10.2752/175174112X13340749707123.

Koszewska, M. (2011). Social and eco-labelling of textile and clothing goods as a means of communication and product differentiation. *Fibres and Textiles in Eastern Europe, 87*(4): 20–26.

Liggett, B. (2010). *How do you define 'Sustainable Fashion', exactly?* Ecouterre [online], retrieved from: http://www.ecouterre.com/how-do-you-define-sustainable-fashion-exactly/ [accessed on: 15/07/2012].

Mintel. (2009). *Ethical clothing – UK Feb 2009*. Mintel: London.

Niinimäki, K. (2015). Ethical foundations in sustainable fashion. *Textiles and Clothing Sustainability*, 1(1): 1.

Oh, H. J. (2002). Clothing involvement and clothing information source on personality types. *Journal of the Global Academy of Marketing Science*, 9(1): 1–17.

Pookulangara, S., Shephard, A., & Mestres, J. (2011). University community's perception of sweatshops: a mixed method data collection. *International Journal of Consumer Studies, 35*(4): 476–483.

Pookulangara, S., & Shepard, A. (2013). Slow fashion movement: Understanding consumer perceptions – An exploratory study. *Journal of Retailing and Consumer Services*, 20: 200–206.

Sharma, T. D., & Hall, C. (2010) *Green PLM for fashion & apparel.* White Paper, Infosys [online], retrieved from: http://www.infosys.com/industries/retail/white-papers/Documents/green-plm-fashion-apparel.pdf [accessed on: 01/02/2012].

Shen, B., Richards, J., & Liu, F. (2013). Consumers' awareness of sustainable fashion. *Marketing Management Journal*, 23(2): 134–147.

Textiles Exchange. (2015). *2014 organic cotton market report.* Textile Exchange [online], retrieved from: http://textileexchange.org/resource-center/media-room/2014-organic-cotton-report [accessed on: 15/01/2016].

Watson, M. Z., & Yan, R. N. (2013). An exploratory study of the decision processes of fast versus slow fashion consumers. *Journal of Fashion Marketing and Management*, 17(2): 141–159. doi: 10.1108/JFMM-02-2011-0045.

Weller, I. (2012). Marketing, brands and textile and fashion industry Sustainable consumption and production patterns in the clothing sector Is green the new black ?, in M. A. Gardetti & A. L. Torres (eds.) *Sustainability in Fashion and Textiles: Values, Design, Production and Consumption*, Chapter 11: 183–194, Greenleaf Publishing: Sheffield, UK.

Wigley, S. M., Goworek, H., Fisher, T., Cooper, T., Woodward, S., & Hiller, A. (2012). The sustainable clothing market: An evaluation of potential strategies for UK retailers. *International Journal of Retail and Distribution Management*, 40(12): 935–955. doi: 10.1108/09590551211274937.

Winge, T. M. (2008). 'Green is the new black': Celebrity chic and the 'green' commodity fetish. *Fashion Theory*, 12(4): 511–524.

WRAP (Waste & Resources Action Programme). (2012). *Valuing our clothes: The true cost of how we design, use and dispose of clothing in the UK.* WRAP [online], retrieved from: http://www.wrap.org.uk/sites/files/wrap/VoC%20FINAL%20online%202012%2007%2011.pdf [accessed on: 15/07/2013].

Yip, D., (2010). *What does sustainable fashion mean to you?* BC Living [online], retrieved from: http://www.bcliving.ca/style/what-does-sustainable-fashion-mean-to-you [accessed on: 21/09/2013].

Ms Zhen Lai is a marketing consultant for the internet industry. She has received a merit in her MSc International Management and Marketing from the University of Sheffield in 2015. Silver's Master dissertation focused on sustainability in the fashion industry. Her dissertation was entitled 'An exploration of consumers' perspective towards eco-labelling in the UK's fashion industry', for which she received a distinction.

Dr Claudia E. Henninger is a Lecturer in Fashion Marketing Management at the School of Materials, the University of Manchester. She was awarded her PhD entitled 'Corporate identity in the contexts of the UK's green slow-fashion industry and micro-organisations' from the University of Sheffield in 2015. Claudia's research centres on corporate marketing, sustainability, and green consumer typologies in the context of the fashion industry. She has published in leading journals, contributed to edited books, and presented her work at various national and international conferences. Claudia is the deputy chair of the Academy of Marketing SIG Sustainability.

Dr Panayiota J. Alevizou is a Lecturer in Marketing at University of Sheffield, UK, where she teaches Marketing Theory and Practice, and Retail and Services Marketing. She is the Programme Director of International Business and Management at the University of Sheffield Management School and a member of the Centre for Research in Marketing and Society (CReiMS). She is particularly interested in exploring consumer behaviour, company communication, and labelling strategies by means of qualitative methods. Panayiota is a fellow of the Higher Education Academy and worked as a marketing consultant in Greece.

6

Ethical Consumption Patterns and the Link to Purchasing Sustainable Fashion

Claudia E. Henninger and Pallavi Singh

6.1 Introduction

The fashion industry is based on fast changing consumer trends that – especially within the fast fashion sector – fosters hyper consumption and a need to be up-to-date at all times. Fast fashion is defined in terms of its production turnaround, whereby new collections are created every two weeks, they are mass-produced, affordable for the everyday consumer, and often mimic styles straight off the catwalk (Joy et al. 2012). The industrial revolution, which originated in the UK, has allowed for the fast fashion phenomenon to become a reality, with the invention of new technologies that cut down on working hours and enhanced production times, as well as reducing overall manufacturing costs. The latter aspect is further

C.E. Henninger (✉)
School of Materials, University of Manchester, Manchester, UK
e-mail: Claudia.Henninger@manchester.ac.uk

P. Singh
Sheffield Hallam University, Sheffield, UK
e-mail: P.Singh@shu.ac.uk

C.E. Henninger et al. (eds.), *Sustainability in Fashion*,
DOI 10.1007/978-3-319-51253-2_6

enhanced with the ability to outsource garment production plants to low labour cost countries, such as Bangladesh, Cambodia, and Myanmar (e.g. ILO 2014; Barrie 2015). These low labour costs however, come at a high price – paid by factory workers, who not only work long, unsocial hours, but also work in unsafe environments. The Rana Plaza factory collapse in 2013 saw thousands lose their lives. This is only one example of many tragedies clouding the fashion industry (Parveen 2014).

Against this bleak backdrop a relatively new movement has taken a prevalent role in the industry – the slow fashion 'movement'. Slow fashion is based on sustainable values, thereby taking into account social, environmental, and economic aspects that seek to reduce the overall impact the fashion industry has on the (natural) environment. The slow fashion concept can best be described in terms of having a conscience (Friedman 2010; Liggett 2010), slowing down the production and product life cycle, utilising renewable materials and local resources (Johnston 2012), and showing a commitment to traditional production techniques (Friedman 2010). Although similar to fast fashion, slow fashion can be trendy and 'fashionable', yet it is not trend led, which implies that garments are designed to have a 'classic' style that does not go in and out of season. Moreover, slow fashion collections are released either biannually or at a maximum of four times a year, thus, dramatically decrease the speed of the fashion production cycle (e.g. Fletcher 2008).

The slow fashion 'movement' has not only changed the industry landscape but also brought forward new terminology, such as organic, ethical, sustainable, or eco-fashion, which are often used interchangeably within the academic literature. Baroness Young of Hornsey further highlights in a parliamentary speech that sustainable fashion is:

> [A]bout so much more than the clothes we wear. It may be an expression of our professional and personal identities, [. . .] about where we see ourselves in relation to our peer group, or cultures, our families, our communities, an expression of creativity. [. . .] However consciously we do it, as we dress, we make a statement. (BBC Democracy 2013)

The phrase 'we make a statement' (BBC Democracy 2013) holds even truer for sustainable fashion, a concept that in itself is relatively new and thus far, no common definition has emerged. Whilst some describe sustainable fashion as an oxymoron – with the fashion industry being one of the most polluting industries – others see it as the future for innovation (e.g. BSR 2012).

6.2 The Rise of Sustainability in the Fashion Industry and Aspects of Ethical Consumption

The sustainable fashion movement has led to organisations changing their initial practices to incorporate an enhanced emphasise on sustainability (Black 2008). Fashion organisations are increasingly producing fashion collections that are characterised by the following attributes:

(a) The use of renewable and/or non-harmful materials (Chen and Burns 2006; Poole et al. 2009);
(b) The use of low-impact processes (Allwood et al. 2008; Poole et al. 2009);
(c) The promotion of reused/recycled waste materials (Joergens 2006; Fletcher 2008; Poole et al. 2009).

Yet the supply side in form of fashion organisations are not the only stakeholder groups that have adapted to the changing environment. Consumers are now demanding more environmentally friendly products, as well as show a positive incline to purchase garments that are more eco-innovative in their design (Gam and Banning 2011). This concern is not a new phenomenon, but rather has emerged in the early 1960s when environmental concerns took centre stage. In the 1960s when *eco* and *green* fashion emerged dominantly in the market, these garments had a negative connotation and were described as hippie, tie-dyed, and alternative clothing, not suited for the mainstream consumer (e.g. Brown 2011).

As previously highlighted factory accidents created an unfavourable spotlight on the fashion industry and led to a public outcry for more socially responsible practices to be introduced within the industry as a whole. A question that emerges is whether this public outcry had effects on consumer behaviour and consumers' ethical consumption patterns. Ethical consumption in this chapter is defined in terms of consumers making a conscious, more responsible choice when purchasing products (Adams and Raisborough 2010). The twenty-first century has seen a change in attitude towards sustainability, with the food sector leading the way of fostering local production and educating consumers on ethical and organic alternatives that are available for purchase. The slow fashion movement derived from the slow food movement, thus, it seeks to educate consumers on ideally reducing their consumption behaviour or at least making a conscious choice of purchasing garments and accessories that have been produced in a more 'sustainable' manner (compared to their counterparts) (Jung and Jin 2014). Yet purchasing ethical alternatives has not necessarily translated into the fashion industry, where the ethical clothing market remains underdeveloped (e.g. Lipson 2008; Mintel 2009). To explain, although consumers are more familiar with 'sustainability', as the food industry has made a head start in educating consumers about ethical, organic, and more consciously sourced produce, this thus far, has had either no or little impact on consumers changing their unsustainable consumption patterns (e.g. De Palsmaker et al. 2005).

Extant research indicates that although consumers have shown greater concern for ethical issues in the fashion industry, their ethical decision-making does not necessarily translate into action, which links to the attitude-behaviour gap identified in the literature (e.g. Szmigin et al. 2009; Carrington et al. 2010; Markkula and Moisander 2012). 'When it comes to fashion purchase, the majority of consumers are more interested in their own personal fashion needs than the needs of others involved in the apparel supply chain' (Joergens 2006, p. 369). Only if consumers believe that the price displayed on a garment reflects the benefits associated with the item of clothing, they (consumers) are willing to pay a premium (e.g. O'Cass and Choy 2008). However, if consumers feel they are sacrificing too much monetarily, ecological/green concerns are secondary considerations, and given less importance than, for example, the price and aesthetics of the product (Yan et al. 2012; Fottrell 2013). This implies that there is a clear attitude-behaviour gap in consumer's decision-making process (e.g. Carrigan and Attalla

2001; Carrington et al. 2010; Markkula and Moisander 2012). Whilst this aspect is not new, but rather a variety of key authors have dedicated their attention to the attitude-behaviour gap (e.g. Carrigan and Attalla 2001; Carrington et al. 2014), what thus far has not been researched is whether a consumer who consumes ethically is classifying themselves as being ethical and whether ethical associations are translated into the purchase of clothing. Yet, it was highlighted that age may have an effect on ethical decision-making within the fashion context, thus our proposition is:

> Older consumer are more likely to classify their purchasing behaviour as ethical, and thus, consider themselves as ethical consumers. It is further proposed that gender and work status may have an impact on consumers identifying themselves as ethical consumers.

Extant research (e.g. Young et al. 2010; Sudbury-Riley and Kohlbacher 2016) has focused on either creating a typology of ethical/green consumers, thereby categorising them according to their shopping behaviour and values, or by providing new scales to measure in how far consumers are ethical based on their consumption choices. Within the fashion industry these decisions could be further influenced, as consumers become increasingly knowledgeable about the effects garment manufacturing has on the natural, social, and economic environment. Mirza (2004) and Joergens (2006) point out that young consumers account for the majority of sustainable fashion shoppers, which might be due to the fact that aspects of sustainability are increasingly taught at schools and gain prominence on video and traditional blogs. Moreover, since the economic downturn in 2008 the UK high street as seen the emergence of more independent and local shops (Carven 2010), advertising the 'home-grown, patriotic, and heritage' feel of the UK fashion industry. Although the whole fashion industry cannot be brought back to the UK, individual designers and various small- and medium-sized enterprises actively seek to re-introduce the seamstress job into society and bring back parts of the British fashion heritage. Local production is costly, yet TV series, such as Mary Portas' Mary Queen of Shops, has brought attention to smaller businesses and the need to support these shops to revive the high street. The *locally made* aspect is strongly linked to slow fashion and sustainability, as it focuses on the social aspect of creating a good working environment, paying fair wages, and looking after employees. Although these stores (independent and local) have increased in popularity, thus far they lack further investigations especially from the perspective of linking independent shops and ethical consumer behaviour. In other words, whilst instructive past research fails to clearly highlight who sustainable fashion consumers are and whether they associate shopping at local and independent shops fosters aspects of sustainable development, which is investigated in this chapter.

H1: There is a positive relationship between consumers, who classify themselves as ethical consumers, prefer shopping at independent shops, and support local designers.

H1.1: There is a positive relationship between consumers, who classify themselves as ethical consumers, prefer shopping at local shops, and shop in independent stores.

This chapter contributes to knowledge by investigation whether there is a link between ethical consumption patterns and purchasing sustainable fashion.

6.3 Methodology

6.3.1 Sample and Procedure

The sample for this study constitutes of consumers, who shop in independent shops, in two major Northern cities in the UK, which predominantly sell female fashion clothing and accessories, as well as children's wear. Both stores that gained the researchers access to their consumer base claim that they produce sustainable fashion items, which are created, designed, and manufactured by local designers and makers. To capture a wide age range, paper-based questionnaires were distributed to collect responses from consumers in both shops.

Altogether the researchers gained 302 usable questionnaires, which were completed in-store with the researchers present to clarify any issues participants have had. Consumers partaking in this research were aged between 18 and 66+ and were distributed across the age brackets as follows: 18–21 years: 19.9%, 22–29 years: 35.8%, 30–40 years: 19.2%, 41–55 years: 17.2%, 56–65 years: 6%, and 66+years: 2%. This indicates that the majority of consumers partaking in this research fall into the 22–29 years age bracket. The majority of respondents were female (81.1%), which can be explained due to the fact that these two shops specialise in female and children's wear. Data indicate that a majority of participants were in full-time employment (42.5%), with 11.3% being part-time employed, 10.3% being self-employed, 27% being students, 5% being retired, and 2.3% being currently unemployed.

6.3.2 Measures

The questionnaire utilised for this study was based on existing, validated surveys, which were conducted by the Ethical Fashion Source (EFS), a key organisation in the slow fashion industry between 2009 and 2011. The EFS survey focused on the consumers' awareness of sustainability in the fashion industry (e.g. Levell 2010; Marsh 2012). This research's survey was divided into three key sections: Section 1 provides an overview of various different product aspects/attributes that people deem important when shopping for clothes, which help to gain an understanding of the customers and their needs. The questionnaire used a 5-point Likert scale ranging from very unimportant to very important to measure consumer responses. Section 2 provides an overview of sustainable fashion in more general terms and seeks to gain an understanding of consumers' perceptions of sustainable fashion, slow fashion terminology, and high street versus independent shopping, as well as aspects of supporting local designers. Again, a 5-point Likert scale was utilised to measure responses, which ranged from strongly disagree to strongly agree. Section 3 was designed to collect demographic data from consumers completing the questionnaire, such as gender, age, and work status.

Single item scales were constructed to check if consumers prefer to shop at independent shops or high street shops and if they consider themselves as ethical consumers. Respondents were asked to indicate their agreement on a 5-point Likert scale ranging from strongly disagree to strongly agree. To measure different factors affecting consumers' attitude towards ethical clothing purchase several single item measures were constructed. These factors were identified through an extensive literature review and extant research. Factors utilised to measure the effect they have on consumers' attitudes towards purchasing ethical clothing are: price, quality, availability, trust in ethical claims, tendency to support local designers by purchasing their products, and clarity of the term ethical/sustainable fashion. A 5-point Likert scale was utilised to measure the consumers' responses, by showing their agreement/disagreement to the statements made.

6.3.3 Validity and Reliability

Although the questionnaire for this study is based on a past survey conducted through the EFS, the scales have been validated again for this research. Content and construct validity were ensured by asking 10 experts working within the field of sustainable fashion to comment on the items and rate them according to the items' ability to measure the factors (Howard 2008). A factor analysis was conducted to ensure that all items measure different factors and to ensure discriminant validity of these items.

6.3.4 Analysis and Results

A Classification and Regression Tree analysis (CRT) was conducted to identify the demographic profiling of the ethical consumers and those shopping in independent shops. Further, a correlation analysis was conducted followed by multiple regression analysis to test the propositions made in the previous section.

The proposition posits that older consumers are more likely to classify their garment purchases as ethical. Figure 6.1 shows that age is a significant determinant of the ethical consumers profile within this specific data set. Figure 6.2 clearly highlights that 32.1% of respondents strongly agree with the statement *'I consider myself an ethical consumer'* within the two older age brackets (30–40 and 41–66 years), whereas only 14.3% of respondents in the younger age brackets (18–21 and 22–29 years) classify themselves as ethical consumers. Thus, the proposition posed in this chapter is partially supported, as age emerged as the most important determinant of classifying oneself as an ethical consumer. However, the decision tree did not identify work status and gender as significant determinants of the profile of consumers, who identify themselves as being ethical. Thus, it is concluded that gender and work status do not contribute to profiling determinants for identifying as ethical consumers for this data set.

To further test the profile of people, who prefer shopping at independent shops, a CRT was constructed that looks at gender, age, and work status as profiling variables.

Figure 6.2 identifies age is the most important predictor within the CRT. Figure 6.2 clearly shows that people within the older age brackets (30–40 and 41–66 years) prefer shopping in independent shops, with more than 65.7% strongly agreeing with the statement *'I prefer shopping in independent shops compared to high street shops'*. Similarly, younger respondents within the age brackets of 18–21 and 22–29 years also showed a positive attitude towards shopping in independent shops with 56% of respondents strongly agreeing with the statement of preferring to shop in independent versus high street shops. The second strongest determinant that emerged from the data set is work status. Respondents in either full-time or part-time employment and students indicated that they prefer to shop in independent stores (69.9%), whilst those that are retired or unemployed do not have a strong affinity to do so. The results show a partial support of the proposition made in this chapter, in that age and work status affect whether consumers shop at independent stores, yet gender did not emerge as a profiling determinant.

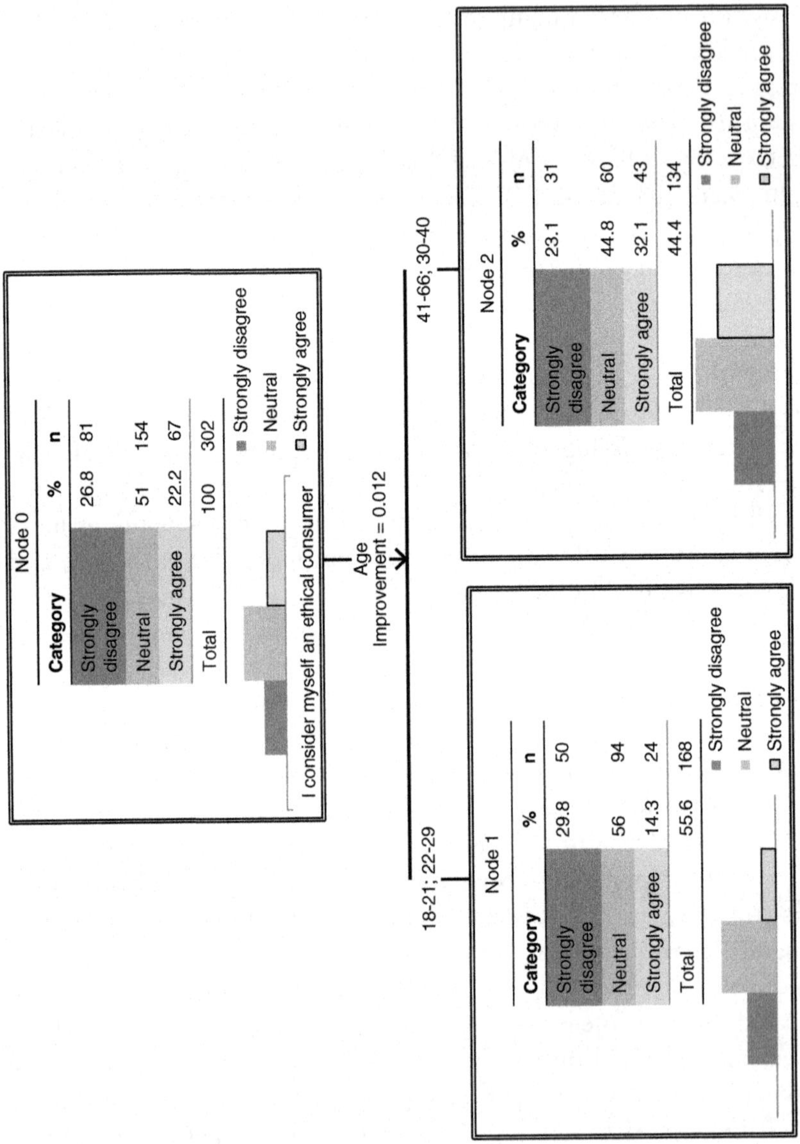

Fig. 6.1 CRT – profiling ethical consumers

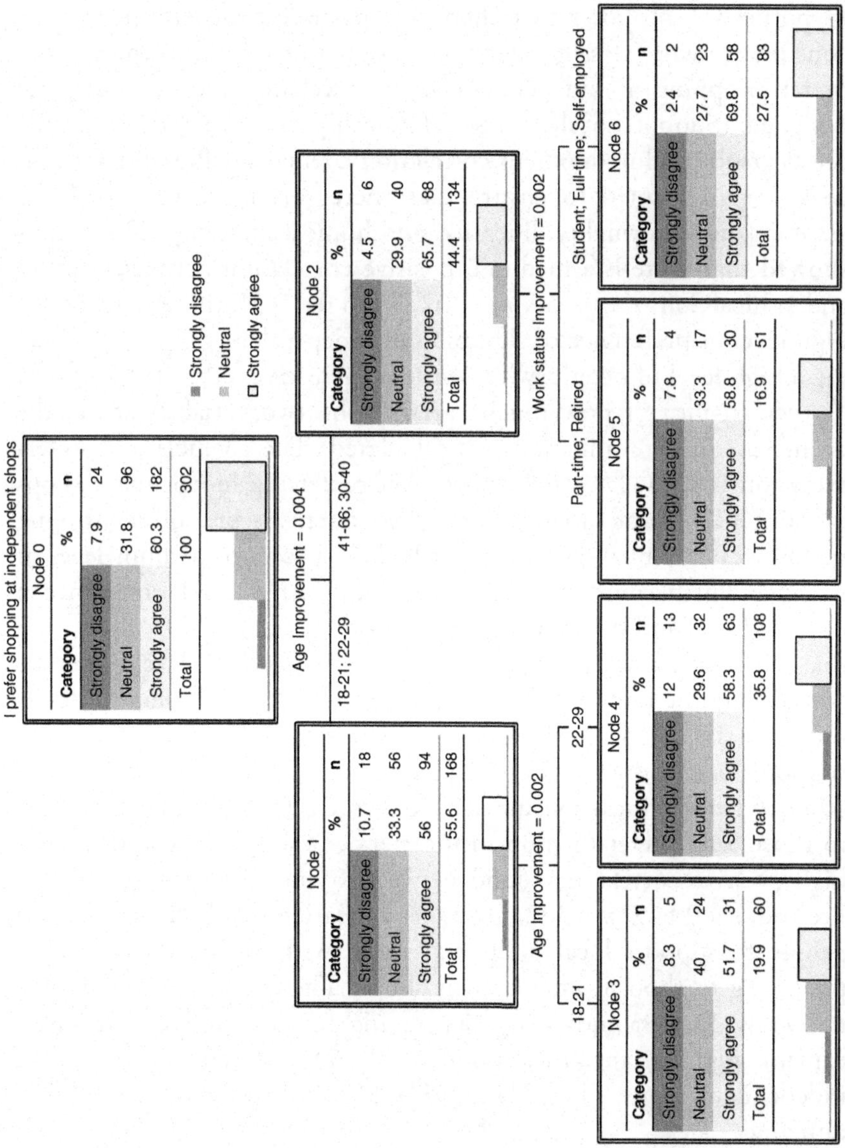

Fig. 6.2 CRT – profiling people, who prefer to shop at independent shops

6.3.5 Hypotheses Testing

Hypothesis 1 proposes that there is a positive relationship between consumers, who classify themselves as being ethical (EthicalCon), prefer shopping at independent shops (PrefInd) and support local designers (SupportLocal). These relationships were investigated using the Pearson product moment correlation coefficient. Preliminary analysis was performed to ensure that there was no violation of the assumption of normality, linearity, and homoscedasticity. The output showed that there is a medium, positive correlation between PrefInd and EthicalCon, $r = 0.368$, $n = 302$, $p < 0.01$, with those that show a high level of preference of shopping in independent shops also showing a high level of people, who consider themselves ethical consumers. To get an idea of how much variance the two variables share, the coefficient of determination was calculated. The coefficient of determination is 13.54%, which shows that preferring independent shops explains 13.54% of variance in the respondents' scores on identifying themselves as ethical consumers, which is a low to medium level of variance. Furthermore, there is a medium positive correlation between SupportLocal and EthicalCon, $r = 0.334$, $n = 302$, $p < 0.01$, indicating that a high tendency to SupportLocal relates to a high level of people considering themselves as ethical consumers. The coefficient of determination is 11.15%, which shows that respondents, who seek to support local designers only explains 11.15% of variance in their score on being ethical consumers. This score is low even in comparison to those who prefer to shop in independent shops. Again, there is a high positive correlation found between trying to SupportLocal and PrefInd, $r = 0.567$, $n = 302$, $p < 0.01$, indicating that high tendency in people to support local designers relates with high level of people preferring to shop in independent shops. The coefficient of determination is 32.14% indicating that trying to support local designers explains high variance in respondents' score in preferring to shop in independent shops. Thus, H1 and H1.1 are supported by the research outcomes.

The correlation analysis shows a positive correlation between the three variables: PrefInd, SupportLocal, and EthicalCon. Although correlation is a useful analysis tool, it does not show any indication of causality and predictive ability of these variables. To test the causality relationship between these variables multiple regression analysis was conducted. A preliminary analysis to ensure no violation of the assumptions of normality, linearity, multicollinearity, and homoscedasticity was undertaken prior to running the linear regression analysis. The hypothesis to test the causal relationship is presented below.

H2: Being an ethical consumer is significantly predicted by PrefInd and SupportLocal.

The total variance explained by the model as a whole was 15.9% $p < 0.001$, shown in Table 6.1.

Table 6.2 shows the coefficient analysis. From Table 6.2 it becomes apparent that both the predictors have a low influence on the dependent variable. Yet, the most dominant one to emerge is *'prefer to shop in independent shop'* ($\beta_{std} = 0.263$, $p < 0.001$, part correlation = 0.216), whereas *'try to support local'* ($\beta_{std} = 0.186$, $p = 0.004$, part correlation = 0.153) contributes less. Calculating the relative contribution of the predictors *'prefer shopping in independent shops'* explains 4.6% variance and *'try to support local'* explains 2.3% variance of the total R^2 of the model. The weak R^2 value of the model indicates that there may be some other variables predicting respondents considering themselves as ethical.

Table 6.1 Regression analysis with EthicalCon as dependent variable

Model summary[a]				
Model	R	R^2	Adjusted R^2	Std. Error of the estimate
1	0.398[b]	0.159	0.153	0.724

[a]Dependent Variable: I consider myself an ethical consumer.
[b]Predictors: (Constant), prefer shopping at independent shops rather than high-street shops, I try to support local designers by purchasing their products.

Table 6.2 Coefficient analysis with EthicalCon as dependent variable

	Coefficients[a]												
		Unstandardised coefficients		Standardised coefficients			95.0% Confidence interval for B		Correlations			Collinearity statistics	
	Model	B	Std. Error	Beta	*t*	Sig.	Lower bound	Upper bound	Zero-order	Partial	Part	Tolerance	VIF
1	(Constant)	1.438	0.209		6.875	0.000	1.026	1.849					
	I try to support local designers by purchasing their products	0.179	0.062	0.186	2.884	0.004	0.057	0.302	0.334	0.165	0.153	0.679	1.473
	Prefer shopping at independent shops rather than High Street Shops	0.228	0.056	0.263	4.080	0.000	0.118	0.338	0.368	0.230	0.216	0.679	1.473

[a]Dependent Variable: I consider myself an ethical consumer

Table 6.3 Regression analysis with PrefInd as dependent variable – model summary

Model Summary[a]				
Model	R	R^2	Adjusted R^2	Std. error of the estimate
1	0.597[b]	0.357	0.352	0.728

[a]Dependent Variable: prefer shopping at independent shops rather than high-street shops.
[b]Predictors: (Constant), I consider myself an ethical consumer, I try to support local designers by purchasing their products.

H3: Preferring to shop at independent shops is significantly predicted by EthicalCon and SupportLocal.

The total variance explained by the model as a whole was 35.7%, $p < 0.001$ (Table 6.3), which shows a good fit.

Table 6.4 shows that the coefficient of the regression analysis brings forward mixed results. Not all predictors have high influence on the dependent variable. The most important predictor emerging from the data set is *'try to support local designers'* ($\beta_{std} = 0.499$, $p < 0.001$, part correlation = 0.471), whereas the second variable *'I consider myself as ethical consumer'* ($\beta_{std} = 0.201$, $p < 0.001$, part correlation = 0.189) contributes less.

Calculating the relative contribution of the predictors *'try to support local designers'* explains 22.18% variance and *'consider myself as ethical consumer'* explains 3.5% variance being ethical consumer, which shows that supporting local designers is a much stronger predictor and contributes more in the R^2 value.

6.4 Discussion

This chapter was laid out to investigate two key aspects: first, to demographically profile the consumers who classify themselves as being ethical and/or who shop in independent shops, and second, to explore in how far

Table 6.4 Coefficient table of regression with PrefInd as dependent variable

Coefficients[a]

Model		Unstandardised coefficients		Standardised coefficients			95.0% confidence interval for B		Correlations			Collinearity statistics	
		B	Std. error	Beta	t	Sig.	Lower bound	Upper bound	Zero-order	Partial	Part	Tolerance	VIF
1	(Constant)	0.987	0.219		4.504	0.000	0.556	1.418					
	I try to support local designers by purchasing their products	0.555	0.055	0.499	10.146	0.000	0.447	0.663	0.567	0.506	0.471	0.888	1.126
	I consider myself an ethical consumer	0.231	0.057	0.201	4.080	0.000	0.120	0.343	0.368	0.230	0.189	0.888	1.126

[a]Dependent Variable: prefer shopping at independent shops rather than high-street shops.

consumers, who identify themselves as ethical, shop at independent shops and support local designers. The results clearly highlighted that age is a major determinant and predicator that profiles people, who consider themselves to be ethical, as well as those who shop in independent shops. The latter was further determined by work status.

Our research has highlighted that older consumers are more likely to consider themselves as being ethical, compared to the younger generation. An explanation that can be provided for this finding is the fact that younger consumers are more involved with aspects of sustainability in the fashion industry and do not necessarily feel that their actions are satisfactory enough to classify themselves as being ethical (e.g. Kagawa 2007; Hill and Lee 2012). Similarly, extant research (e.g. Joergens 2006; Pookulangara and Shepard 2013; Jung and Jin 2014) indicates that younger consumers are predominantly trend-driven, which implies that they prefer to shop at high street retailer and purchase the newest fashion garments on offer, rather than considering ethical aspects in their decision-making process. Future research could investigate when the behavioural shift from being trend-driven to preferring sustainable choices happens. We further found that older consumers are more inclined to shop at independent fashion shops, compared to the younger generation. The literature indirectly concurs with this notion by highlighting that independent and/or local shops are seen to support the community (e.g. Smith and Sparks 2000). This aspect has become prevalent since the credit crisis hit the UK market in 2008 and the high street landscape has seen a dramatic change with independent retailers emerging strongly (Carven 2010).

The second most prominent factor that characterises the demographic profile of consumers shopping at independent shops is work status. People, who are self-employed, in full-time employment, or study for a degree in higher education are most likely to shop in independent stores. This finding extends extant research and contributes to knowledge by clearly being able to profile, who these consumers are that prefer shopping in independent shops. This finding could have managerial implications, as it allows owner-managers of these stores to target their audience more specifically. To explain, students and those in full-time employment may have different financial capabilities and disposable income, thus, lower price ranges may appeal to students, whilst exclusive and premium price garments may appeal to those with full-time employment. Moreover, knowing their target market enables owner-managers to gear their marketing communication messages better to their audience. Those consumers, who may not necessarily be concerned with ethical and/or sustainable issues could be integrated in the consumer pool, by providing a product range that is appealing to a wider audience.

A further objective of this chapter was to investigate the relationship between people's preference of purchasing garments in independent shops and their personal associations and identification of being ethical consumers. As highlighted in the literature review, typologies of ethical consumers have been well researched and common characteristics have been identified (e.g. Young et al. 2010; Sudbury-Riley and Kohlbacher 2016). Within the food industry, ethical and organic choices are well established, with the fashion industry slowly establishing themselves within the 'slow movement' (e.g. Joergens 2006; Jung and Jin 2014). With local and independent shops becoming a common occurrence on the high street, investigating the relationship between ethical consumer behaviour and shopping at local and independent stores attracts attention. We found that the correlation and regression analysis point towards consumers, who shop in independent stores do consider themselves to be ethical. Yet, consumers who classify themselves as ethical do not necessarily prefer independent shops, as the correlation and regression analysis only show a weak correlation. These results have various implications: first, consumers, who shop in independent shops could be seen as ethical, as they support individual designers/makers rather than mass-produced garments, thereby following deep rooted aspects of social sustainability. Second, consumers, who shop locally and or independently actively contribute to ethical consumption behaviour. Our research findings imply that consumers do not seem to be aware that their actions of supporting local and independent shops could be classified as being ethical. This suggests that thus far, there seems to be a lack of communication and education to clearly highlight the beneficial aspects of shopping and supporting local and independent shops especially in the fashion industry.

Our results further indicate that consumers, who support local designers, prefer shopping in independent shops. Our research suggests that these people have a strong affiliation with the local aspect and are proud of the heritage that stands behind local production. Yet, these consumers do not seem to make a connection between being ethical and shopping locally. This finding is interesting, as extant research highlights that consumers, who shop for food, are aware that local production and small independent shops implies contributing to the local community and fostering ethical consumption. However, this link is not yet rooted in the fashion industry, which indicates that retailers need to enhance their communication and make stronger alignments between the fashion and food industry, by learning from the latter. This result contributes not only to our current knowledge of ethical consumers and their decision-making process/ethical choices, but also provides an insight into how to communicate ethical consumption within the fashion industry, by revising current promotion strategies and policies.

6.5 Conclusion

This chapter was laid out to investigate ethical consumption patterns and the link to purchasing sustainable fashion. The questionnaire data collected allowed profiling consumers, who identify themselves as being ethical or who prefer to shop at independent shops through the CTR analysis. Age emerged as a major determinant, with work status further providing an indication on whether consumers are shopping at independent shops. This has wider managerial and practical implications, as the profiling process provides shop owners with a better understanding of whom their target audience is. Identifying those that shop in store will make it easier to send out targeted messages through age appropriate channels, such as offline communication (e.g. newspaper, magazine) or online communications (e.g. Twitter, Facebook). Moreover, the findings indicate that especially younger consumers do not necessarily describe themselves as ethical consumers. Thus, communicating buzzwords, such as ethical, sustainable, or organic could potential alienate this target segment. On the other hand, older consumers are more inclined to identify themselves with ethical consumer characteristics, thus, advertising messages could feature 'ethical' terminology, thereby making the store in itself more attractive.

References

Adams, M., & Rainsborough, J. (2010). Making a difference: Ethical consumption and the everyday. *British Journal of Sociology, 61*(2): 256–274.

Allwood, J. M., Laursen, S. E., Russell, S. N., De Rodrıquez, C. M., & Bocken, N. M. P. (2008). An approach to scenario analysis of the sustainability of an industrial sector applied to clothing and textiles in the UK. *Journal of Cleaner Production, 16*: 633–638.

Barrie, L. (2015). *Sourcing: Low labour cost countries linked to highest risks*. Just-Style (online), retrieved: http://www.just-style.com/analysis/low-labour-cost-countries-linked-to-highest-risks_id124482.aspx, accessed: 13/08/2016.

BBC Democracy. (2013). *Peers urge support for sustainable fashion*. BBC (online), 20 March 2013, retrieved: http://www.bbc.co.uk/democracylive/house-of-lords-21850300, accessed: 05/07/2013.

Black, S. (2008). *Eco-chic: The fashion paradox*. Black Dog Publishing Limited: London.

Brown, S. (2011). *Future factory: Sass Brown is coming to NTU*. Future Factory (online), retrieved: http://futurefactory.weebly.com/live-event-streams.html, accessed: 20/03/2012.

BSR (Business of a Better World). (2012). *Sustainable fashion design: Oxymoron no more?*, BSR *(online)*, retrieved: http://www.bsr.org/reports/BSR_Sustainable_Fashion_Design.pdf, accessed: 05/07/2013.

Carrigan, M., & Attalla, A. (2001). The myth of the ethical consumer – Do ethics matter in purchase behavior? *Journal of Consumer Marketing, 18*(7): 560–577.

Carrington, M. J., Neville, B. A., & Whitwell, G. J. (2010). Why ethical consumers don't walk their talk: Towards a framework for understanding the gap between the ethical purchase intentions and actual buying behaviour of ethically minded consumers. *Journal of Business Ethics, 97*: 139–158.

Carrington, M.J., Neville, B. A., & Whitwell, G. J. (2014). Lost in translation: Exploring the ethical consumer intention-behaviour gap. *Journal of Business Research, 67*: 2759–2767.

Carven, N. (2010). *Britain's independent high street shopping boom: Extra 10,000 retailers launch in 'biggest revival' since the 2008 crash*. Mail on Sunday (online), retrieved: http://www.thisismoney.co.uk/money/news/article-2888614/10-000-retailers-launch-boomtime-Britain.html, accessed: 29/08/2016.

Chen, H.-L., & Burns, L. D. (2006). Environmental analysis of textile products. *Clothing and Textile Research Journal, 24*: 248–261.

De Pelsmacker, P., Driesen, L., & Rayp, G. (2005). Do consumers care about ethics? Willingness to pay for fair-trade coffee. *Journal of Consumer Affairs, 39*(2): 363–385.

Fletcher, K. (2008). *Sustainable Fashion and Textiles Design Journeys*. Earthscan: London, UK.

Fottrell, Q. (2013). *Would you pay more for fair-trade socks? – Why shoppers don't care about Bangladesh*, Marketwatch (online), retrieved: http://www.marketwatch.com/story/why-shoppers-dont-care-about-bangladesh-2013-05-14, accessed: 28/01/2014.

Friedman, V. (2010). *Sustainable fashion: what does green mean?*, Financial Times (online), 4 February 2010, retrieved: http://www.ft.com/cms/s/2/2b27447e-11e4-11df-b6e3-00144feab49a.html#axzz1z1DRM8Y9, accessed: 27/06/2012.

Gam, H. J., & Banning, J. (2011). Addressing Sustainable Apparel Design Challenges With Problem-Based Learning. *Clothing & Textiles Research Journal, 29*(3): 202–215.

Hill, J., & Lee, H. H. (2012). Young generation y consumers' perceptions of sustainability in the apparel industry. *Journal of Fashion Marketing Management, 16*(4): 477–491.

Howard, K. (2008). *Validating Questionnaires*, Kestrel Consultants Inc. (online), retrieved: http://kestrelconsultants.com/reference_files/Validating_Questionnaires.pdf, accessed: 28/02/2013.

ILO (International Labour Organization). (2014). *Wages and working hours in the textiles, clothing, leather and footwear industries*. ILO (Online), retrieved: http://www.ilo.org/wcmsp5/groups/public/@ed_dialogue/@sector/documents/publication/wcms_300463.pdf, accessed: 13/08/2016.

Joergens, C. (2006). Ethical fashion: Myth or future trend? *Journal of Fashion Marketing and Management, 10*: 360–371.

Johnston, A. (2012). *The first steps towards considerate design incorporating Cradle to Cradle principles*. London: College of Fashion (online), retrieved: http://innovatingsustainablefashion.files.wordpress.com/2012/07/cradle-to-cradle_copenhagen_final_small.pdf, accessed: 05/07/2013.

Joy, A., Sherry, J. F., Venkatesh, A., Wand, J., & Chan, R. (2012). Fast fashion, sustainability, and the ethical appeal of luxury brands. *Fashion Theory, 16*(3): 273–296.

Jung, S., & Jin, B. (2014). A theoretical investigation of slow fashion: Sustainable future of the apparel industry. *International Journal of Consumer Studies, 38*: 510–519.

Kagawa, F. (2007). Dissonance in students' perceptions of sustainable development and sustainability: Implications for curriculum change. *International Journal of Sustainability, 8*(3): 317–338.

Levell, K. (2010) *Ethical Fashion Survey*, Ethical Fashion Forum (online), retrieved: https://spreadsheets.google.com/a/sheffield.ac.uk/viewform?formkey=dHVvb2lnbFZ2cWs3Z0VBNFNLM0E0b0E6MA, accessed: 28/02/2013.

Liggett, B. (2010). *How do you define 'Sustainable Fashion', Exactly?*, Ecouterre (online), retrieved: http://www.ecouterre.com/how-do-you-define-sustainable-fashion-exactly/, accessed: 15/07/2012.

Lipson, E. (2008). *International market for sustainable apparel.* Packaged Facts: Rockville, MD.

Markkula, A., & Moisander, J. (2012). Discursive confusion over sustainable consumption: A discursive perspective on the perplexity of marketplace knowledge. *Journal of Consumer Policy, 35*(1): 105–125.

Marsh, P. C. (2012). *Consumer awareness of sustainability – A survey*, Ethical Fashion Source (online), retrieved: http://source.ethicalfashionforum.com/digital/consumer-awareness-of-fashion-and-sustainability-a-survey, accessed: 28/07/2013.

Mintel. (2009). *Ethical Clothing – UK- Feb 2009.* Mintel: London, UK.

Mirza, K. (2004). *Is green this season's colour?*, Drapers, November 13: 21–22.

O'Cass, A., & Choy, E. (2008). Studying Chinese Generation Y consumers' involvement in fashion clothing and perceived brand status. *Journal of Product and Brand Management, 17*(5): 341–352.

Parveen, S. (2014). *Rana Plaza factory collapse survivors struggle one year on*, BBC (online), retrieved: http://www.bbc.co.uk/news/world-asia-27107860, accessed: 06/08/2014.

Pookulangara, S., & Shepard, A. (2013). Slow fashion movement: Understanding consumer perceptions – an exploratory study. *Journal of Retailing and Consumer Services, 20*: 200–206.

Poole, A. J., Church, J. S., & Huson, M. G. (2009). Environmentally sustainable fibers from regenerated Protein. *Biomacromolecules, 10*: 1–8.

Smith, A., & Sparks, L. (2000). The role and function of the independent small shop: the situation in Scotland. *The International Review of Retail, Distribution, and Consumer Research, 10*(2): 205–226.

Sudbury-Riley, L., & Kohlbacher, F. (2016). Ethically minded consumer behaviour: Scale review, development, and validation. *Journal of Business Research, 69*(8): 2697–2710.

Szmigin, I., Carrigan, M., & McEachern, M. G. (2009). The conscious consumer: Taking a flexible approach to ethical behaviour. *International Journal of Consumer Studies, 33*: 224–231.

Yan, R.-N., Hyllegard, K. H., & Blaesi, L. F. (2012). Marketing eco-fashion: The influence of brand name and message explicitness. *Journal of Marketing Communication, 18*(2): 151–168.

Young, W., Hwang, K., McDonald, S., & Oates, C. J. (2010). Sustainable consumption: green consumer behavior when purchasing products. *Sustainable Development, 18*(1): 20–31.

Dr Claudia E Henninger is a Lecturer in Fashion Marketing Management at the School of Materials, the University of Manchester. She was awarded her PhD entitled 'Corporate identity in the contexts of the UK's green slow-fashion industry and micro-organisations' from the University of Sheffield in 2015. Claudia's research centres on corporate marketing, sustainability, and green consumer typologies in the context of the fashion industry. She has published in leading journals, contributed to edited books, and presented her work at various national and international conferences. Claudia is the deputy chair of the Academy of Marketing SIG Sustainability.

Dr Pallavi Singh is a Senior Lecturer in Marketing at Sheffield Business School, Sheffield Hallam University, Sheffield, UK. Before commencing her academic career, she was a Civil Servant in India. She obtained her PhD in Ethical Marketing from University of Sheffield Management School, Sheffield, UK; her MBA in Marketing also from University of Sheffield Management School (SUMS) UK; her Masters in Hindi Literature (Silver Medallist) and her Bachelors in Physics from the prestigious University of Allahabad in India. Her research interest includes environmental education in schools, and higher education institutions, sustainable consumption in families, socialization theory, green consumer behaviour, and child influence in family purchase decision-making. Her work has been presented at the Academy of Marketing

Conference, World Environmental Education Congress and many more conferences across Asia and Europe. She is a reviewer with number of publications like the *Journal of Consumer Behaviour, South Asian Journal of Global Business Research*, and *Journal of Consumer Ethics*. She serves as consultant for social businesses, charity organisations, and not for profit organisations.

7

Determining Effective Sustainable Fashion Communication Strategies

Sara Li-Chou Han, Claudia E. Henninger, Phoebe Apeagyei and David Tyler

7.1 Introduction

On a daily average a consumer is exposed to over 3,500 marketing messages, of which only a small number of actual adverts and products/services can be recalled without prompting (Gibson 2005). This has various implications: first, a majority of messages are lost and do not reach the intended audience. Second, there is an information overflow, which makes it challenging to design an advert that has an impact in terms of being recalled. Third, consumers will only notice messages that are relevant to them. Thus, to increase the efficacy of product and brand recall and overcome challenges faced with information overload,

S.L.-C. Han (✉) · P. Apeagyei · D. Tyler
Manchester Fashion Institute, Arts and Humanities,
Manchester Metropolitan University, Manchester, UK
e-mail: S.Han@mmu.ac.uk; P.Apeagyei@mmu.ac.uk; D.Tyler@mmu.ac.uk

C.E. Henninger
School of Materials, The University of Manchester, Manchester, UK
e-mail: Claudia.Henninger@manchester.ac.uk

C.E. Henninger et al. (eds.), *Sustainability in Fashion*,
DOI 10.1007/978-3-319-51253-2_7

fashion companies seek to broadcast their core values through a variety of channels; such as flickering billboards, web pop-ups, social media messages, in-store communication, magazine adverts, A-boards, and garment labels. To communicate their message more efficiently, retailers need to identify, measure, and understand their market, and target a specific segment with a unique offering, which provides features and benefits to that group not available elsewhere (Webb 2007). Messages communicated are ideally short, creative, and distributed through a variety of channels, to stand out from competitive brand advertising. For fashion marketing communications, a major part is visual or non-verbal and thereby easily identified (Solomon and Rabolt 2004); however, campaigns must also be underpinned by research to establish the goals for an effective promotional strategy (Lea-Greenwood 2013).

After one of the worst garment factory accidents in the history of the fashion industry at Rana Plaza in Bangladesh, in which thousands lost their lives (Parveen 2014) – aspects of social and environmental sustainability have regained centre-stage. A new wave of sustainability concern has emerged that re-emphasises key issues from the 1990s, namely worker rights and safety conditions in factories, and, more generally, labour laws. Sustainability in itself is a fuzzy concept that lacks a clear-cut definition, yet it is intuitively understood (Markusen 2003; Gunder 2006). Key aspects of sustainability presented within this chapter follow the Triple Bottom Line (TBL) (Elkington 2004) and encompass social, environmental, and economic aspects. The social aspect includes, but is not limited to providing workers with safe working conditions and fair wages, as well as a focus on improvements that can be made to strengthen a society, in terms of investments in public facilities, such as outdoor spaces, schools, and community centres (Harris 2003). Environmental sustainability links to utilising less harmful raw materials and the reuse or recycling of materials. Economic sustainability relates to preventing any imbalance that could damage or destroy the agricultural and/or industrial production within a country. To be 'fair' and 'sustainable' the production process must produce goods/services on a continuous basis and be financially viable for stakeholders at every level (Harris 2003).

The fashion industry has seen a dramatic change in its industry landscape, with increasing numbers of fashion companies incorporating sustainability practices throughout their daily business routines and in their supply chain at large (e.g. Henninger et al. 2015; Hendriksz 2016). These practices include the use of organic materials, the re-use and recycling of materials through upcycling processes, acquisition of eco-labels, and looking after employee welfare. The industry distinguishes between two types of fashion production processes: slow- and fast-fashion. The latter facilitates hyper-consumption and mass-production and continuously fosters a fashion appetite by producing new collections every two weeks (Sharma and Hall 2010). By contrast, slow-fashion takes a different philosophical stance in that it centres on sustainability values, reflected in the use of environmentally friendly raw materials and production techniques, consideration of workers' rights and safety, as well as a slowing down of the production life cycle to produce new fashion lines either biannually or quarterly (Fletcher 2008; LeBlanc 2012). Such emerging fashion collections have been described as 'eco', 'green', 'ethical', or 'sustainable' fashion, with each of these terms being used interchangeably to describe the same phenomenon (Brown 2011; Dickson et al. 2011). To explain, Fletcher (2008) associates sustainable fashion with strong and nurturing relationships between consumers and producers, in which garments encourage versatility, inventiveness, personalisation, and individual participation. Eifler and Diekamp (2013) echo this sentiment, characterising sustainable fashion by slow trends with long-lasting value and compelling design. This change in the business routine and overall supply chain is actively promoted in the companies' messages and incorporated as an integral part of their communication strategies. In its most basic form communication theory states that the organisation (source) is encoding a message and forwards it to a transmitter, before being picked up by the receiver (audience/stakeholders), who then decodes the message to make sense of it (Fill 2009). Social and environmental sustainability cues can indicate to the consumer that the company is producing garments that are less negatively impactful on the environment compared to their counterparts.

The ulterior motive of sustainability communication is to alter the course of current consumption patterns, moving away from the insatiable consumer fashion appetite (Sharma and Hall 2010), which puts pressure on manufacturers to cut corners and overlook worker safety. Instead conscientious, sustainable fashion consumption is promoted, with regard to all actors in the supply chain. The Nordic Initiative defined sustainable fashion consumption as the use of clothing for purposes beyond utilitarian needs, including 'identity making'; achieved without jeopardising the ability of future generations to meet their needs (Eder-Hansen et al. 2012). This definition and understanding of sustainable consumption links with the Brundtland Commissions' understanding of sustainable development (World Commission on Environment and Development 1987), which is a key priority for governments and other non-governmental organisations – the UK being no exception.

Sustainable fashion consumption is outlined as a sub-set of the sustainable fashion system. Consumer attitude and behaviour change that leads to reductions in the negative TBL impacts from buying, wearing, using, maintaining, and eventually disposing of fashion goods is emphasised. Demanding sustainable alternatives, caring for garments in less impact intensive ways and the responsible disposal or recycling of obsolete goods are also key practices (Eder-Hansen et al. 2012). Gam et al. (2010) highlight that consumers are more likely to buy products made by companies with an environmentally friendly business ethos, and are likely to pay a price premium. However, environmentally friendly products become successful only if customers perceive the regular product attributes as superior to competitors' conventional offerings. Research indicates that consumers predominantly choose cheap fashion alternatives, as price is a major determinant in the purchase decision-making process (Joergens 2006; Pookulangara and Shephard 2013). Similarly, Goworek et al. (2012) suggest that there is a 'values-action' gap between consumers stating that they want to purchase green alternatives and actually translating their intentions into purchasing behaviour. For consumers to be able to make an informed decision, especially when purchasing sustainable fashion, information needs to be broadcasted to the audience in a clear and coherent manner. Yet, past studies highlight that the information provided predominately focuses on environmental aspects of sustainability (e.g. Sheth et al. 2010; Ha-Brookshire and Norum 2011). Potential conflicting messages portrayed across different media lead to confusion and consumer scepticism (e.g. Gam and Banning 2011), and negative consequences overall, which warrant further investigation.

Han et al. (2015) focused on consumer perceptions of sustainable fashion and remarked that sustainable fashion has been perceived to consist of basic, unremarkable styles or of out-dated, 'hippie' fashions, nonetheless consumers indicated that they would be inclined to purchase upcycled garments if the styles were relevant to them. Consumer perceptions within the context of sustainable fashion have been widely studied, yet current research lacks an understanding of how organisations that are producing sustainable fashion not only communicate their message to their audience, but also analyse how their consumers perceive their messages. This research addresses this gap by investigating how sustainable fashion brands understand their consumers' perceptions of sustainable fashion.

7.2 Methodology

This research utilises a qualitative research approach to investigate what the current techniques employed by upcycled and sustainable fashion brands are to communicate the ethos behind their products and the benefits to consumers and society. Data from fourteen in-depth semi-structured interviews form the basis of this research. Informants were selected from nine ethical fashion brands with experience of designing, producing, and retailing upcycled or ethical fashion; and an additional five sustainable fashion experts provided further insights to the study. The purposive sampling procedures offered a representation of the range of market levels and expertise present in the fashion industry. Brands and designers ranged from higher profile labels that show regularly on and off schedule at London Fashion Week, to medium-sized enterprises with their own bricks and mortar premises, smaller labels and start-ups, producing limited collections for loyal customer bases, mainly reached through social media. Ethical fashion experts were selected based on their specialist knowledge and experience of the industry and their distinct and varied perspectives, to give a broad range of viewpoints from the most forward thinking areas. Table 7.1 provides an overview of participants.

Table 7.1 Study participants

Brand 1	A well-established Berlin-based business that displayed and retailed upcycled fashion and jewellery from all over Europe and provided a network hub for the local sustainable design community.
Brand 2	A micro-sized ethical cycle wear enterprise based in London. The owner and director of this brand had previously held roles designing collections for two different London-based upcycled fashion brands.
Brand 3	A London upcycled fashion label of a UK-based charity raising money for vulnerable children in Romania. Both the head designer and creative director were interviewed.
Brand 4	A well-established organic clothing line from London, produced under ethical conditions in China and printed in the UK. The brand specialised in printed organic cotton and hemp t-shirts.
Brand 5	A high-profile upcycled fashion brand based in Spain and the UK, with production in Bulgaria. The brand also functions as a consultant and facilitator for outsourced ethical and upcycled production in Bulgaria.
Brand 6	A collaborative studio shop in London that is used to design, showcase, and sell sustainable and ethical fashion and accessories, focusing on high-quality handmade craftsmanship, fair trade, and transparency of production.
Brand 7	A well-established micro-enterprise upcycling brand based in Bristol with a background in academic research informing sourcing decisions. This brand manufactured and produced through a network of local UK makers and artisans.
Brand 8	A high-profile upcycling brand, known for campaigning and public engagement, and pioneering collaborations between educational institutions and upcycling innovators. Based in London with production in Italy.
Brand 9	A London-based charity which raised money to fund international development projects to improve working conditions in the global textile industry. The charity operates an award-winning in-house upcycling label.

(continued)

Table 7.1 (continued)

Expert 1	Expert 1 had a background in sustainable business practice in the fashion industry, having devised and implemented the first corporate social responsibility strategy for a major UK-based online retailer. Now based in New York and working as an independent advisor.
Expert 2	Expert 2 had a background in fashion design and academia, and was currently working as an artist and mending activist, having founded organisations to map mending practice and devise a critical agenda for mending research. Now based in Cuba.
Expert 3	Expert 3 was an ethical fashion educator and writer, with a background in design and academia, having published several well-received books on sustainable design practice. Now based in New York and pursuing further research into artisanal craft skills.
Experts 4 and 5	Experts 4 and 5 were a researcher and a founding executive from a closed-loop production company based in London, researching and developing a technique to enable end-of-use clothes and textiles to be processed back into new yarn, textiles, and clothing.

Semi-structured interviews were conducted with brands and designers on how they currently communicate their ethos to their consumers, what information is important to know about consumers, and areas in which they felt more understanding was needed. Interview schedules provided a flexible guide to the order and flow of questioning for each interview. A mixture of different kinds of questions allowed to explore the way interviewees understood issues related to the research topics, whilst still being flexible in following alternative areas of enquiry during the course of the interviews (Bryman 2012). Interviews with sustainable fashion experts covered topics pertaining to each informant's area of expertise, such as corporate social responsibility in the mainstream fashion industry, consumer understanding, media and communication, design, and closed-loop production. In flexible semi-structured interviewing style that included critical incidents and applications, questions varied between respondents to reflect what data could most appropriately be collected from each specific informant and how interviewees were directing the flow and emphasis of the data gathering. Thematic analysis allowed key themes to emerge from the data, broken down into single units of analysis, such as a sentence or phrase. From these indicators, concepts could then be generated to build theories (Bryman 2012).

7.3 Results

Presented in this section are the findings from key sustainable fashion industry informants. Perspectives on what the brands and designers believed consumers already knew, and the implications of this for design and production issues were highlighted. Areas in which brands and designers felt more clarity was needed have also been presented.

7.3.1 Consumers

Informants expressed the opinions that consumers were, on the whole, unwilling to acknowledge or unaware of how their consumption behaviour contributed to wider problems caused by the fashion industry (Table 7.2). The idea of cognitive dissonance, in which individuals experience discomfort when holding two conflicting beliefs (Sun and Guo 2013) was discussed in relation to continued consumption in the face of growing ethical awareness. When asked about what is important to know about consumers, the consensus from key informants was that design and price were the most important factors for consumers. Knowing what they were willing to spend and what sort of designs and styles they were looking for, as well as other aspects of their lifestyles, which could identify their preferences, were vital. Informants were of the view that ethics were unimportant for most consumers and would only be viewed as a secondary benefit. To make sustainable fashion desirable for consumers, it was felt that the right designs had to be offered at competitive prices. Unique designs and limited edition supply created by upcycling can also create an appealing exclusivity for consumers.

Table 7.2 Key theme: consumers

Sub-theme	Summary	Illustrative quote	Informant cited
Consumers own knowledge	Consumers are unwilling to or unaware of how to change	'...this consumer focused industry creates cognitive dissonance...'	Expert 1
What it is important to know about consumers	Design and price come first. Ethics are a bonus.	'What they really want is just to know that everything is OK without them having to do anything to find that out.'	Brand 2
Consumers don't care	Design and price can convert consumers to sustainable purchases	'...you've got people that don't really care, and they are buying it for design and price.'	Brand 5
Knowing what consumers want	What would appeal to consumers in these markets in terms of wants, needs, and preferences	'It's whether they like the product at the end of the day. And are they willing to part with their hard earned cash for it?'	Brand 6
Knowing what consumers will spend	What price ranges consumers are looking for	'I think our garments are priced comparatively to the high street. Our price point goes from £30 to £100 /£120...'	Brand 7
How to design for consumers	How products are designed and how they look was the most effective way of appealing to consumers.	'You've just got to make a really great product. It's got to be what people want.'	Brand 2
Uniqueness of designs	The one of a kind exclusivity of upcycled designs was appealing for consumers.	'People like the fact that is it limited edition, which is inherently connected to the fact that it is upcycled.'	Brand 7

(continued)

Table 7.2 (continued)

Sub-theme	Summary	Illustrative quote	Informant cited
Do they buy for quality?	How do consumers view the quality of fast fashion?	'That would be very interesting, to know people's opinions towards fast fashion and quality.'	Brand 5
Do they buy for function or need?	Do consumers seek functionality and high performance from their clothing?	'I am interested in whether people want things to perform that well.'	Brand 2
Social status and stigma	Social stigma still exists towards second hand clothing	'But then a lot of people don't like buying second-hand clothes because they think it's dirty. They just don't like it.'	Brand 5
Do they care about ethics?	Do consumers care about the ethics of how their clothes were made?	'The consumer that is not interested in who makes your clothes or ethical issues is a very difficult consumer to sway.'	Brand 8
The values-action gap	How to convert customers who expressed sustainable consumption intentions into actual sales	'What do we need to close that gap? Is it better marketing? Is it better advertising? Is it better sex appeal? Is it better kudos with your friends?'	Expert 1

Questions were raised by informants on what extra qualities consumers were seeking in garments, such as high quality, longevity, functionality, and ethics, and if any of these things were important to consumers. The idea of social status from designer brands and labels was also discussed, as well as the inverse of the social stigma attached to buying second-hand clothes. Such opprobrium presents a challenge for designers creating garments from post-consumer textiles, as a negative connotation may be attached to these materials. A challenge is presented in how to best communicate the desirable qualities of such garments to consumers. A further challenge is also presented to sustainable fashion designers when attempting to convert expressed sustainable consumption intentions into actual sales. As highlighted by Goworek et al. (2012), various studies have shown that consumers who profess to hold ethical views often do not transfer their intentions into ethical purchase behaviour, thus forming a 'values-action gap'. In both these instances, understanding current strategies used by designers and brands in presenting information, and how consumers receive this information is key to the success of promoting sustainable fashion consumption.

7.3.2 Communication

Informants outlined current sustainable fashion communication strategies for brands and designers, including in-store dialogue, social media content, public relations (PR) agencies, and editorials (Table 7.3). In-store dialogues for brands with their own premises presented a chance to connect with consumers and share stories of how items had been produced. This provides a unique shopping experience and enables brands to equip consumers with information about the fashion industry in an engaging and non-confrontational manner. It also provides an opportunity to gauge consumer reactions to new products, services, price points, and information provided, offering vital feedback for these businesses.

Social media was conceivably the most commonly used strategy to connect with a wider audience. Sharing related content and stories allowed brands to communicate their ethos and non-product related posts. These posts also communicate a lifestyle, ethos, and experiences to an audience, which has already shown an initial interest in sustainability issues. Social media was mentioned time and again by the key informants as their main communication strategy, allowing brands to collect feedback and market research, and to tell the story of their company by openly associating with issues and causes they found important, and other brands and designers, which they supported. By more easily gauging audiences through social media, directed marketing strategies could be put in place by the brands to offer consumers

Table 7.3 Key theme: communication

Sub-theme	Summary	Illustrative quote	Informant cited
In-store dialogue	Knowledgeable brand owners on hand to advise and share the stories of the products that appeals to their customers.	'So I think for us it's just having a shop. We just start getting direct feedback. We know customers like and what they don't like.'	Brand 6
Social media, PR and press	Social media was cited as the main method communication with consumers	'Obviously since social media has come along it has been a lot easier to kind of gauge who your audience are and directly market to them.'	Brand 4
Big brands using social media	For large multi-national brands, customers are providing market information and asking questions.	'Quite often it seems to be coming from the feedback mechanisms they have on their social media, through their blog, through their website.'	Brand 7
Communicating upcycling to consumers	Appealing to consumers through the design and style rather than the ethics was the most successful approach.	'Then the best is to start from the design side and show how cool the design is. And how you can use materials that were already used.'	Brand 1
Story and emotional link	Consumers found human stories about workers easier to connect with than more abstract ideas about climate change and environmental degradation.	'I think people are more interested in knowing who has made it, where the fabric came from, if it had a story.'	Brand 2

(*continued*)

Table 7.3 (continued)

Sub-theme	Summary	Illustrative quote	Informant cited
Market research	Talking to their current market was their main form of market research.	'We always try and work out who they actually are and why they are motivated to buy.'	Brand 7
Media and communication	Although the mainstream press has been covering the issue, it was still falling short.	'I think we need a lot more kind of support from media in general... to help people understand what they can do, what they should be doing, and why.'	Expert 1
Integrating into the mainstream	Ethical fashion needs to be integrated instead of being treated as a novelty.	'You just don't get a Goodone piece put alongside a Chanel jacket in deep summer in Elle magazine. It doesn't happen, it's still so segregated.'	Brand 7

the most appropriate products. Social media also offers brands the opportunity to respond expressly to questions from customers in an open forum.

In communicating upcycled fashion to the public and emphasising its appeal, informants tended towards an opinion that establishing qualities of design and style before ethics would be a more successful strategy in engaging consumers. Once desirable fashion aesthetics had been achieved, it would then be possible to inform consumers about sustainable credentials, provenance, and garment care practices. Using language and terms, which consumers easily understand and can engage with was seen as vital, as for some consumers, psychological barriers to accepting second-hand textiles may exist. In creating engaging information around sustainable fashion, it was also felt that consumers found emotional stories concerning those working in the fashion industry easier to connect with rather than more abstract ideas about climate change and environmental degradation. The latter are seen as intangible aspects that are hard to grasp and make sense of and may not affect everyone in the same manner.

To find out more about their present and potential customers, current forms of market research ranged from social media and in-store feedback to expressions of regret at a lack of market research or complete disconnection from the marketing side of their business altogether. For the majority of key informants, talking and connecting with their customers was their main form of market research, although there was a recognised need to appeal to a wider audience than just those who were engaged with issues of sustainability. For some brands it was not explicitly clear how to go about this, and a certain measure of scepticism was expressed once again regarding the 'values-action gap'. Queries were raised about how to close the gap between expressed intentions and actual purchasing behaviour.

Informants also felt that efforts from the mainstream media and fashion press to cover sustainable fashion were disappointing. On the one hand, the media have covered stories about working conditions and labour rights abuses in Asia, but on the other hand, responsible alternatives to consuming products made by the companies creating injustice were not shown in any meaningful way. It was felt that sustainable alternatives were often shown as a novelty and not integrated into mainstream media and fashion as equal and viable options to the current offerings and methods of consumption.

7.4 Analysis and Discussion

In many ways, what is true for standard and mainstream fashion (fast-fashion) is also true for sustainable and circular economy fashion (slow-fashion). For effective communication, messages should be underpinned by relevant research to identify the intended audience and most effective forms of transmission. Short, creative messages, delivered through a wide variety of media, often using highly engaging visual or non-verbal forms target the predetermined audience (e.g. Solomon and Rabolt 2004). In mainstream and value fashion, promotional messages encourage hyper-consumption through a high turnover of new product lines. For sustainable and circular economy fashion, a paradoxical challenge arises in conveying a message, which aims to reduce consumption impacts and change consumer behaviour, yet also sell more products at the right price for the target market (Black 2011). Circular economy fashion communication aims to nurture relationships between consumers and producers and encourage responsible consumption choices which make use of products designed with long-lasting value and enduring style (Fletcher 2008; Cooper et al. 2013). Personal creativity is emphasised, in which non-purchase related lifestyle choices offer greater versatility, inventiveness, and personalisation through practices such as mending, customising, and swapping (Busch 2008). Information about company supply chains, ethics, and sustainability ethos must be communicated in a clear and coherent manner as an integral part of each brands' communication strategy, in a way which connects and is relevant to consumers. It is in this departure of intended outcomes where mainstream strategies and those of the circular economy begin to deviate. Circular economy fashion brands have less environmental impacts than their mainstream rivals, and must combine this message with a compelling presentation of well-designed and desirable products. We found eight key elements that can be summarised in the circular economy fashion communication canvas (Table 7.4):

The brands and designers interviewed had taken the stance of offering more conscientious choices to responsible fashion consumers. Products offered were designed for lasting style and versatility, incorporating socially and environmentally aware materials and production. Although extensive research had often been carried out in how to source reused, recycled, or secondary and sustainable raw materials, not all brands carried through the message of the full extent of their sourcing efforts into their communications strategy. Sustainability ethos was often highlighted by brand websites; however, style and design preferences and correct pricing were noted as being the most important points to be aware of when communicating with consumers, which the relevant research into consumer opinion, lifestyle, and behaviour would reveal.

Table 7.4 The circular economy fashion communication canvas

Relevant research For example, industry trends, competitor analysis, current issues in industry, market research	**Target audience** Clear consumer profile (e.g. age, occupation, income, interests)	**Clear message** For example, what is the brand ethos? Key values? Key attributes?	**Multi-channel** Reaching a wide audience by combining online and offline channels
Coherent values Core values must be clearly communicated and followed through across the supply chain	**Visually engaging** Use of creative, short, unique text, images, and symbols	**Compelling products** Unique pieces that attract consumers to buy into the slow-fashion movement	**Feedback loops** Creating feedback loops, which incorporate suggestions from stakeholders across the supply chain

Informants also highlighted further queries regarding consumers for which appropriate research was still necessary; such as whether consumers were interested in quality, functionality, or ethics, and how it would be possible to close the 'values-action gap' and convert expressed good intentions into sustainable behaviour.

To communicate their company ethos and the features and benefits of their products to consumers, informants outlined two main strategies of social media content and in-store dialogue. In identifying a target audience, the advantages of social media lay in enabling brands direct access to individuals with a prior expression of interest in sustainability issues. In-store dialogue also enabled brands to target individuals who were actively engaged in sustainable consumption by their visit to specific sustainable fashion shops; however, a clear idea of the target audience for sustainable fashion or circular economy fashion was not readily available to the informants. Brands involved with academic research were able to take advantage of the collaborative opportunities to gather more information about their target audience, creating open and effective communication and assisting positive developments into the industry as a whole.

Messages communicated through social media enabled brands to re-post non-fashion related sustainability content which aligned closely with their company ethos, demonstrating a clear message about their beliefs and values, and reaching out to a wider audience. Barriers to communicating this message beyond the Internet and social media were the lack of coverage from mainstream media and mainstream fashion. Inadequate exposure and a lack of integration of sustainable alternatives left many brands unable to connect with a mainstream fashion audience. Despite growing consumer awareness, the fashion industry shows a marked reluctance towards transparency. Leadership and support from larger well-established brands in the industry was felt to be vital to instigate any sort of change.

As well as websites, blogs, social media, and in-store dialogue, some brands had experience of utilising PR agencies and placing editorials in fashion publications, enabling a multi-channel communication approach; however, full utilisation of this approach was limited by the micro and small sizes of each enterprise. Increased availability of information online has resulted in individuals being more informed than in the past, and it is through these channels of online and social engagement that consumers seem most ready to receive these messages. Using social comparison and peer-to-peer dialogue may also provide a platform to engage individuals through more positive messages of social change and clean technologies than in guilt inducing judgements of previous behaviour, as well as offering fresh opportunities for individuals to make the right decisions going forward.

A coherent message about company values was often demonstrated through each brands' website, and through online articles by sustainable fashion bloggers. Information on the provenance of materials and production was given, highlighting the ethos behind each brand's activities in creating enduring and sustainable fashion. For a fully functioning circular fashion system to be in place, understanding of the entire life cycle by all participants is required, including consumers. This can only be achieved through clear and coherent communication of values; demonstrating the best alternatives and responsible choices to consumers, rather than pointing out what they were currently doing wrong. Informants felt that feelings of guilt would not be helpful in changing consumer attitudes. Converting the way individuals think about consumption is balanced very finely between communicating the right message and going too far, making individuals feel judged and guilty for their consumption behaviour. Research by Zane et al. (2015) has shown that consumers who wilfully ignore ethical product attributes often denigrate other, more ethical consumers who seek out and use this information in making purchase decisions; but that denigration becomes less strong if the wilfully ignorant consumers have a second opportunity to act ethically after initially ignoring the ethical product information.

Brands and designers interviewed created design-led, fashion forward garments, modelled in styled images and product shots. Each brand had a distinctive style, logo, and graphic design approach. These elements all worked together to create a visually engaging identity, often presented through a strong online presence; however, many informants felt that mainstream media coverage was lacking in provision. Informants were frustrated that sustainable fashion was often shown as a novelty and not integrated alongside other fashion editorials. Not enough was being done to highlight responsible alternatives to continued fashion consumption or to show sustainable style as being equally desirable as high-street fashion. Informants were unanimous in their opinion that style and design were the most effective ways to appeal to consumers, who would only regard ethics as a bonus addition. Connecting with consumers through aesthetics was vitally important to create a platform on which to engage individuals on the sustainable credentials and human stories regarding garment workers and the fashion industry.

The distinctive style of each brand resulted in design-led fashion pieces and highly compelling products; however, the extra work in sourcing materials and smaller production runs ensuring ethical standards often led to higher prices. Successfully communicating the wider global benefits of producing in this way to consumers was key to generating sales of products and services for circular economy brands. The strongest results reported in gaining this level of understanding and acceptance, including sales and repeat custom, were again through online interactions and in-store dialogue in dedicated ethical fashion stores. Providing enough information about the ethical product credentials and origin of the source materials needed to be carefully balanced against showing garments for their aesthetic appeal.

Once again, social media and in-store dialogue also presented opportunities for feedback from consumers, allowing individuals to express opinions and reactions towards new products, production information, and the presentation of the message communicated. Feedback can also take the form of product returns and take back schemes, in which the opportunity to identify product failures or to assess life cycle impacts is presented. Retail feedback from wholesale customers is also key to developing and growing circular economy fashion, and integrating collections into a wider variety of outlets. Limited understanding from UK-based retail buyers regarding the variability of upcycled stock and fears of inconsistency and poor quality have also presented barriers to wider acceptance. Identifying the most effective retail strategy for sustainable fashion has been an on-going challenge to the industry. Barriers include sourcing solely from one stream, such as post-consumer textiles. Brands utilising a variety of sources such as pre- and post-consumer textiles, recycled textiles, and sustainably sourced fabrics have shown more success in scaling up their operations for wholesale supply. A constant process of open dialogue and feedback between suppliers, designers, producers, makers, retail buyers, consumers, users, and those dealing with the use-phase and end-of-life stages is vital to share information essential to the development of a successful circular economy fashion industry.

7.5 Conclusions

Current understanding in the business practices of sustainable and circular economy fashion brands points towards a communication strategy built around emphasising the design, style, and aesthetics of products, without leaning too heavily on the provenance and ethical credentials of supply chains, or holding in mind a clear target audience. Products must certainly be compelling and design led to compete with the mainstream; however, under-pinning consumer research and strategic considerations must also be included in business activities to ensure effective communication of a brand's ethos, values, and messages in a way which connects with the target audience. It is clear that circular economy fashion communication strategies would benefit from further research into how to identify target consumers, and profile current patrons, to determine strategies to close the 'values-action gap'. Small and micro enterprises are often limited in their resources to carry out vital research, which would under-pin all business and communication activities; however, collaborations with academic research partners with shared sustainability goals offer greater scope for developing the pool of knowledge available. Key areas for further inquiry include identifying the target audience, their wants, needs, and lifestyle preferences, including how best to communicate with these individuals, and how to integrate sustainable fashion into mainstream media and garment industry to reach a wider market and make best practice more commonplace.

References

Black, S. (2011). *Eco-Chic: The Fashion Paradox*. Black Dog Publishing: London.

Brown, S. (2011). Future factory: Sass Brown is coming to NTU. *Future Factory [online]*. Available from: http://futurefactory.weebly.com/live-event-streams.html [Accessed March 20, 2012].

Bryman, A. (2012). *Social Research Methods*, 4th ed. Oxford University Press: Oxford.

Busch, O. V. (2008). *FASHION-able: Hacktivism and Engaged Fashion Design*. Art Monitor: Gothenburg.

Cooper, T., Hill, H., Kininmonth, J., Townsend, K., & Hughes, M. (2013). *Design for Longevity: Guidance on Increasing the Active Life of Clothing, WRAP [online]*. Available from: http://www.wrap.org.uk/sites/files/wrap/Design%20for%20Longevity%20Report_0.pdf [Accessed January 23, 2017].

Dickson, M., Cataldi, C., & Grover, C. (2011). The slow fashion movement. *Not Just a Label*, pp. 1–6. [online]. Available from: https://www.notjustalabel.com/editorial/slow-fashion-movement [Accessed July 20, 2016].

Eder-Hansen, J., Kryger, J., Morris, J., Sisco, C., Watson, D., Kiorboe, N., Dahlgren, S., Larsen, K.B., Burchardi, I. (2012). *The NICE Consumer Research Summary and Discussion Paper, BSR. [online]*. Available from: https://www.bsr.org/reports/BSR_NICE_Consumer_Discussion_Paper.pdf [Accessed January 23, 2017].

Eifler, C., & Diekamp, K. (2013). Consumer acceptance of sustainable fashion in Germany. *Research Journal of Textile and Apparel*, 17: 1.

Elkington, J. (2004). Enter the triple bottom line, in J. Henriques & A. Richardson (eds.) *The Triple Bottom Line: Does it all Add Up?* Earthscan: London.

Fill, C. (2009). *Marketing Communications: Interactivity, Communities and Content*, 5th edn. Prentice Hall: Harlow, UK.

Fletcher, K. (2008). *Sustainable Fashion and Textiles: Design Journeys*. Earthscan: London.

Gam, H. J. et al. (2010). Quest for the eco-apparel market: A study of mothers' willingness to purchase organic cotton clothing for their children. *International Journal of Consumer Studies, 34*(6): 648–656.

Gam, H. J., & Banning, J. (2011). Addressing sustainable apparel design challenges with problem-based learning. *Clothing and Textiles Research Journal, 29*(3): 202–215.

Gibson, O. (2005). Shopper's eye view of Ads that pass us by. *The Guardian*, pp. 3–5. [online]. Available from: http://www.theguardian.com/media/2005/nov/19/advertising.marketingandpr [Accessed June 11, 2016].

Goworek, H. et al. (2012). The sustainable clothing market: An evaluation of potential strategies for UK retailers. *International Journal of Retail & Distribution Management, 40*(12): 935–955.

Gunder, M. (2006). Sustainability: Planning's saving grace or road to perdition? *Journal of Planning Education and Research, 26*: 208–221.

Ha-Brookshire, J., & Norum, P. (2011). Cotton and sustainability. *International Journal of Sustainability in Higher Education, 12*(4): 369–380.

Han, S. L.-C., Tyler, D., & Apeagyei, P. R. (2015). Upcycling as a design strategy for product lifetime optimisation and societal change. In *Conference Proceedings – Product Lifetimes and the Environment.*

Harris, J. M. (2003). Sustainability and sustainable development. *International Society for Ecological Economics* [online]. Available from: http://isecoeco.org/pdf/susdev.pdf [Accessed July 15, 2013].

Hendriksz, V. (2016). 55 fashion companies sign 'milestone' sustainability covenant. *Fashion United*, pp. 1–20 [online]. Available from: https://fashionunited.uk/news/fashion/55-fashion-companies-sign-milestone-sustainability-covenant/2016070420984 [Accessed June 11, 2016].

Henninger, C. E., Alevizou, P. J., Oates, C. J., & Cheng, R. (2015). Sustainable Supply Chain Management in the Slow-Fashion Industry, in T. M. Choi & T. C. E. Cheng (eds.), *Sustainable Fashion Supply Chain Management: From Sourcing to Retailing*. Springer: London.

Joergens, C. (2006). Ethical fashion: Myth or future trend? *Journal of Fashion Marketing and Management, 10*(3): 360–371.

Lea-Greenwood, G. (2013). *Fashion Marketing Communications*. Wiley: Chichester.

LeBlanc, S. (2012). *Sustainable Fashion Design: Oxymoron No More?, BSR [online]*. Available from: https://www.bsr.org/reports/BSR_Sustainable_Fashion_Design.pdf [Accessed January 23, 2017].

Markusen, A. (2003). Fuzzy concepts, scanty evidence, policy distance: The case for rigour and policy relevance in critical regional studies. *Regional Studies, 37*(6–7): 701–717.

Parveen, S. (2014). Rana Plaza factory collapse survivors struggle one year on. *BBC News* [online]. Available from: http://www.bbc.co.uk/news/world-asia-27107860.

Pookulangara, S., & Shephard, A. (2013). Slow fashion movement: Understanding consumer perceptions-An exploratory study. *Journal of Retailing and Consumer Services, 20*(2): 200–206.

Sharma, T., & Hall, C. (2010). Green PLM for fashion & apparel – White Paper. *Infosys* [online]. Available from: http://www.infosys.com/industries/retail/white-papers/Documents/green-plm-fashion-apparel.pdf [Accessed February 1, 2012].

Sheth, J. N., Sethia, N. K., & Srinivas, S. (2010). Mindful consumption: A customer-centric approach to sustainability. *Journal of the Academy of Marketing Science, 39*(1): 21–39.

Solomon, M. R., & Rabolt, N. J. (2004). *Consumer Behaviour in Fashion*, 2nd edn. Pearson Education Ltd: New Jersey.

Sun, Y.-S., & Guo, S. (2013). Media use, social comparison, cognitive dissonance and peer pressure as antecedents of fashion involvement. *Intercultural Communication Studies, 1*: 117–139.

Webb, B. (2007). Retail brand marketing in the fashion industry, in T. Hines & M. Bruce (eds) *Fashion marketing: Contemporary issues*, 324. Elsevier: Oxford.

World Commission on Environment and Development (1987). *Our Common Future (The Brundtland Report)*. World Commission on Environment and Development, Oxford University Press: Oxford, UK.

Zane, D. M., Irwin, J. R., & Reczek, R. W. (2015). Do less ethical consumers denigrate more ethical consumers? The effect of wilful ignorance on judgments of others. *Journal of Consumer Psychology* [online]. Available from: http://linkinghub.elsevier.com/retrieve/pii/S1057740815001011.

Sara Li-Chou Han is a Research Associate at Manchester Metropolitan University. Her background lies in fashion design, styling, and social enterprise, and she is currently researching how circular economy fashion strategies can re-value post-consumer textiles and close 'values-action gaps' in supply chains.

Dr Claudia E Henninger is a Lecturer in Fashion Marketing Management at the School of Materials, the University of Manchester. She was awarded her PhD entitled 'Corporate identity in the contexts of the UK's green slow-fashion industry and micro-organisations' from the University of Sheffield in 2015. Claudia's research centres on corporate marketing, sustainability, and green consumer typologies in the context of the fashion industry. She has published in leading journals, contributed to edited books, and presented her work at various national and international conferences. Claudia is the deputy chair of the Academy of Marketing SIG Sustainability.

Dr Phoebe Apeagyei is a Senior Lecturer in Fashion Technology and Anthropometrics at Manchester Metropolitan University. Her experiences and research interests lie in body scanning technology, anthropometrics, body image, sizing, plus consumer perceptions and attitudes towards fashion, innovation, and sustainability.

Dr David Tyler is a Reader in Fashion Technology at Manchester Metropolitan University. With many years of experience in the garment industry and in Higher Education, he has developed research interests using UK and EU funding. His current projects include new product development, impact protection, apparel sustainability, and wearable technologies. He is involved with Resyntex: an EU-funded initiative to extend the circular economy to fashion products.

8

Fashion in a Circular Economy

Kirsi Niinimäki

8.1 Introduction

In the near future, the fashion field will need to overcome new challenges, as sustainable development moves towards more holistic and systemic understanding and further knowledge on circular economy models emerges. A Circular Economy (CE) is regenerative by nature, based on principles of closed loops. The foundation for this closing the loop approach is based on McDonough and Braungart's (2002) cradle-to-cradle principle. According to this principle a product is designed to have multiple life cycles or it is biodegradable. Accordingly, after the use phase, the product will continue in technical or biological cycles. Composting is not a realistic option for garments and textiles, which include many harmful chemicals, and further composting causes methane, which contributes to greater greenhouse gas emissions and global warming (Niinimäki 2013). Therefore, in the fashion sector, closing the loop must occur in a technical cycle.

K. Niinimäki (✉)
Aalto University, Helsinki, Finland
e-mail: kirsi.niinimaki@aalto.fi

C.E. Henninger et al. (eds.), *Sustainability in Fashion*,
DOI 10.1007/978-3-319-51253-2_8

A CE approach in fashion aims to develop a more sustainable and closed-loop system where the goal is to extend the use time of garments; furthermore, all materials will be recycled in several rounds. Products are designed to be included in a system where all aspects are considered: the original design and its suitability for several lifecycles, material flows in the system, appreciating waste as a valuable resource and even collecting back all products after their use. Accordingly, moving towards a CE means taking a system perspective on fashion, where all actors are included: designers, producers, manufacturers, suppliers, business people and even consumers. Moreover, building a CE system and transformative business for fashion requires a new system level and radical innovations.

8.2 Design for Longevity, Quality and Design for Long-Term Satisfaction

In a CE, system design has a different role compared to that in a linear economy. In the former, design has to contribute strongly to minimising the environmental impact of the garment, through, for example, four different paths, as presented in Fig. 8.1 from the Great Recovery report (RSA 2016). The model starts from a new kind of consumer understanding, and the principle is that a company creates a new kind of relationship with the end user. The company has to know the end user and his/her needs and desires much better if it is to offer a longer use-time of the garment or better and more stable satisfaction with the product.

The first principle of design for CE is to extend the use-time of products (see Fig. 8.1). Therefore, consumer satisfaction has to be the focus of design. How, then, to do this in practice? When considering consumer satisfaction, quality is a critical aspect: the quality of the textile material, all details, dyes and sewing work. Our earlier study (Niinimäki 2014) has shown that product satisfaction correlates strongly with quality issues, but quality is neither a simple aspect nor a one-level approach regarding garments. On the other hand, clothing offers us a certain performance, which can be seen as instrumental or expressive (Swan and Combs 1976; Niinimäki 2011). Instrumental performance is linked to the product's physical properties while expressive performance

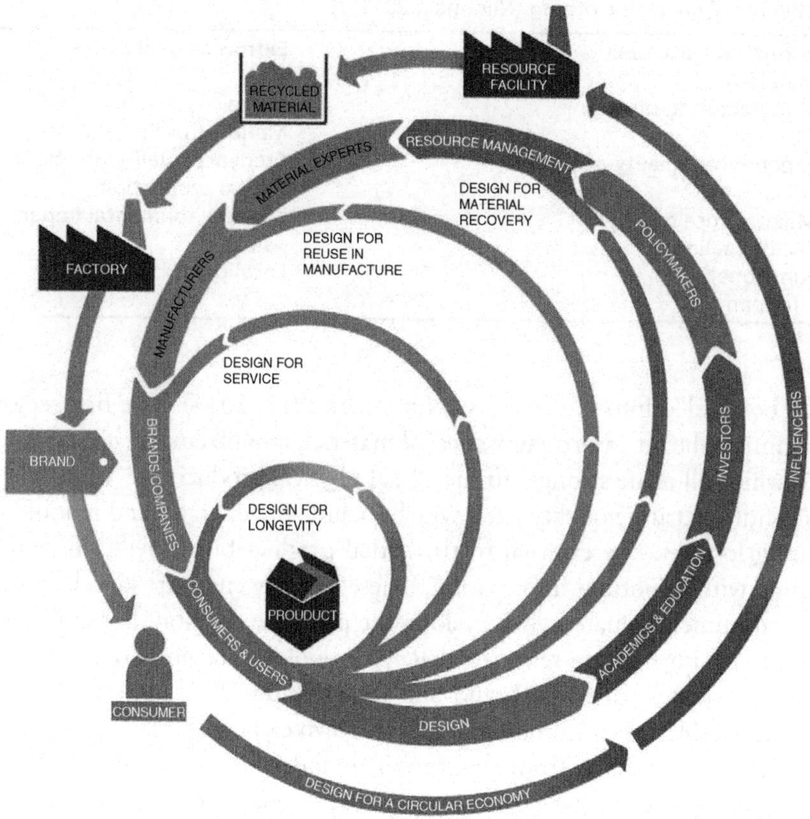

Fig. 8.1 The four models of DCE, design in a circular economy (RSA great recovery, used with permission)

is linked to consumers' psychological response to the garment, the emotional side of the satisfaction. To offer satisfaction to the consumer, the product needs to fulfil expectations at both levels: if first the instrumental performance expectations are met (e.g. durability, fit, quality) and then the expressive performance (e.g. beauty) pleases, the result is deep product satisfaction.

But let us start the investigation from clothing quality. Ophuis and Trijp (1995) argue that in perceived quality, evaluation depends on the consumer's judgement. Quality in garments from the consumers' viewpoint

Table 8.1 Quality in clothing (Niinimäki 2011)

Intrinsic quality cues	Extrinsic quality cues
Material	Price
Manufacturing quality	Brand
Fit	Manufacturing location
Experienced quality attributes	**Credence quality attributes**
Fit	Ethical production
Maintenance quality	Low environmental impact
Tactile feeling	Safety
Functionality	Local production
Life span	

can be divided into four sectors (Niinimäki 2011, 2014). The first sector comprises the intrinsic quality cues, of material, manufacturing quality and fit, which all relate strongly to the actual physical product (see Table 8.1). Secondly, extrinsic quality cues, which include price, brand and manufacturing location, are external to the actual product but provide the consumer with important information. These "quality cues" are key elements the consumer evaluates when making the purchase decision. For example, many consumers have reported that when looking for good quality they strongly trust a particular brand and its reputation for high-quality garments. In this case customers rely on their own earlier experiences with the life span of garments from this certain brand (Niinimäki 2011, 2014); therefore, product quality is an important value for a brand and its reputation. Jackson and Shaw (2009, p. 125) argue that price is forgotten not long after purchase, while the quality of the product is remembered long after. Therefore good experienced quality can lead to brand loyalty.

Quality *cues* are product characteristics that can be observed without actual use experience. In contrast, quality *attributes* can only be evaluated in use. Quality attributes experienced in garments are fit (experience in long-term use), maintenance quality, tactile feeling, functionality and life span (Niinimäki 2011, 2014). In consumer satisfaction with garments, when the aim is extend the life span of a garment, the use experience is most critical. A critical aspect for consumers' dissatisfaction, leading to a very short use-time of a garment, is low maintenance quality. Such a garment has lost its fit, size or colour or the material simply looks worn out after laundering, which leads to early disposal of the garment (Niinimäki 2011, 2014).

There are quality attributes that link to a consumer's own value base, and thus stay at a cognitive level, and these are called credence quality attributes (Ophuis and Trijp 1995). In the clothing sector, such attributes can include ethical production, low environmental impact, safety issues (e.g. no toxic chemicals) and local production, if the consumer's values are grounded on environmental and ethical interest (Niinimäki 2011, 2014).

But increasing the quality of the product to achieve garment longevity is not enough. Especially in fashion, symbolic values are important. Fashion is linked to our emotional needs, our individuality and the need to express ourselves and gain social acceptance (Kaiser 1990). The emotional aspects of fashion consumption therefore need to be addressed through design when aiming to extend the longevity of a garment. This is quite a challenging task. The aesthetic aspects and emotional experiences are important in clothing, and therefore aiming for better quality alone does not guarantee the longevity of a product. The aesthetic experience with clothing includes multisensorial dimensions: A garment's beauty is experienced through visual, tactile, olfactory and kinetic experiences, resulting in feelings of beauty, comfort, a pleasant weight or sensual movement of the material against our body (Niinimäki 2010). The experience of beauty with a garment can be above average, making this kind of garment special to us and leading to deep product satisfaction or even to person-product attachment. Therefore this kind of experience helps to extend the use-time of garments (Niinimäki 2011, 2014).

Different garment types and use situations emphasise different satisfaction attributes (Niinimäki and Armstrong 2013). For garments in frequent use, the functional aspects might be much more important than the aesthetic ones. Here, active use defines the satisfaction attributes that need to be at the core of the design. For example, for sport clothing in frequent use, the critical satisfaction attributes are durability, high performance and high functionality, and good quality in maintenance (frequent washing). For festive dresses, for example, on the other hand, aesthetic experiences are more important, which may not be as functional or even pleasurable to use. A festive dress is not in active, frequent

Table 8.2 Design attributes for long-term satisfaction

Design for satisfaction	
Quality aspects	Good fit (size and cut)
	Durable materials
	Durability A) in use
	B) while laundering (stability in fit, material, colour)
	High quality in manufacturing (sewing work)
Aesthetic aspects	Beauty
	Style
	Colour
	Fit
	Tactile feeling (material and fit)
Functional aspects	Performance
	Suitability in use
	Use experience
	Easy maintenance
Emotional aspects	Satisfaction
	Emotional experiences
	Fulfilling the need for change in a sustainable manner

use, and we can tolerate much more uncomfortable experiences if we seldom wear the dress. Here, the beauty experience might be the most important aspect for consumer satisfaction. To include a satisfaction offering in design, designers and companies have to know their customers better than currently, and this conclusion is also the basis for the service aspect that will be discussed in the next section (Table 8.2)

8.3 Design for Services: Offering Satisfaction and Change in a Sustainable Way

In Product-Service Systems, the PSS approach, one aim is to move the focus from personal ownership to alternative utilisation options to decrease total material consumption. This can be effected through offerings that mix tangible products and intangible services, and the goal is to offer satisfaction and fulfilment of consumers' needs and desires in a more sustainable and less materialistic way (Briceno and Stagl 2006; Mont 2002; Tukker and Tischner 2006). Depending on the service offering, product design in PSS can include features such as durability, flexibility, modularity and ease of use (Mont 2002; Pawar et al. 2009; Van Halen et al. 2005). Moreover the service model can aim for less material-intensive consumption as in renting or leasing models (collaborative consumption), in clothing swaps or in using consultancy to update the wardrobe (Armstrong et al. 2015). Change is fundamental to fashion, and services can provide a solution to fulfilling customers' need for change. In these kinds of service offerings, upgrading and modifications can deliver change experiences for consumers while preventing the desire to buy new clothing.

In PSS offerings, a critical point is consumers' readiness to accept and use services to extend the use-time of garments. Therefore, the service has to be designed according to the target customer group's values and wishes. Armstrong et al. (2015) studied consumers' attitudes to services in the fashion sector, to define barriers as well as pathways to viability. Findings from this study indicated a moderate level of interest in a variety of clothing-related PSS features, with the highest level of interest in clothing take-back, swaps and consultancy services. PSS concepts including experiential, innovative and social approaches (renting, swapping and fashion result) were evaluated as best suited for younger consumers. Clothing services that emphasised product satisfaction (e.g. redesign, repair/maintenance, customisation and consultancy) were seen to be most suited for older consumers with their more stable value base and less need for appearance change (Armstrong et al. 2015).

In developing a PSS, the service element has to be included in the product design and business model from the beginning. This approach changes the design criteria, for example, the need for high quality in renting services to keep the product in use for an extended time. From the business viewpoint, the PSS will not succeed if the service is a simple add-on and not a fundamental goal in product design and in the business model.

8.4 Design for Reuse in Manufacture

Taking the remanufacturing approach necessitates a completely new model for garment design and construction. Here, the garment construction should be based on modularity and it should be able to be updated or modified. In principle, broken components should be able to be replaced and the product be restored to its original state (Action and Centre 2016). In the fashion sector this is a big challenge. Here, PSS thinking offers the possibility to create services to mend damaged garments, update them or modify them, and these aspects could be included in the business model.

In the ideal case the original garment has to be designed and manufactured in a manner that makes it possible to recycle all parts. One example of modularity is a modular concept design created by Essi Karell for her MA thesis in 2014 in Aalto University (Fig. 8.2). The outcome is a combination of a fashion design concept based on modularity and PSS. The core value is in the service, where a customer can take back the garment to the store so it will be updated or transformed. The idea is to create fashion design that includes a service aspect; this creates a new kind of system that is not linear (i.e. make-use-dispose). The garment is constructed from modules, which enable the garment to be unstitched and reassembled, resulting in different looks. The service can offer sustainable satisfaction for fashion change based on modular design, and moreover the model can provide new profit-making possibilities for the fashion designer (in the reassembling stage) (Karell 2013, 2014).

In CE, products should be able to be disassembled, and thereafter components should be able to be separated into different flows. Components should be separated into consumable or durable elements, which could be used later in remanufacturing processes. Components that cannot be reused could go into a material recovery process. This principle challenges current garment design and manufacturing practices, where most of the materials in garments are blends that are complicated or impossible to separate. Designing garments for disassembly also needs new innovations: for example, thread that can easily be broken apart in the disassembly stage or a durable textile material that can go through a disassembly process.

The remanufacturing principle may be impossible in the garment sector, as scalability is a critical issue. Modular principles might be possible to implement only in a small scale. In the industrial scale, it is quite challenging, and therefore the next principle of design for material recovery might be more relevant for the fashion sector.

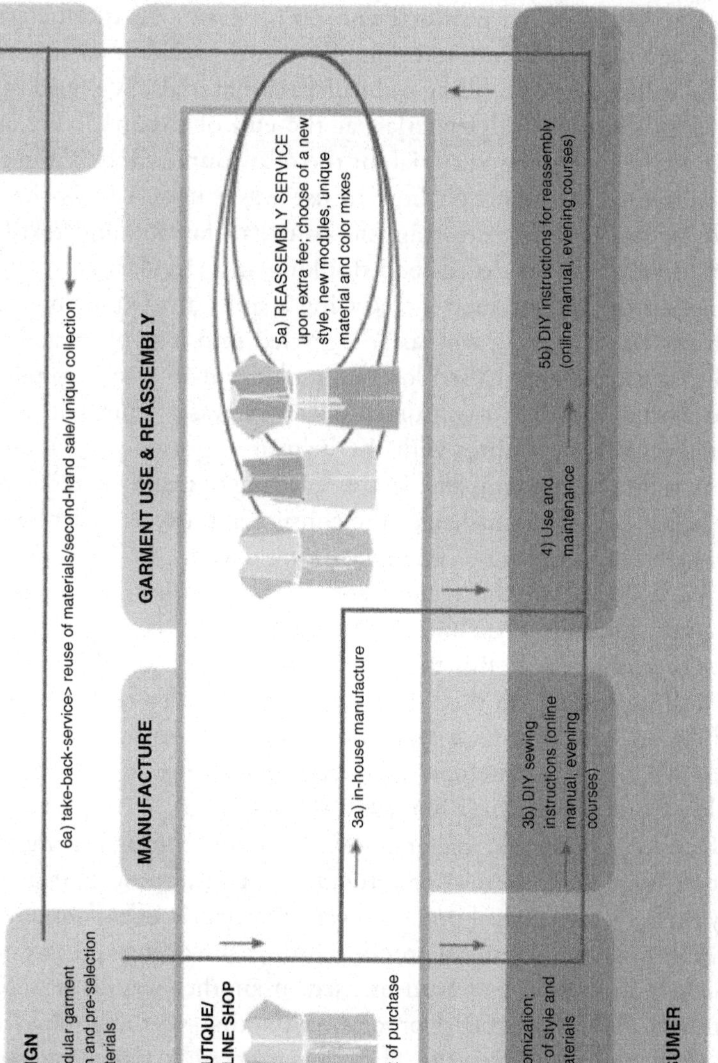

Fig. 8.2 Essi Karell's system for modular fashion design (Karell 2013, p. 117)

8.5 Design for Material Recovery

In a linear system, all products end up as waste. Textile material has long been recycled, but it is mainly down-cycled into lower value products, for example, filling or insulation materials. We need to foster new appreciation of all materials at the end of products' life and see waste as a valuable raw material for the next round. Here, we need new innovative technologies on how to use waste material. As the textile waste stream is ever increasing, the future of fashion and textiles will need to be based on closed-loop thinking and circularity.

Closing the fashion loop by recycling is quite a new phenomenon. In a closed-loop system, garments are recycled into new fibres and further into yarns. Currently closed-loop examples remain rare (e.g. the Teijin factory that turns post-consumer polyester waste from the company Patagonia into new fibres with the help of virgin polyester), and scalability is by and large missing. In the recycling of textile material, the loss of quality is a clear challenge. Pre-consumer waste is easier to recycle than post-consumer waste. Manufacturing offcuts (pre-consumer waste) can be collected in the factory and re-spun with the help of virgin materials into new yarn, and this practice is more common than using post-consumer waste. But the amount of post-consumer waste is huge and still increasing, so this waste stream should also be used. Here the problem is collecting and separation, where issues include chemicals, unknown fibre content, low quality, and therefore the predicted end quality from this origin is uncertain (Hvass 2016).

Recycling of textile material can be done through a mechanical process (e.g. wool, cotton) or through a chemical process (e.g. viscose, polyester). A mechanical process means that fabric is broken down into fibres through a mechanical process, cutting, shredding and carding, and then it is spun into new yarn or used in another way in new product manufacturing. A chemical process means that synthetic fibres can be dissolved and thereafter the fibre is regenerated. Chemical recycling processes have recently been developed to be suitable also for cotton, cellulose materials and blends (cotton-polyester), but it remains quite challenging and needs further development.

In 2013, researchers at the University of Helsinki and Aalto University in Finland were successful in developing a novel cellulose spinning solvent, which revealed excellent spin stability resulting in outstanding fibre properties. This innovation is called Ioncell-F, and it enables the production of man-made cellulosic fibres by dry-jet wet spinning. It offers an alternative to viscose processes, which have high environmental impact. The Ioncell-F process is a green, non-toxic and environmentally friendly technology for dissolving waste cotton utilising an ionic liquid. The waste-cotton solution is then extruded through spinnerets and finally regenerated into cellulose fibres. This innovation opens up new ways to use cotton and cellulose textile waste as a resource for fibre production (Aalto University, 11.2.2016).

Scientific development work to find the best technical solutions to transform waste materials (cotton, cellulose, polyester and blends) into high-quality textile fibres are currently been investigated in "T2C", the Trash to Cash project (2015–2018). Paper waste or cardboard waste can also be used to produce high-quality textiles in the project (T2C 2015). Recycled paper and cardboard are good raw materials for textiles because of the reuse of material and the low level of processing needed. This method with waste uses less chemicals and energy than pure, virgin birch cellulose (Aalto University, 27.10.2015). The T2C project objectives offer a good example of how, in a CE, all raw waste streams should be considered anew and their capability to be used as material for the next product cycle should be tested.

The closed-loop remanufacturing approach does not only challenge product and material design but also there needs to be consideration of chemical compounds in textiles. The purity and nontoxicity of materials, chemicals and colours are essential if textiles are to be remanufactured from waste materials. We need further research on what kinds of chemicals can be recycled in the system and what cannot. This means that only those chemicals can be used in the original product that can be safely recycled in a closed-loop way. Smirnova et al. (2016), for instance, have been studying the recycling of colours in the Ioncell-F process. The results show that it is possible to recycle some textile colours in a stable way while other colours change or disappear in this fibre regeneration process. The material recovery approach in fashion needs further research and new guidelines for the design and manufacturing of the original product so that it is suitable for recycling in a closed-loop way.

8.6 New Business Models in a Circular Economy

> The "take, make and dispose" model of production has long relied on cheap resources to maintain growth and stability. That world no longer exists. By applying the principles of a CE – a system that is regenerative by design – forward looking companies can seize growth opportunities while laying the groundwork for a new industrial era that benefits companies and economies alike (Nguyen et al. 2014, pp. 16–17).

The linear economic system is based on fast material throughput and a mind-set of "take, make, use and dispose" in very fast and unsustainable way. The business thinking in fast fashion emphasises low quality, fast production and a short use-time of garments to maximise sales and profit. The mind-set has to change and slower cycles have to be created, but this needs new business principles. In the buy-and-consume economy, the simple goal is to sell the product. In a CE, the goal must be different; it can propose renting the product to ensure the return of the product's materials into the material flow, as the responsibility of the product producer (Nguyen et al. 2014). Alternatively, a deposit system or incentives must be included in the business model to guarantee the product's return. Therefore, rethinking the system has to start from materials, which have to be seen as a valuable source that will be used in multiple cycles through disassembly and reuse – and not as material that quickly flows through the economy only once (Nguyen et al. 2014).

The approaches of design for longevity, for services, for reuse or for material recovery do not only challenge the current industrial design and manufacturing principles but also business models in the current linear fashion system. The whole business thinking has to change, and profit making has to be based on totally different grounds. Antikainen and Valkokari (2016) have argued that CE needs radical and systemic innovation, and therefore the whole value chain has to be redesigned through new business thinking. Circularity can be seen as a threat or an opportunity for a fashion business. New business opportunities can be created, for example, with a PSS approach or in take-back schemes. If aiming for a PSS, the service aspect has to be included in the business model from the beginning.

The service has to increase the customer satisfaction or extend the use-time of the garment, but it can also be a clear strategy to make profit. For example, if the product is meant to be rented, it has to be durable and long lasting, and the profit comes from rent, not from selling the product. The business model in CE thereby has to change from ownership of the product to performance-based payment models (EMF 2012).

Reverse-logistic providers (collectors, sorters, remanufacturers) will have an ever more important role in the CE if the future norm is material return into remanufacturing and material recovery. All these new business approaches need new networks and totally new thinking in the global context. In Sustainable Business Model Innovation (SBMI), the aim is not only to create economic value but also environmental value, for example, through creating value from waste or societal value and through re-purposing the business existence (Antikainen and Valkokari 2016). Therefore, considering SBMI might provide a good starting point for building new understanding for a CE business model.

8.7 Who Is Needed and How to Make the Transformation

This chapter began by presenting the model for a CE (Fig. 8.1). It is good to notice that the diagram also presents stakeholders and different knowledge holders who need to be included in this system. Starting from the centre, Design for longevity, the critical stakeholders are the consumers and their willingness to participate in using garments longer with their own actions and consumption habits. The second level is Design for service, and here companies are the stakeholders who carry the responsibility to develop the product-service offering so that it extends the use-time of garments and offers consumers a more sustainable way to fulfil their needs in the fashion arena. The third level is Design for reuse, and here the main stakeholders are manufacturers. With the help of new design understanding, the product should be designed and manufactured in a manner where reuse of components is possible. The fourth level is Design for material recovery, where material experts' and resource management experts' knowledge is needed.

Policymakers have a critical role in speeding up the change process. Policymakers could push business to move towards transformative, creative and circular business models. Extended Producer Responsibility (EPR) could be used to push business towards closed-loop thinking where products have to be collected back after their life span. If virgin materials were more expensive than today because of green taxation, this would have a positive effect on the price of recycled materials. This development could be accelerated with the help of taxation on the use of virgin materials or with regulations.

Textile waste legislation and EPR principles can speed up the transformation. For example, in Finland a new regulation for recycling all waste and preventing organic waste from ending up in landfills came into force in 2016. EPR is a policy that requires the original manufacturer or producer to take back the product after its use. It can be a mandatory system, as exists in, for example, France. There, producers, distributors and importers of clothes, linens and footwear have had to take back old products since 2008. A company has to have a take-back system itself or it can join a scheme, which is accredited by the French government, and pay to participate in it (Tojo et al. 2012; cited in Niinimäki 2013). Voluntary EPR is driven by industry, and we have seen examples of this lately in the fashion business. Companies proactively take back old clothes and mainly donate them to charity. The companies see these actions as improving brand value more than emphasising closed-loop systems. Some positive examples do exist, mainly in the Research & Development sector. In Finland, the Relooping Fashion project collected back old cotton clothes with the help of the Recycling Centre and a fashion company. Waste was thereafter sorted, processed into new fibres and manufactured as new garments (Relooping Fashion 2016). The project is a good example of the experimental collaboration among academy, industry, a fashion company and stakeholders we need to build new knowledge for CE (Fig. 8.3)

EPR does not yet cover the fashion and textile field, but it soon might, as EU policy increasingly aims at waste prevention and closing landfills. This would change fashion companies' actions and

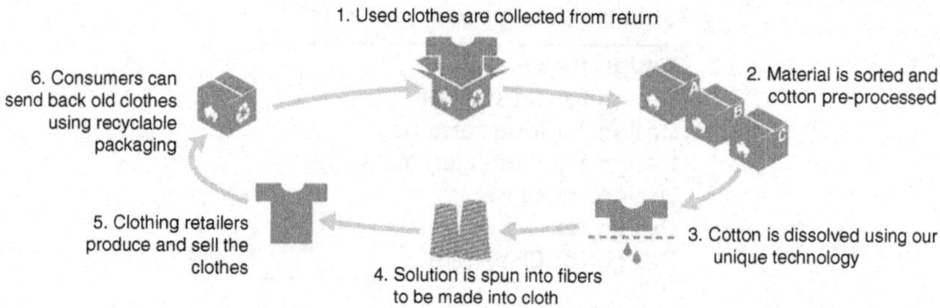

Fig. 8.3 Relooping Fashion project (Relooping Fashion 2016, used with permission)

business logic, as old garments mean extra cost through waste treatment. Therefore an effective material recycling system needs to be established (Niinimäki 2013).

The transformation towards CE requires systemic and multilevel thinking, as well as radical innovations. Innovations are needed at the macro level (trends and drivers), the meso level (ecosystem and value co-creation) and the micro level (company, customer, consumer) (Valkokari et al. 2014). As Hvass (2016) has pointed out, all stakeholders and members of the value chain have to be included in this CE system, which necessitates global thinking. Currently "... [c]hain members, such as garment producers, brands, collectors, sorters, fabric spinners and recyclers are diffused over different countries and continents, which challenge global closed loop supply chain management and its integration" (p. 134). There are political obstacles in, for example, legislation in different countries, which prevents the import of used textiles. This is the reality in, for example, Turkey, which is a significant textile producer. Local legislation thereby prevents the global transformation towards CE. Hvass (2016) further argues that a critical mass of closed-loop material is needed to create a functional system; this also needs global thinking. Moreover much coordination, collaboration and transparency is needed across the total value chain with the support of textile waste legislation to make this happen (Krikke et al. 2004, cited by Hvass 2016, p. 134).

How this can all happen at the product, manufacturing, use, material recovery and system levels should be the target of new research, with the

Table 8.3 Design approaches for CE

Design for quality
Design for satisfaction
Design for long-term use
Design from recycled materials
Design for reuse
Design for recycling
Design for CE system

support of design examples. To initiate the change with fashion designers, some design approaches for a CE are therefore highlighted in Table 8.3.

References

Aalto University. (27.10.2015). Luxury fibre from recycled cardboard, retrieved from http://chem.aalto.fi/en/current/news/2015-10-27-005/ [accessed on: 01/06/2016].

Aalto University. (11.2.2016). A process revolutionising cotton recycling wins the H&M Global Change Award, retrieved from http://www.aalto.fi/en/current/news/2016-02-11/ [accessed on: 01/06/2016].

Antikainen, M., & Valkokari, K. 2016. *Framework for sustainable circular business model innovation*. ISPIM Innovation Forum, 13–16 March 2016, Boston, USA, retrieved from http://search.proquest.com/openview/bbdc162809e5430c6a3d151bb65e657d/1?pq-origsite=gscholar&cbl=2040562 [accessed on: 01/05/2016].

Armstrong, C., Niinimäki, K., Kujala, S., Karell, E., & Lang, C. (2015). Sustainable product-service systems for clothing: Exploring consumer perceptions of consumption alternatives in Finland. *Journal of Cleaner Production, 97*: 30–39. DOI: 10.1016/j.jclepro.2014.01.046.

Briceno, T., & Stagl, S. (2006). The role of social processes for sustainable consumption. *Journal of Cleaner Production, 14*(17): 1541–1551.

EMF. (2012). Towards the circular economy: Economic and business rationale for accelerated transition. Ellen MacArthur Foundation, UK, retrieved from https://www.ellenmacarthurfoundation.org/assets/downloads/publications/

Ellen-MacArthur-Foundation-Towards-the-Circular-Economy-vol.1.pdf [accessed on: 05/03/2016]

Hvass, K. K. (2016). *Weaving the Path from Waste to Value: Exploring Fashion Industry Business Models and the Circular Economy*. Doctoral dissertation, CBS, Copenhagen, Denmark.

Jackson, T., & Shaw, D. (2009). *Mastering Fashion Marketing*. Palgrave Macmillan: New York.

Kaiser, S. (1990). *The Social Psychology of Clothing: Symbolic Appearances in Context*, 2nd ed. Macmillan Publishers: New York.

Karell, E. (2013). Planned continuity; multi-life garments through modular structures & supplemental services, in K. Niinimäki (Ed.) *Sustainable Fashion: New Approaches*, 110–123, Aalto ARTS Books: Helsinki, Finland.

Karell, E. (2014). *Planned Continuity: Design of Sustainable Clothing Service Concept*. MA thesis, Aalto University. https://aaltodoc.aalto.fi/handle/123456789/13401. [accessed on: 01/06/2016]

Krikke, H., le Blank, I., & van de Velde, S. (2004). Product modularity and the design of closed loop supply chains. *California Management Review, 46*(2): 23–39.

McDonough, W., & Braungart, M. (2002). *Cradle to Cradle: Remaking the Way We Do Things*. North Point Press: New York.

Mont, O. K. (2002). Clarifying the concept of product-service system. *Journal of Cleaner Production*, 10(3): 237–245.

Nguyen, M., Stuchtey, M., & Zils, M. (2014). Remaking the industrial economy. *McKinsey Quarterly*, February, retrieved from http://vuggetilvugge.dk/wp-content/uploads/2015/12/Circular_economyEMF-Newsletter-februar-2014.pdf [accessed on: 01/05/2016].

Niinimäki, K. (2010). Forming sustainable attachments to clothes, in The Proceedings of the 7th International Conference on Design & Emotion, 4–7 October 2010, Chicago, USA.

Niinimäki, K. (2011). *From Disposable to Sustainable. The Complex Interplay between Design and Consumption of Textiles and Clothing*, Doctoral dissertation, Aalto University: Helsinki, Finland.

Niinimäki, K. (Ed.) (2013). *Sustainable Fashion: New Approaches*, Aalto ARTS Books: Helsinki, Finland. retrieved from https://aaltodoc.aalto.fi/handle/123456789/13769 [accessed on: 01/03/2016].

Niinimäki, K. (2014). Sustainable consumer satisfaction in the context of clothing, in C. Vezzoli, C. Kohtala, A. Srinivasan, J. C. Diehl, S. M. Fusakul, L. Xin, &

D. Sateesh (Eds) *Product-Service System Design for Sustainability*, 218–237. Greenleaf: Sheffield, UK.

Niinimäki, K., & Armstrong, C. (2013). From pleasure in use to preservation of meaningful memories: A closer look at the sustainability of clothing via longevity and attachment. *International Journal of Fashion Design, Technology and Education*, 6(3): 190–199.

Ophuis, P., & Trijp, H. (1995). Perceived quality: A market driven and consumer oriented approach. *Food Quality and Preference*, *6*: 177–183.

Pawar, K. S., Beltagui, A., & Riedel, J. C. K. H. (2009). The PSO triangle: Designing product, service and organization to create value. *International Journal of Operation and Production Management*, *29*(5): 468–493.

RSA Action and Research Centre. (2016). *Designing for a Circular Economy: Lessons from the Great Recovery 2012–2016*, RSA Action and Research Centre: London, UK.

Relooping Fashion. (2016). What is the relooping fashion initiative? retrieved from http://reloopingfashion.org/ [accessed on: 08/07/2016]

Smirnova, E., Elina Ilén, E., Sixta, H., Hummel, M., & Niinimäki, K. (2016). *Colours in a Circular Economy. Circular Transitions – Mistra Future Fashion Conference on Textile Design and the Circular Economy*. 23–24 November 2016. Chelsea College of Arts & Tate Britain. London UK.

Swan, E., & Combs, L. (1976). Product performance and consumer satisfaction: A new concept. *Journal of Marketing*, *40* (2, April): 25–33.

T2C. (2015). Trash2Cash: Utilising zero-value waste textiles and fibres with design-driven technologies to create high quality products, retrieved from http://trash2cashproject.eu/ [accessed on: 05/06/2016].

Tojo, N., Kogg, B., Kiørboe, N., Kjær, B., & Aalto, K. (2012). *Prevention of Textile Waste: Material Flows of Textile in Three Nordic Countries and Suggestions on Policy Instruments*. Nordic Council of Ministers: Copenhagen, Denmark.

Tukker, A., & Tischner, U. (2006). Product-services as a research field: Past, present and future. Reflections from a decade of research. *Journal of Cleaner Production*, *14*(17): 1552–1556.

Valkokari, K., Valkokari, P., Palomäki, K., Uusitalo, T., Reunanen, M., Macchi, M., Rana, P., & Liyanage, J. P. (2014). Road-mapping the business potential of sustainability within European manufacturing industry. *Foresight*, *16*(4): 360–384.

Van Halen, C., Vezzoli, C., & Wimmer, R. (2005). *Methodology for Product Service System Innovation*. Koninklijke Van Gorcum: The Netherlands.

Dr Kirsi Niinimäki is an Associate Professor in Fashion research in Aalto University. Her research focuses on holistic understanding of sustainable fashion and textile fields and connections between design, manufacturing, business models and consumption. In Aalto University Niinimäki runs the Fashion/Textile Futures research group. The research group is involved in several significant research projects, which integrate closed loop, bioeconomy and circular economy approaches in fashion and textile systems. Her work is widely published in top scientific journals.

9

Investigating the Relationship Between Consumer Attitudes and Sustainable Fashion Product Development

Angharad McLaren and Helen Goworek

9.1 Introduction

This chapter investigates the relationship between consumers and sustainable fashion products, revealing consumer views which are closely intertwined with the product offering provided by clothing retailers and brands, through mutual influence. The chapter draws both from the literature and from a research project which aimed 'to explore the technical, behavioural and strategic obstacles to implementing innovative and sustainable product development processes that could enhance clothing longevity' (Oxborrow et al. 2017). Low and Davenport (2006) suggest that ethical consumers' actions could potentially be significant

A. McLaren (✉)
Nottingham Trent University, Nottingham, UK
e-mail: angharad.mclaren@ntu.ac.uk

H. Goworek
Management School, University of Leicester, Leicester, UK
e-mail: hg77@leicester.ac.uk

C.E. Henninger et al. (eds.), *Sustainability in Fashion*,
DOI 10.1007/978-3-319-51253-2_9

enough to be transformative, but a study by Shaw et al. (2006) revealed that cost, fashionability and availability were key barriers for consumers when purchasing ethical clothing. The identification of a difference between people's attitudes and actual practice has been termed an intention-behaviour gap, a phenomenon which was explored in various studies (see, e.g. Carrington et al. 2010). In their ground-breaking work in this field, Carrigan and Attalla (2001) stated that marketers who behave ethically were unlikely to be rewarded in commercial terms, although the market for sustainable clothing has improved somewhat in the intervening years. The perception that ethical clothing is unfashionable (Tomolillo and Shaw 2003) has been challenged by many brands more recently, since London Fashion Week launched an ethical fashion exhibition (Estethica) and Berlin Fashion Week offered three separate ethical fashion trade fairs in January 2013 (Ethical Fashion Show, Green Showroom and the green section of Premium). A broader offer of ethical choices in clothing purchases has become available for consumers. During the past decade, well-known fashion designers such as Vivienne Westwood and Katharine Hamnett have launched product ranges with sustainable features, Zandra Rhodes has collaborated with ethical fashion brand People Tree and specialist designer collections based on ethical principles have become established (e.g. Edun and Linda Loudermilk). These developments demonstrate that ethical fashion is gaining more mainstream acceptance, culminating in the Copenhagen Fashion Summit (CFS) in May 2016, organised by the Danish Fashion Institute, which attracted in excess of 1,300 delegates from industry, academia and other sectors, attending presentations about ethical aspects of fashion from organisations including Diesel, Nike, Patagonia, H&M and Vogue (Copenhagen Fashion Summit 2016). Additionally, an international group of students gave a series of presentations at CFS which exhorted those in the fashion business to take action to meet the UN Global Compact Principles.

Empirical experience within the team of authors tells us that fashion retailers and brands can acquire information about consumer attitudes via formal methods organised by consumer insights teams, such as retailers' regular online questionnaires to selected consumers and focus groups between buyers and consumers to discuss new product samples face to face. Additionally, more informal methods include in-store visits from product development-orientated Head Office staff, such as designers and buyers, to receive feedback about consumer behaviour from store sales staff or more covertly, through spending periods of time working in store changing rooms (Goworek 2009). The information acquired by these methods is exclusive to the companies concerned however, and would usually be closely guarded, remaining with the large organisations who can afford to employ their own market research teams or consultancies, whereas our study comprises findings which are freely available and applicable to companies of all sizes. This research can therefore potentially have a wider impact upon the fashion industry. The extant literature has identified a gap for an improved understanding of consumer perspectives on sustainable clothing (e.g. Oxborrow and Claxton 2016; WRAP 2012), which this chapter seeks to address by investigating views on purchase, maintenance and disposal of garments. The phases of production, distribution and disposal within the clothing life cycle all impact upon the environment but the extension of the lifetime of clothing through effective product development, maintenance and re-use assist in lessening their impact on the environment, hence the emphasis on clothing longevity in our study. If the average life of clothes were to be extended by three months, carbon, water and waste footprints could be reduced by 5–10% (WRAP 2012; McLaren et al. 2015). An extensive study by Allwood et al. (2006) also identified that the maintenance stage of the clothing life cycle generally had the most significant impact upon the environment, largely through the usage of energy and water for laundering.

The chapter's overall aim is to examine consumers' behaviour towards sustainable clothing determining potential barriers and methods by which they could be overcome through design and product development processes. The research questions that the study seeks to answer are:

- What are consumers' attitudes towards sustainable clothing?
- Which aspects of product development could encourage consumers to behave more sustainably in relation to clothing?
- How can consumer engagement in making clothes more sustainable be improved?

This research project was carried out by an interdisciplinary team comprising members with experience of marketing, product sustainability, design, clothing technology and supply chain management. Funding was supplied by the UK government's Department for Environment, Food and Rural Affairs (DEFRA). At the end of the study, feedback from consumers was compiled alongside views from fashion industry practitioners in a report to be disseminated to designers and colleagues involved in clothing product development (Oxborrow et al. 2017) in combination with a tool-kit to facilitate design that lessens sustainability impacts by prolonging the life of clothing.

9.2 Influences on Consumer Behaviour Towards Sustainable Clothing

Consumer attitudes towards sustainability can be reflected to some extent via their clothing purchase decisions. Using a framework of pro-environmental behaviour, consumers can be segmented into groups according to their behaviour in relation to sustainability, from 'positive greens' (group 1) through to 'honestly disengaged' (group 7) based on their willingness and ability to act (DEFRA 2008), which thus assists organisations in categorising consumers without relying solely on demographic characteristics.

9.2.1 Purchase

Consumers in the UK market have a broad range of choices of garment styles and price ranges from retailers or brands, yet there is a relatively low level of choice for clothing with more sustainable characteristics. During product development and production, improved sustainability can be engineered into clothing in various ways such as classic styling or using durable fabric and components (Cooper et al. 2010; Goworek et al. 2012). The most high-profile ways to improve sustainability at the purchase stage would be to offer consumers organic clothing (i.e. made from cotton grown without the use of toxic pesticides) or Fair Trade manufacturing (where the producers are paid a premium price). People Tree is an example of a company which combines both environmental and social sustainability via these methods (Goworek 2011). However, there are several other approaches available to brands and retailers in order to enhance product sustainability to meet consumer needs. For example, 'Keep and Share' offers garments with interesting and classic styling for sale or hire, intentionally avoiding mainstream fashion trends, to increase their wearable life cycle (Goworek et al. 2012; Keep and Share 2016) and hoodies by Flint and Tinder (Huckberry 2016) are backed by a 10-year guarantee. These sustainable elements can be communicated to consumers through promotion before or at the point-of-sale and on relevant labelling. Although consumers can tend to discard clothing more frequently due to the prevalence of fast fashion (Barnes and Lea Greenwood 2010; Birtwistle and Moore 2007), research conducted by WRAP (2013–2014) identified demand for longer-lasting clothes, both from low earners and higher social grades.

9.2.2 Maintenance: Wear, Care and Repair

Consumers' maintenance of clothing is often driven by their perceptions of cleanliness, for example, hygiene and freshness and there are social stigmas and norms that encourage fresh clothes being worn each day and a lack of repetition of outfits, thus leading to unnecessary volumes of laundering. Low-wash materials can be a way of discouraging overly frequent washing of clothes. For example, Jaeger is a brand that was originally built around ideas of clothing hygiene and natural fibres, based on Dr Gustav Jaeger's 'scientific' theories in the nineteenth century about the use of hygienic dress and of wearing wool next to the body, believing it would keep you clean and lead to better wellbeing. There is also the potential for new brands to develop from using the processes and practices of consumer clothing care as a starting point for sustainable fashion design. Reduced washing is preferable for certain fibres, such as merino wool, which has anti-bacterial qualities and is used for these properties by clothing companies including Icebreaker (Icebreaker 2016) and Toad&Co (Toad&Co 2016). Washing abstinence can therefore be facilitated by the selection of suitable fabrics during product development. For example, Hiut Denim is a brand based in Wales which promotes a low-wash policy for its jeans, offering advice on how to keep them bacteria-, odour- and dirt-free in between. Labelling is another method of influencing consumers to maintain clothes more sustainably. Clevercare is an information campaign by the International Association for Textile Care labelling in collaboration with H&M to promote better care, which was launched by Stella McCartney in 2014, with advice on how to avoid pilling and using the correct detergent. The label can be used by any fashion company using Ginetex's care labelling system (Just-Style 2014). There is also potential for Radio Frequency Identification (RFID) tags to help in future, by being embedded in clothes and communicating with 'smart' washing machines to set the right temperature and spin cycle for the clothes it contains.

When garments require repairs, they are often discarded by consumers (YouGov 2012; Birtwistle and Moore 2007), yet clothing's useful life could often be extended relatively easily. Certain retailers have begun to offer repair services to accommodate busy lifestyles or workshops that offer skills training in social settings, to help overcome the lack of sewing skills within the school curriculum and a reduction in sewing being taught by parents (Fisher et al. 2008). Repair cafés can also be set up by grass-roots movements to support participants in mending used items, an idea that originated the Netherlands and which is now being used by sustainability-orientated transition towns in the UK (Centre For Sustainable Design 2016; Leeds Inspired 2016; Less Waste 2016; Repair Café 2016). Similarly, craft practitioner Bridget Harvey has set up a 'Department of Repair' as a social repair space (Department of Repair 2015), as have various hackerspaces, and FabLabs have instigated mending libraries around the world (Fablabs 2016). Visible repairs can also be made, that could be considered to enhance the appearance and uniqueness of garments (McLaren and McLauchlan 2015) as craft practitioner Tom of Holland's visible repair programme (Tom of Holland 2015) champions.

Other innovative methods of approaching clothes in more sustainable ways have been developed. Film-maker Sheena Matheikin began 'The Uniform Project', by wearing the same dress for 365 days, to challenge people to think about the size and versatility of their wardrobe, and how frequently they wear items (Matheiken 2009). The No Wash sweatshirt was a pioneering concept developed by academics Becky Earley and Kate Fletcher, taking the idea of no laundering to extremes, by designing knitwear not to resist or repel dirt, but to wear it like a badge. Developed in response to a laundry diary that had been kept over the previous six months, which showed the majority of odour in the underarm area and dirt on the cuffs, elbows and front panels of garments, this jumper had wipe-clean surfaces and extra underarm ventilation, designed to be worn for over six months without washing (UAL 2003; Hix 2014).These two examples are somewhat extreme, but show 'what might be' in a move towards an alternative, more sustainable future that transcends trends and engages consumers in emotional longevity with clothing to form more enduring attachments. Such strategies seek to enhance the user-garment relationship to encourage consumers to value their clothes and to take better care of them.

Consumers' understanding and use of washcare instructions can impact significantly upon the lifespan of clothing. Key problems include selecting incorrect wash cycles and abrasive detergents (ASBCI 2013), unnecessary use of fabric conditioner (Chiwese and Cox Crews 2000) frequent excessive washing and tumble drying (Laitala et al. 2011). Male consumers, younger people and relatively high earners were the most significant market segments lacking ability to care for clothing effectively, according to the results of a study by Langley et al. (2013). Research into clothing care is somewhat limited and literature on this topic concentrates largely on the reduction of energy, water or chemicals, with the aim of being more environmentally sustainable or economical (e.g. Bain et al. 2009; Dombek-Keith and Loker 2011). Consequently, a literature gap exists with regard to consumers' behaviour in the care and maintenance of clothing in relation to sustainability.

Previous research has explored social and technical aspects of clothing use and maintenance, investigating wear and laundering, identifying ways in which consumers could be encouraged to adopt behaviour changes in these respects (Shove 2002). Other studies have suggested that stronger awareness of social and experiential aspects of usage, maintenance and repair of garments assists in the retention of clothing use (Fletcher 2012; Laitala and Boks 2012; Niinimaki and Armstrong 2013). The perception of value is another significant factor in influencing consumers to retain clothing, not only in terms of price but also in relation to practical, aesthetic, emotional and social value (Pink 2005; Fletcher 2012; Laitala and Boks 2012; Niinimaki and Armstrong 2013; McLaren and McLauchlan 2015).

9.2.3 Re-use and Disposal

Consumers exhibit various behaviours in deciding when clothing should be disposed of (Bide 2012:126). Clothing can therefore be discarded prior to the end of its useful life when consumers consider it to be outdated, making new purchases seem preferable (Cooper et al. 2013; Laitala and Boks 2012; You Gov 2012). Such clothing could have its useful life extended by being donated to charitable organisations, although this type of merchandise may be viewed by some as socially unacceptable and unhygienic (Fisher et al. 2008). Despite this, second-hand clothing is gaining wider acceptance with consumers, particularly through selling via eBay, borrowing clothes from fashion libraries (Pedersen and Netter 2015) or 'swishing' events for exchanging clothing with other consumers. Whilst disposal of garments may seem rather distanced, or even disconnected, from the product development stage, decisions made by designers and buyers, as well as fabric and garment technologists, can ultimately have a vital impact upon the complete lifecycle of garments in the latter stages of the clothing lifecycle. Such initiatives can be applied to a variety of price ranges, for example, Asda's '100 days guarantee' and advertising campaigns to discourage over-consumptions from Patagonia 'Don't Buy This Jacket' to Jigsaw's 'For Life, Not Landfill'.

Textiles recycling can take place through various routes and discarded garments can be revitalised as carpet underlay or furniture fillings (WRAP 2012). Raising consumer awareness that used textiles can be of further value by increasing the level of repurposing, could therefore contribute to a reduction in the volume of waste in landfill sites. Retailer-led schemes can also provide consumers with the motivation to recycle products (Goworek et al. 2012). For example, the Marks & Spencer 'shwopping' scheme was launched in 2012, offering free store vouchers in exchange for donations of clothes to the charity Oxfam (Smithers 2012). H&M Conscious launched a similar system in 2013 by collecting used clothes at their stores for re-wear, re-use or recycling (H&M 2016) and US brand The Reformation takes this concept beyond stores by providing the option to send back used clothing for recycling in the packaging from each online purchase (Sorrel 2015).

9.3 Methodology

The primary research in this chapter adopted an exploratory approach using mixed qualitative research methods to examine consumers' attitudes towards sustainability in relation to clothing, particularly longevity, focusing on purchase, wear, care, repair and maintenance, to investigate the barriers and opportunities for sustainable product development.

9.3.1 Sampling

Qualitative research was carried out via focus groups with 29 participants in three consumer segments:

- Consumers aged 18–35 associated with 'fast fashion' consumption (F1 & F2)
- Parents with children of school age (P)
- Consumers aged 30–60 with a focus on classic clothing (S)

The three segments were selected to represent market segments with different approaches to shopping, different demands of clothing and lifestyles that affect their behaviour towards clothing.

Purposive sampling was used to recruit participants in the three consumer segments. The sample was selected via a combination of demographic and behavioural segmentation. Groups F1 and F2 consisted of students from mixed disciplines and young, full-time professionals aged 18–35, who shopped frequently in high-street fast fashion outlets, such as Topshop, H&M and Zara. In group P, participants were all parents and the discussion focused on garments purchased for their children. Group S consisted of respondents aged between 30–60 in a range of job roles and one who had recently taken early retirement.

Snowball sampling was used for the clothing diaries to acquire respondents with a variety of backgrounds and lifestyles who were willing to commit to these tasks over a series of weeks. The samples for the focus groups and clothing diaries consisted mainly of female consumers, to reflect the fact that almost twice as much women's wear as men's wear is sold in the UK (Mintel 2014) and that women are also typically responsible for purchasing most children's clothing.

9.3.2 Focus Groups

Four focus groups were conducted to gain a variety of consumer perspectives, located in cities in the UK Midlands. The focus groups included discussion facilitated by members of the research project team and additional interactive tasks. The schedule of questions prompted discussions on four main stages of the clothing lifecycle, that is, purchase, use – including wear, care, maintenance and repair – re-use and disposal. Interactive tasks explored participants' relationships with clothing through a favourite garment exercise and perspectives on a range of potential sustainability strategies and influences. The focus groups involved 29 participants in total. The discussions were transcribed before being analysed by the research team.

9.3.3 Clothing Diaries

Ethnographic research was also carried out via the compilation of clothing diaries by a small sample to assess everyday garment care including records of wash, wear and care patterns of an individual garment for each participant, followed by interviews to provide further detail.

9.4 Findings

This section considers the main aspects discussed in the literature: purchase, usage and disposal, to offer insights into ways in which consumer behaviour can influence clothing product developers and the organisations in which they work.

9.4.1 Purchase

The results of this research revealed a certain level of willingness for consumers to purchase more sustainable clothing, yet numerous respondents did not feel that they had enough room in their wardrobe, thus supporting the existence of the intentions-behaviour gap in practice (Carrington et al. 2010). For example, one respondent had bought an extra clothing rail 'temporarily' seven years previously. Generally, value for money was the most important priority for all groups when purchasing clothing. Assessment of sustainability aspects such as longevity at point of purchase was based on a combination of experience, touching and trying on garment.

All of the focus groups revealed experiences of garments that had failed in a short time period and not met expectations. Participants associated certain brands with cheap, throwaway clothes that are unlikely to last, and were considered by some to be avoided, whereas other brands were valued, associated with quality, style, customer service, good fit and selection (e.g. Nike, Gap, M&S and Next), resulting in a level of trust for their products. Purchase price was, predictably, of the least importance for the 30–60-year-old focus group and more of a priority for parents and younger fast-fashion consumers. It was found that people did not generally bother to return low-priced faulty items. Although expectations of more expensive items were higher, as Bide (2012) also found, consumers felt price did not always positively correlate with quality. In general though, they had a higher level of trust in more expensive brands, and brand value was understood beyond the purchase price, as this statement shows:

> I feel like because I've spent more money, I have trust in that brand. If something went wrong with it, I'd be happier to go back and say, 'This has happened. Would you mind replacing the garment?' And I feel like that's the kind of quality, whereas if that happened to me in the T-shirt from Primark I would probably throw it away. (F1:CT)

Comfort was also important and consumers said that they would avoid fabrics that had caused negative experiences, such as being scratchy, having no 'give' or making them feel sweaty. Comfort had different interpretations: comfortable to wear, a comfortable, relaxed style of casual wear for the younger market or an outcome of feeling confident in styles that suit a person's body shape and sense of personal identity. Emotion-driven purchases, although sometimes impulsive, may be preferable to encourage clothing longevity, as the garment is better loved by the owner from the start, leading the owner to value it and take more care of it. Purchase strategies based on whether garments will go with other items in their wardrobe emerged in both the 30–60 focus group and the student group.

In relation to longevity, online shopping was considered a risk, as it was not possible to assess the quality of a garment and several in the sample said that they preferred interacting with clothing before buying. This was a typical comment from one of the participants:

> I think shopping for clothes online is always going to be a little bit of a gamble as well because it might look all right on the actual image but when you try it on, it could be a different case scenario, so you are taking a gamble with it, rather than going in the shop and physically having that item there. (F1:LM)

One of the most direct ways for consumers to behave more sustainably would be to purchase second-hand clothing. The respondents' attitudes to buying and wearing second-hand clothes varied with reasons cited being similar to those mentioned in previous research (Fisher et al. 2008), including hygiene; not being comfortable wearing strangers' clothes; questions of quality and disliking the shopping experience. The younger fast fashion group were the most likely to shop second-hand, including online, reflecting a rising trend towards vintage clothing and possibly due to this group having the lowest income. The other groups were less likely to buy second-hand, due to lack of time and being able to afford new (F2), or having adequate supply of hand-me-downs for children from friends and family (P). Some of the participants in the focus group aged 30–60 said that they would buy second-hand if items were viewed as particularly valuable or rare, for example, designer pieces, but they believed that the quality of clothing in charity shops had decreased. The younger (F1) group discussed how they thought older clothes were better quality, made with more craftsmanship and care to last longer. Some of their comments suggested they felt trapped by the current cheap, fast system of short-life garments as it made them feel obliged to buy new clothing frequently. Although certain branded clothes, such as Fruit of the Loom T-shirts, were praised by participants, some of the respondents were pleased to have found that in some cases cheaper clothes could be surprisingly durable, as these comments demonstrate:

> This little top that I talked about came from what used to be called Quality Seconds... and it was ridiculously cheap at the time but it still looks exactly the same as the day I bought it and that's a good 20 years ago. (S:HF)

> I bought a Henri Lloyd polo shirt, it was only about £40... I took it on holiday... and it faded quite badly. And I wore a George top for about £5/£10, it didn't fade, it was fine. So, you know, you don't always get what you pay for really. (S:GB)

9.4.2 Usage: Care, Maintenance and Repair

Easy care, convenience and cost of laundry were top priorities for parents and working people, demonstrated by this statement:

> I mean with washing, I used to separate darks and lights, now it all just goes in in a mixed wash, everything. Yeah, I haven't got time to be messing whites darks and also it's cheaper, isn't it to put one massive wash than two separate washes. (P:TO)

Care labels were rarely followed by the research participants beyond first wash and many found them difficult to understand. Wash and wear frequency was affected by deeply embedded social norms and habits, such as washing after one wear. The clothing diary exercise revealed that detergents were chosen largely due to brand familiarity, such as those used in the family home by parents. Price also affected the care relationship: consumers were more likely to hand-wash, separate colours, maintain and repair higher priced items. The value of an item was understood beyond purchase price though and the emotional value, exchange potential, social value, aesthetics and use value were also important.

> I think if it's expensive or if it has a sentimental value, then I'll try and take more care of it whereas if... they're a cheap pair of leggings, then you just throw them away and get another pair of them. (F1: CT)

As well as straightforward cleaning, washing was also viewed as a method of 'freshening up' clothing. The cost of care was judged financially, for example, dry cleaning, but also in terms of energy and water. Additionally, washing was seen as having a material cost to the garment's fibres that, whilst prolonging their active life in the short-term, ultimately leads to their deterioration. Pilling was viewed as a key problem for clothing at various price points, although surprisingly one respondent found that a jumper with cashmere content that she had bought from a supermarket did not pill after 10 years of wear. One of the participants in the diary exercise said that she did everything she could to maintain clothes and used eco detergents, low energy cycles, and washed only when needed but she would like to know more, to be able to sew and fix everything. The natural ageing process of clothes becoming faded was viewed in a positive light by some of the study's participants, with one having had a favourite T-shirt for 20 years, although it was now worn only at home. Another respondent in the same group commented:

> Something like fading, it doesn't necessarily always mean a bad thing. Sometimes, particular shirts or jeans or something like that, the fading can actually enhance them sometimes. (S:HF)

Clothing repairs were not generally undertaken by many of the participants, being viewed as expensive in comparison to the cost of buying new garments, but one of the respondents explained how she persevered with repairing garments:

> I've been to the launderette... where you get this quick stitch repair if it's something I really want to keep and extend. Yes, I did that in the past. If it's something I can't do then I will try and get it repaired if possible... repair costs a lot of money. (S:SF)

Some of the parents in the focus groups had been creative in the past with repairs, even transforming garments from one type to another, for example, trousers to skirts, but often they no longer had the time nor the inclination to do so. Participants tended to delegate clothing repairs to older female relatives, as identified in previous research by Fisher et al. (2008), even when participants had sewing skills themselves. One of the participants suggested reasons for consumers' reluctance to repair clothes:

> There's not really places you can get repairs done. I mean, that's half the problem. There are very few and again, particularly if you work full-time, you haven't really got much free time available... To be honest, it's easier to replace it. I would repair more if it was easier and cheaper to do it. (S:HF)

9.4.3 Re-use/Disposal

Those who were trend-driven would pass on or sell clothes before they wore out so that they could find replacements and keep up-to-date. All of the focus groups discussed donating items to charity shops. Most had a hierarchy of disposal methods, with expensive items being sold online (via eBay and Facebook selling groups, dress agencies or exchanging sites) or at car boot sales. Good quality items were passed on to friends or family, especially children's clothes. In Nottingham, the council had a 'red bag' textiles collection scheme, and this was seen by some of them as a convenient way to dispose of items, especially when they did not feel these were good enough to be worn:

> So my hierarchy goes: nice things for people I know, wearable, but not that nice to charity shop and complete rubbish into the red bag. (P:HM)

Pilling affected satisfaction of user experience and led to low active use and disposal. Other examples of reasons for disposal of clothing were T-shirts that had shrunk after three washes; zips and lining going on expensive garments when the rest of the garment was fine and leaching colours onto other items (due to colour transfer or hairy fibres). Failure of garments prior to their expected useful life caused emotional responses of frustration, annoyance and disappointment in our participants. One of the respondents had considered swapping garments with friends, but she felt it unlikely that there would be a large enough pool of people of the same age and clothing size to make this viable, but another participant felt that swapping could work well if it was planned at the purchase stage:

> Sometimes, I swap with this guy and we get Vivienne Westwood clothes. And so, I'll swap with him and he'll swap with me so we never have the same thing each night. (S:MM)

Overall, the findings revealed a range of different approaches to sustainability from consumers, with key barriers being the expense and time involved in behaving more sustainability, combined with a lack of knowledge and access to sustainable practices, which could be facilitated by retailers, brands and other organisations.

9.5 Conclusion

The research findings showed that numerous factors affect consumer attitudes towards the sustainability of clothing during the different stages in the garment life cycle during purchase, usage and disposal, from the consumers' perspective, supporting the findings of previous studies (e.g. Fisher et al. 2008; Laitala and Boks 2012; Langley et al. 2013). The conclusion addresses how these factors can influence product development practice in the fashion industry. Product developers and consumers can influence each other and this iterative process can potentially lessen sustainability impacts in relation to clothing. This study found that a key way in which fashion products could be designed to encourage consumers to prolong the lifetime of clothing would be to ensure that customers would perceive garments as good value for money (although not necessarily cheap). Practical considerations such as ensuring clear and convenient washcare instructions, avoiding fabrics that pill and incorporating functional, long-lasting features during product development, could improve maintenance, and therefore durability of clothing. Inventive approaches to new product development (NPD) such as those discussed in the literature could inspire media attention and engage consumers' interest in buying such products.

Various aspects of product development could encourage consumers to behave more sustainably in relation to clothing. Firstly, there is pressure on NPD process to produce garments within a short timescale, thus leaving limited time and resources to consider sustainability. Secondly, designers and their colleagues may lack information about consumers' attitudes towards sustainable clothing, which can mean that they are not addressed sufficiently during the product development process. Increased support from marketing teams and managers in this area and guidelines for those involved in NPD could assist towards facilitating sustainable design, to better meet consumer needs.

The implications for clothing companies are that they can provide product sustainability guidelines for their product development teams and investigate their own customers' opinions of sustainable clothing, particularly in relation to longevity, either supplying them to designers or involving the design/product development team in the discussion. Workshops on sustainability-related activities such as clothing repair could also be offered to consumers by fashion brands and retailers. To facilitate these options, additional time and financial resources may need to be allocated by management. Clearly, this would be likely to affect price in certain respects, so price ranges may need to be reviewed in relation to consumers' perceptions of value. Implications for theory are that new models of the consumer decision-making process and the NPD process could be developed to incorporate steps which address the sustainability of clothing.

A limitation of this study is that it was based in one country. Therefore, the research topic could also be applied in future research in the context of other locations. Future research in this field could add an extra dimension by investigating how links between technical knowledge and skills in industry and education impact upon consumers' clothing longevity attitudes.

Acknowledgement The primary research study discussed in this chapter is a DEFRA-funded research project EV0553 'Strategies to improve design and testing for clothing longevity'. Findings from this study were presented at the Design Research Society in Conference at Brighton University in June 2016 and the British Academy of Management Conference at Newcastle University in September 2016.

References

Allwood, J. M., Laursen, S. E., De Rodriguez, C. M., & Bocken, N. M. P. (2006). *Well Dressed? The Present and Future Sustainability of Clothing and Textiles in the UK.* Cambridge University Institute of Manufacturing: Cambridge, available online at: http://www.ifm.eng.cam.ac.uk/resources/sustainability/well-dressed/.

ASBCI. (2013). *Caring for Your Clothes (3rd edition)*, Industry Manual from the Association of Suppliers to the British Clothing Industry: UK.

Bain, J., Beton, A., Schultze, A., Mudgal, S., Dowling, M., Holdway, R., & Owens, J. (2009). Reducing the Environmental Impact of Clothes Cleaning. Final Report to the Department for Environment, Food and Rural Affairs (DEFRA): London.

Barnes, L., & Lea-Greenwood, G. (2010). Fast Fashion in the Retail Store Environment. *International Journal of Retail & Distribution Management, 38*(10), 760–772.

Bide, M. (2012). Testing Textile Durability, in P. Annis (Ed.) *Understanding and Improving the Durability of Textiles.* Woodhead: Cambridge.

Birtwistle, G., & Moore, C. M. (2007). Fashion Clothing – Where Does it all End Up? *International Journal of Retail & Distribution Management, 35*(3), 210–216.

Carrigan, M., & Attalla, A. (2001). The Myth of the Ethical Consumer: Do Ethics Matter in Purchase Behaviour?' *Journal of Consumer Marketing, 18*(7), 560–578.

Carrington, M. J., Neville, B. A., & Whitwell, G. J. (2010). Why Ethical Consumers Don't Walk Their Talk: Towards a Framework for Understanding the Gap Between the Ethical Purchase Intentions and Actual Buying Behaviour of Ethically Minded Consumers. *Journal of Business Ethics, 97*, 139.

Centre for Sustainable Design. (2016). *Farnham Repair Café*, available online at: http://cfsd.org.uk/events/farnham_repair_cafe/

Chiwese, A., & Cox Crews, P. (2000). Influence of Household Fabric Softeners and Laundry Enzymes on Pilling and Breaking Strength. *Textile Chemist and Colorist & American Dyestuff Reporter, 32*(9), 41–47.

Cooper, T., Fisher, T., Hiller, A., Goworek, H., & Woodward, S. (2010). Excessive Speed/Short Lives: Attitudes to Clothing Longevity and Disposal, in V. Ceschin Zhang (Eds.) *Sustainability in Design: Now! Proceedings of the LeNS Conference, Bangalore, India*, pp. 728–737, Greenleaf Publishing Limited: Sheffield. Available online at: http://bura.brunel.ac.uk/bitstream/2438/6726/3/Ceschin%20Vezzoli%20Zhang_2010_LeNS%20proceedings_vol1.pdf.

Cooper, T., Hill, H., Kininmonth, J., Townsend, K., & Hughes, M. (2013). Design for Longevity: Guidance on Increasing the Active Life of Clothing, A report for WRAP: Banbury, available online at: http://www.wrap.org.uk/sites/files/wrap/Design%20for%20Longevity%20Report_0.pdf.

Copenhagen Fashion Summit. (2016). *Video*, available online at: http://www.copenhagenfashionsummit.com/video/#video

Defra. (2008). *A Framework For Pro-Environmental Behaviours*. Defra: London. Available online at: https://www.gov.uk/government/uploads/system/uploads/attachment_data/file/69277/pb13574-behaviours-report-080110.pdf.

Department of Repair. (2015). *Department of Repair*, available online at: https://thedepartmentofrepair.wordpress.com/

Dombek-Keith, K., & Loker, S. (2011). Sustainable Clothing Care by Design, in A. Gwilt & T. Rissanen (eds) *Shaping Sustainable Fashion: Changing the Way We Make and Use Clothes* (pp. 101–116). Routledge: London.

Fab Labs UK. (2016). *Fab Labs*, available online at: http://fablabsuk.co.uk/

Fisher, T., Cooper, T., Woodward, S., Hiller, A., & Goworek, H. (2008). *Public Understanding of Sustainable Clothing*, A Research Report Completed for the Department for Environment, Food and Rural Affairs by Nottingham Trent University and Sheffield Hallam University. DEFRA: London.

Fletcher, K. (2012). Durability, Fashion, Sustainability: The Processes and Practices of Use. *Fashion Practice Journal, 4*(2), 221–238.

Goworek, H. (2009). Oasis Consumer Behaviour Case Study, in D. Jobber & J. Fahy (2009) (eds.), *Foundations of Marketing*. 3rd ed. McGraw Hill.

Goworek, H. (2011). Social and Environmental Sustainability in the Clothing Industry: A Case Study of a Fair Trade Retailer. *Social Responsibility Journal, 7*, 74–86.

Goworek, H., Cooper, T., Fisher, T., Woodward, S., & Hiller, A. (2012). The Sustainable Clothing Market: An Evaluation of Potential Strategies for UK

Fashion Retailers. *International Journal of Retail and Distribution Management, 40*(12), 935–954.

H&M. (2016). Recycle Your Clothes, available online at: http://about.hm.com/en/sustainability/get-involved/recycle-your-clothes.html

Hix, L. (2014). 'Could the Clothes On Your Back Halt Global Warming?', *Collectors' Weekly*, available online at: http://www.collectorsweekly.com/articles/could-the-clothes-on-your-back-halt-global-warming/

Huckberry. (2016). 10 Year Hoodie, available online at: https://huckberry.com/store/shop/flint-and-tinder-10-year-hoodie

Icebreaker. (2016). Why Icebreaker Merino? available online at: http://uk.icebreaker.com/en/why-icebreaker-merino/why-icebreaker-landing.html

Just-Style. (2014). H&M Partners with Ginetex on New Care Label. *Just-Style*, available online at: http://www.just-style.com/news/hm-partners-with-ginetex-on-new-care-label_id120679.aspx

Keep and Share. (2016). *About Keep and Share*. Available online at: http://www.keepandshare.co.uk/about/what-keep-share

Laitala, K., Boks, C., & Klepp, I. G. (2011). Potential for Environmental Improvements in Laundering. *International Journal of Consumer Studies, 35*, 254–264.

Laitala, K., & Boks, C. (2012). Sustainable Clothing Design: Use matters. *Journal of Design Research, 10*(1/2), 21–139.

Langley, E., Durkacz, S., & Tanase, S. (2013). Clothing Longevity and Measuring Active Use. A Summary Report by Ipsos Mori for WRAP: London, available online at: http://www.wrap.org.uk/content/clothing-longevity-measuring-active-use

Leeds Inspired. (2016). *Leeds Repair Café*, available online at: http://www.leedsinspired.co.uk/events/leeds-repair-cafe

Less Waste. (2016). *Repair Café, Fearon Hall, Loughborough*, available online at: http://www.lesswaste.org.uk/events/repair-cafe-fearon-hall-loughborough/

Low, W., & Davenport, E. (2006). Mainstreaming Fair Trade: Adoption, Assimilation, Appropriation. *Journal of Strategic Marketing, 14*, 315–327.

Matheiken, S. (2009). *The Uniform Project*, available online at: http://matheiken.com/uniform-project/

McLaren, A., Oxborrow, L., Cooper, T., Hill, H., & Goworek, H. (2015). Clothing longevity perspectives: exploring consumer expectations, consumption and use, in T. Cooper, N. Braithwaite, M. Moreno, G. Salvia (eds.), Product Lifetimes And The Environment (PLATE) Conference Proceedings,

17–19 June - Nottingham (pp. 229–235), UK. Nottingham Trent University: CADBE. ISBN 978-0-9576009-9-7.

McLaren, A., & McLauchlan, S. (2015). 'Crafting Sustainable Repairs: Practice-based Approaches to Extending the Life of Clothes', *PLATE Conference*, 17th–19th June 2015, Nottingham Trent University, available online at: http://irep.ntu.ac.uk/7526/1/220771_PubSub2645_McLaren.pdf

Mintel. (2014). *Clothing Retailing UK.* October 2014, Mintel Group: London.

Niinimaki, K., & Armstrong, C. (2013). From Pleasure in Use to Preservation of Meaningful Memories: A Closer Look at the Sustainability of Clothing via Longevity and Attachment. *International Journal of Fashion Design Technology and Education, 6*(3), 190–199.

Oxborrow, L., & Claxton, S. (2016). Extending clothing lifetimes: an exploration of design and supply chain challenges, in P. Lloyd & E. Bohemia (eds.), Proceedings of DRS2016: Design + Research + Society - Future-Focused Thinking, Volume 10, pp 3815–3830, DOI 10.21606/drs.2016.XXX.

Oxborrow, L., McLaren, A., Cooper, T., Hill, H., Goworek, H., & Claxton, S. (forthcoming 2017) *Strategies to Improve Design and Testing for Clothing Longevity*, Report for Defra.

Pedersen, E. R. G., & Netter, S. (2015). Collaborative Consumption: Business Model Opportunities and Barriers for Fashion Libraries. *Journal of Fashion Marketing and Management, 19*(3), 258–273.

Pink, S. (2005). Dirty Laundry. Everyday Practice, Sensory Engagement and the Constitution of Identity. *Social Anthropology, 13*(3), 275–290.

Repair Café, R. (2016) *About Repair Café*, available online at: https://repaircafe.org/en/about/

Shaw, D., Hogg, G., Wilson, E., Shui, E., & Hassan, L. (2006). Fashion Victim: The Impact of Fair Trade Concerns on Clothing Choice. *Journal of Strategic Marketing, 14*, 427–440.

Shove, E. (2002). Converging Conventions of Comfort, Cleanliness and Convenience, Published by the Department of Sociology, Lancaster University, Lancaster, UK, available online at http://www.comp.lancs.ac.uk/sociology/papers/Shove-Converging-Conventions.pdf

Smithers, R. (2012) M&S Launches 'shwopping' Scheme, *The Guardian*, 26th April 2012, available online at: https://www.theguardian.com/money/2012/apr/26/marks-spencer-shwopping-scheme

Sorrel, C. (2015) Send Your Old Clothes Back in the Box Your New Clothes Came In. *fastco.exist*, 12th May 2015, available online at: https://www.fastcoexist.com/3050214/send-your-old-clothes-back-in-the-box-your-new-clothes-came-in#1

Toad&Co. (2016). *Sustainability Update*, available online at: https://www.toadandco.com/blog/tag/merino-wool/

Tom of Holland (2015). The Visible Mending Programme: making and re-making. (online). Available from: https://tomofholland.com/about/

Tomolillo, D., & Shaw, D. (2003). Undressing the Ethical Issues in Clothing Choice. *International Journal of New Product Development and Innovation Management, 15*(2): 99–107.

UAL. (2003). *No Wash Sweatshirt*, available online at: http://ualresearchonline.arts.ac.uk/839/

WRAP. (2012). *Valuing Our Clothes: The True Cost of How We Design, Use and Dispose of Our Clothing in the UK*, A report for WRAP: London. available online at http://www.wrap.org.uk/sites/files/wrap/VoC%20FINAL%20online%202012%2007%2011.pdf

You Gov. (2012). Bored with Your Clothes? A report by You Gov for M&S, available online at: https://yougov.co.uk/news/2012/06/27/bored-your-clothes/

Angharad McLaren is a Lecturer in Textile Design, Sustainable Clothing Research Coordinator and former Research Fellow in Design for Clothing Longevity, at Nottingham Trent University, UK, with research interests in sustainable fashion and textiles, sustainable consumption, consumer behaviour and clothing longevity.

Dr Helen Goworek is MSc Marketing Programme Leader at Leicester University, UK, and chair of the British Academy of Management's Sustainable and Responsible Business conference track. She is the author of three books about the fashion business and retailing, and has also written book chapters and articles on retail buying, product development and sustainability. She is a member of the organising committees for the Management and Environmental Sustainability conference and the International Colloquium on Design, Branding and Marketing (ICDBM).

10

Social Sustainability in Apparel Supply Chains: Organizational Practices for Managing Sub-Contracted Homework

Archana and Marsha A. Dickson

10.1 Introduction

While the apparel industry is an immense source of employment on a global scale, long supply chains are also rampant with human rights abuses like poor wages, long hours, child labor, health and safety concerns, and discrimination. One area of concern in recent years has been the persistence of subcontracting and its relationship to poor working conditions. Subcontracting is on a steady rise due to various global and economic factors. As the lowest level in the subcontracted supply chain, homework tends to be hidden and homeworkers, often including children, are invisible and subject to exploitation. Existing codes of conduct and monitoring schemes favor the rights of the visible workforce employed in industrial settings in tier 1 factories. This fact, coupled with the invisible nature of homework, leaves workers open to exploitation, poor pay, ambiguous

Archana · M.A. Dickson (✉)
Department of Fashion and Apparel Studies, University of Delaware, Newark, DE, USA
e-mail: archana@udel.edu; Dickson@udel.edu

C.E. Henninger et al. (eds.), *Sustainability in Fashion*,
DOI 10.1007/978-3-319-51253-2_10

employment status, irregular work, and without documentation of work hours, employee benefits, and an understanding of their rights (Hurley and Miller 2005; Marian 2013).

Brands and retailers tend to shy away from acknowledging the existence of subcontracting and homework in their supply chains due to the potential for a number of critical issues like child labor and the inherent difficulty of effectively monitoring the informal segment. As a result, brands and retailers often make subcontracting a contractually illegal practice, claim it does not exist in their supply chains, and are sometimes unaware that their contractors have in fact outsourced their order to a sub-contractor or homeworkers. Unfortunately, this does nothing more than hide the problem or possibly give brands and retailers a false sense of security about conditions in their supply chains (Marian 2013). This study focuses on understanding the sustainable management systems that have been put in place by an embroidery center to assure global buyers that homework can be carried out in ways consistent with standards for labor and human rights.

10.2 Review of Literature

Despite concerns of brands and retailers, homework is a controversial topic in the apparel industry with benefits and challenges. By the nature of its construct, homework allows for freedom of organization of work thereby providing a source of employment to workers who would have been excluded from the work force (Green 2003). Other factors like legal employment status (McCormick and Schmitz 2001) and lack of employment opportunities in the formal sector (Freeman 2003; Buttle 2008) make homework the only viable option for many workers. Evidenced by previous research (McCormick and Schmitz 2001; Freeman 2003; ETI 2010; Green 2003; Littrell and Dickson 2010), predominantly women stand to benefit from homework as it allows them to manage their household effectively while offering a source of livelihood and added household income. More so, cultural restrictions render homework as the only available option for many women who want to earn a livelihood (Wilkinson-Weber 1997; Freeman 2003; Green 2003; ETI 2010). While these subcontracting arrangements create an environment that allows violations against workers' rights (Wills and Hale 2005, p. 189), the advantages to making homework an acceptable part of the supply chain are stronger. Littrell and Dickson (2010) found that this kind of work not only offered the women a source of income but also created empowerment and enhanced material, social, and psychological well-being.

With homework being a form of sub-contracting, there is rampant exploitation by contractors who manage this tier of the supply chain. Workers are dependent on middlemen and contractors and constantly face conditions of poor pay, irregular workflow, and lack of worker benefits (Boris 1989; McCormick and Schmitz 2001; Delaney 2004; ETI 2010; Littrell and Dickson 2010). To add to these terrible working conditions, their ambiguous employment status is coupled with almost no awareness or knowledge of worker rights, thereby extending their exploitation at the hands of the contractors. Seldom do homeworkers have access to information or an understanding of market mechanisms, which keeps them under the control of the middlemen (Bhatt 2006).

Lack of structured work hours is another issue that makes it hard to monitor this sector. Irregular work hours cause an unpredictable work flow and erratic hours with tight deadlines for the workers (Littrell and Dickson 2010). Furthermore, this work mostly being of a seasonal nature only compounds the irregularity of work and pay. Working with contractors also means these homeworkers are not offered any worker benefits and are not aware of their rights to such benefits. All these aspects and issues within homework call for the need to include corporate social responsibility (CSR) to this lower tier of the supply chain to improve the status of homeworkers.

10.2.1 Managing Corporate Social Responsibility from a Homework Perspective

One approach to increasing visibility in supply chains involves adopting management systems that integrate CSR policies and practices into day-to-day business (Castka et al. 2004; Castka and Balzarova 2007). Based on longitudinal case study research with several companies based in the UK,

Castka et al. (2004) proposed a model for a CSR system that incorporates continuous improvement. Taking into consideration the views of stakeholders, including shareholders, the researchers proposed a cycle incorporating strategic planning; management of resources, processes, and systems; measurement and analysis; and managing change and continuous improvement. This is preferable to a stand-alone system that isolates CSR efforts. Determination of the adequacy of the programs established and implemented is based on whether stakeholders are satisfied.

Management systems providing standards or guidance to companies for implementing quality, environmental, and social responsibility programs are key elements in international standards established by the International Organization of Standardization (ISO), such as ISO 9000, ISO 14000, and their newest standard on CSR (ISO 26000) (Castka and Balzarova 2007). In qualitative research of CSR professionals for major companies, Dickson and Chang (2015) found that management systems were the most frequently cited characteristic of apparel manufacturing companies with "world class" CSR programs. The management system approach to CSR could be a useful approach to managing homework in ways that are acceptable to stakeholders, including brands and retailers.

With the rise of CSR in the apparel industry since the 1990s, a few entities have attempted to systemize homework. The International Labour Organization (ILO) adopted Convention 177 on Homework in 1996 defining homework and articulating the rights of homeworkers worldwide (American Society of International Law 1997). However, with only seven countries having ratified this convention, it remains a placeholder in the absence of hard laws. The Pentland Group plc, based in Pakistan, tried to centralize its football production to mitigate child labor but this operation was not fully successful due to the initial exclusion of women, who accounted for the majority of the workers, from these centers (Freeman 2003). The Body Shop attempted to improve its supply chain transparency by registering homeworkers (Freeman 2003).

In Australia where homeworkers account for 20 percent of the workforce; the Textile, Clothing and Footwear Union of Australia (TCFUA) introduced the Homeworkers Code of Practice in light of the increasing homework trend (Brill 2002). Another initiative deemed successful has been the Australian Fairwear Campaign's attempt in using media-friendly tactics to highlight the homeworkers' cause (Burchielli and Delaney 2009). In the UK, the Ethical Trading Initiative (ETI) Homeworker Project, utilizing the ETI Base Code as its starting point, assembled a collaborative approach by involving brands, NGOs, government, and the public as a strategy of improving homeworker rights. This approach to homeworker rights seems to have an effective strategy as illustrated by Williams' (2005) UK Change Influence Model.

Even with the few trial and error efforts to address homework, this lower tier of the supply chain remains largely uncontrolled. In light of this, research studies have brought attention to the need for extending CSR to homework (Freeman 2003; Hensman 2005; Burchielli and Delaney 2009; Delaney n.a.; Littrell and Dickson 2010). We focused on homework from a CSR perspective in an attempt to identify the practices necessary to make it an acceptable and protected component of the apparel supply chain.

10.2.2 Self Employed Women's Association

Embroidery centers operated by the Self Employed Women's Association (SEWA) in Delhi, India served as the field sites for this research study. SEWA, established in 1971 in Ahmedabad, Gujarat, has been working to organize and empower workers in the informal sector. While the main objective of SEWA is to function like a trade union and organize women workers, the organization also focuses on providing social services like banking, legal aid, child care services, and technical training to its members (Spodek 1994; Datta 2003). The programs are always centered on the work and women are leaders of their own programs (SEWA Bharat 2008–2009).

10.3 Theoretical Framework

For a theoretical framework, we adapted Williams' (2005) model for change that posits better conditions of employment for homeworkers can be influenced with an integrated strategy of labor rights campaigning, organizing homeworkers, strengthening company codes of conduct and government regulation, and bringing homeworkers' rights to the attention of the public.

This adapted model proposes how homework can be integrated into the supply chain and made a visible and unexploited component of the production process by involving brands, retailers, government, and the public to influence better terms of employment for the homeworkers (see Fig. 10.1). The scope of this study remained on the top and the bottom tiers of the model pertaining to the brands and retailers as well as homeworker empowerment. Williams' (2005) model maintained that unions and NGOs were core to improving working conditions for homeworkers. This adapted model conceives the role of SEWA Delhi as a point of influence in integrating homework into the supply chain and making it a visible and unexploited component of a brand's production process, as illustrated in the Fig. 10.1.

SEWA albeit registered as a trade union acts as an NGO in much of its functioning, with a focus on worker empowerment through education, training, and support services. SEWA Delhi replaces the unions and NGOs from the original model and is the core component to be

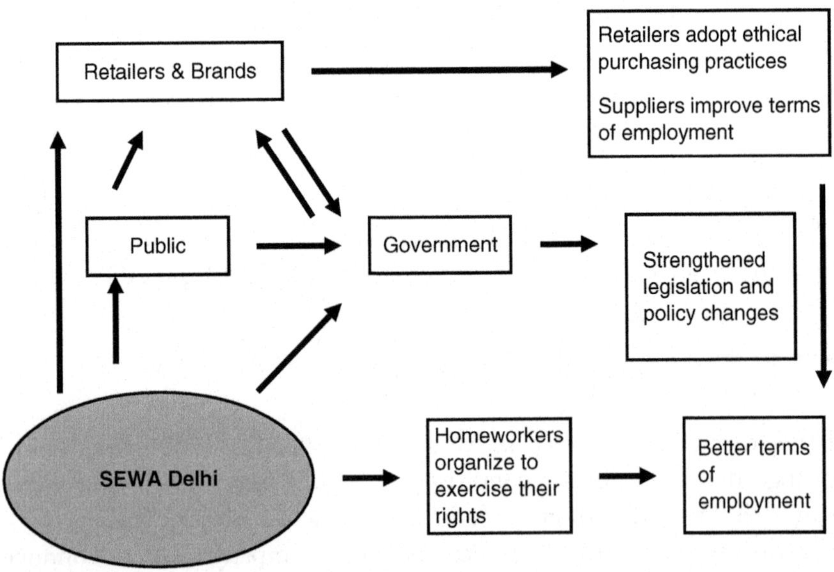

Fig. 10.1 Homework change model

studied. We focus on the effect of SEWA Delhi's CSR initiatives and practices, efforts made for homeworkers' empowerment, and the organization's influence on retailers and brands in adopting better supply chain practices concerning homework. Studying the CSR initiatives at SEWA's embroidery centers at one end and understanding the basic way that they work to empower workers, while looking into SEWA's strategic engagement of the brands and the public on the other provided a clear picture of the unique homework phenomenon at the embroidery center and its influence in changing homework conditions.

10.4 Methods

A field study was carried out in New Delhi, India. The qualitative field research involved documentation review, researcher observations, and first hand semi-structured interviews with five members from SEWA Delhi management, five homeworkers, and four external stakeholders. We examined the ways SEWA works to organize and empower homeworkers, the organization's CSR practices regarding homework, SEWA's impact on issues associated with homework, how the organization engages brands and retailers in improving homework conditions, and how SEWA engages with the public (e.g., consumers, civil society, others) about homework. Narrative data from the interviews were coded using the constant comparative data analysis method, which allowed for the development of broader conceptual themes (Strauss and Corbin 2008).

10.5 Findings

SEWA Delhi launched a livelihood promotion project in 2005 to organize homeworkers in the embellishment sector, establish a mode of income generation, eliminate middlemen, and enable more visibility in the supply chain. With a large Muslim population in the neighborhoods where SEWA was working, the women workers were restricted to piece-based embellishment work through contractors who exploited their immobility. SEWA's embroidery centers eliminated much of this immobility with the opening of the sub-centers located closer to the women's homes, thereby allowing them to access employment via the SEWA's project. SEWA Delhi currently organizes three clusters of homeworkers in Sunder Nagri, Rajiv Nagar, and New Ashok Nagar in the Delhi area, and two clusters in Richola and Faridpur in the Bareilly area totaling approximately 500 registered members.

SEWA, while trying to remain competitive in the market, has also been trying to maintain the essence of homework by ensuring the core advantage of working at home. Modelled closely after the ETA's Homework Project guidelines (SEWA Bharat 2008–2009), SEWA Delhi formed Ruaab SEWA Artisans Producer Company Limited (Ruaab) as the business front for the livelihood promotion project in December 2010. Ruaab is owned and operated by the women workers who buy shares of the company.

Ruaab's organizational structure consists of a board of directors, CEO, and design, merchandise, production, and accounts departments, which function in a systemized process focused on industry quality parameters and timely delivery of goods. Six women workers, two SEWA representatives, and one external representative form the nine-member board of directors. Other key employees at Ruaab are the in-house sampling unit of nine highly skilled women workers, who were formerly engaged in homework with SEWA, along with SEWA Saathis (field organizers) who help with neighborhood organizing efforts.

10.5.1 Integrated CSR Management Systems

The livelihood promotion project follows a system of processes that maintain visibility into production, payment, and other key elements of the work. The management systems cover the following areas of work: order initiation, issue-receipt (IR), production, quality control, and billing and payment. The embroidery centers are the main point of contact between the homeworkers and the export house while the sub-centers help with constant organizing efforts that is central to SEWA's initiatives.

Order initiation. After the export house initiates an order with the merchandiser, the sampling supervisor directs the sampling unit in a time-motion study. The sampling unit makes notes about the entire sampling process, including amount of time, skill requirements, average material consumption, and quality control measures involved in the production of the sample and maximization of output. The CEO, quality supervisor, and the merchandiser analyze this time-motion study to calculate the piece rate. After the export house approves the in-house sample, the price is negotiated and the order is booked. The export house then dispatches the materials along with the approved sample with a purchase order and a challan (transfer invoice).

Issue-Receipt. After the order is booked, it is received in the IR department, where the quality supervisor notes the quality parameters required for the order. The next step in the process is pre-production approval of about 1–5 percent of the first lot of the order, which is produced by the sampling department and checked for quality parameters by the export house's quality supervisor. After approvals are received, planning for production based on lead-time and worker capacity at the centers and sub-centers is carried out.

Production. During the production phase, the SEWA Saathis (field organizers) inform the homeworkers about the availability of work at the centers. Workers gather at the center and sampling is carried out under the supervision of the center in-charge or the quality supervisor to ensure understanding of the style and quality measures. When the workers finish sampling and the management is satisfied with the quality, the production order is distributed at the centers and sub-centers along with the challan (transfer receipt). The center in-charge makes a record of the work allotted to each worker in both, the worker's pass book and the register. All workers carry a passbook containing their membership information including address, occupation, age along with a detailed record of the work allotted, date of acceptance, date of delivery, alterations, and other pertinent information. The center in-charge also maintains a record of all this information in the register. In time for the monthly payment, the passbook and register are checked to calculate the wages earned by the member.

Quality control. When the production is underway, the SEWA Saathis carry out house-to-house monitoring to ensure quality control. The workers bring in finished pieces to be collected by the center in-charge, who checks for quality parameters before accepting the pieces. The finished pieces are then tagged and bundled for dispatch to the IR department along with a challan. After the production order reaches the IR department, the quality supervisor inspects the pieces.

The in-house sampling team carries out minor alterations but in case of multiple changes, the production is sent back to the centers. Approved quality production is dispatched to the exporter with a challan. Per the export house quality control, the order is accepted or returned for alterations. Alterations performed by the export house are debited onto Ruaab's account.

Billing and payment. The challan from the export house is tallied with the external challan issued by the IR department and conveyed to the exporter. If the tally does not match, it is debited onto Ruaab's account. The IR department hands the approved bill over to the runner, who submits it to the export house ensuring it issues a receiving note. The accountant then follows up with the billing cycle, a range of two weeks to three months. The runner is responsible for the bank deposits and the accountant maintains the hard copies of the payment checks received from the clients.

The workers are paid their wage earnings on a monthly cycle, with the payment cycle calculated from the 21st to 20th of each month and payments made in the first week of the month. There are two formats for payment procedures based on the workers' membership: cooperative, for the members who buy shares, and non-cooperative, for the members who choose not to buy shares in Ruaab or take on work orders with SEWA occasionally. Different payment sheets are prepared for the cooperative and non-cooperative members and handed over to the respective departments via e-mail. An authorized hard copy is sent to the head office on the 26th of each month. The head office prepares the checks for both the departments. After cashing a check from the head office to the accountant, a runner delivers cash for the payment of the non-cooperative members against the payment sheet. The center in-charge receives the cash and disburses the non-cooperative payments after making a record, which is filed by the accountant. The cooperative payments are directly deposited to the members' bank accounts as soon as the department receives the check, usually around the 3rd of each month. However, it is not clear if the workers receive a payment stub other than the calculated details in their notebook.

10.5.2 Improvement of Homeworker Working Conditions

SEWA, via the embroidery centers, has an impact on critical issues in homework like child labor, pay issues, work hours, health problems, and benefits and the overall quality of life of the workers. External stakeholders we interviewed identified child labor as a key issue in homework and pointed out that brands do not wish to associate with homework because of the risk of related negative reporting in the media, so often a no homework policy works best. The embellishment sector by and large includes child labor, in part due to skill training that begins at an early age.

SEWA has been working via its strict age policy that allows employment of workers 18 or over, continued education of the workers, and constant monitoring, carried out by SEWA Saathis while out in the field, to mitigate child labor from its work force. All the homeworkers interviewed understood the importance of eliminating child labor and expressed they would prefer their children receive an education instead of entering the embellishment industry. However, SEWA also encourages skill training for young girls to keep the traditional skills alive; when children above the age of 14 years shows an interest in the art form they are allowed to work up to two hours per day. One external stakeholder indicated that the training period would not be considered child labor, saying that:

> Even ILO says, when a child is actually working with his parents, there is no question of exploitation and it is not called child labour but it is called child help or child work.

Research revealed certain inconsistencies in management members' views on critical issues like child labor, with a couple of them expressing lenient views on the topic. A work in progress, SEWA is working to better its processes.

In competing with other vendors, SEWA's workers now face tighter industry deadlines and as a result Ruaab is focused on timely deliveries and quality to remain competitive in the market. A management member said, "If we satisfy the supplier and brand in these two things [delivery and quality], then we don't have to go to them to get orders, they are the ones who actually give us a call and give us work." Yet, another management member said that deadlines do require that some pressure be maintained on the workers, explaining that, "Because I also have pressure to meet production and delivery deadlines then I maintain the pressure on them." But in this case at Ruaab, there is no quota to be met and homeworkers only take on as many pieces as possible for them to complete by the order deadline. So, they are not under as much pressure as when working with contractors who may not allow workers to choose the amount of work they can reasonably handle.

While there can be periods of heavy work, underemployment is the larger problem with seasonal export orders causing a fluctuation in the regularity of work for the homeworkers. This leads the women to take on domestic work from local contractors, which pays very poorly and prolongs the exploitation of the workers at the hands of the contractors. SEWA management said that getting continuous work has been the biggest challenge in a fashion driven industry where embellishment is not in demand all the time. SEWA management indicated they were trying to find ways to remediate underemployment by taking on domestic orders and possibly launching their own brand in the future. SEWA is working to improve its processes and entering the domestic market will most likely fill the gap during the export off-season. Whether this move will garner SEWA members with sufficient employment as their membership continues to grow remains unanswered.

Irregular workflow can create difficulties for the workers, especially during low production periods, but so can regular work with a terrible pay scale. Interviews also confirmed the prevalence of issues of non-payment, back-pay, and gender-based suppression from the middlemen in the homeworker and contractor dynamic. SEWA attempts to alleviate pay-related issues by negotiating for better prices with the suppliers, informing the workers of the piece-rate before an order goes into production, and timely monthly payment of earned wages. By doing so, SEWA has ensured the women are always informed of their pay scale and wage cycle.

These women workers are paid piece-based wages and market mechanisms still tend to take a toll on the piece-based sector. A management member said that the women do complain about lack of work and low rates and it is mainly due to seasonal trends and low rates in the market. The management member spoke of the homeworkers' concerns regarding pay:

> A lot of the women aren't happy with the payments and piece-rates they get; so then I have to explain things to them. When I visit the centres, there are a lot of women who complain that the rates aren't good but then I have to explain to them that the market rates are running low right now. Or that the time study costing allowed only for this rate, or that the market itself is down and there isn't much work coming in, then in such a situation, we have to take orders that do come in at lower rates.

SEWA has had a positive impact on the pay scale of the workers by removing middlemen who pay low rates and homeworkers indicated access to better pay at SEWA than when working with contractors. All the homeworkers interviewed said the pay was much better with SEWA than when employed with the contractors. One homeworker said, "Like, say the contractor pays you Rs. 20; SEWA pays Rs. 40 for the same, that's how much you get paid. There is a difference between working for a contractor and working with SEWA." Several of them also noted that even though the pay was better, it was not always sufficient in meeting their monthly expenditure. Nonetheless, SEWA's practices are causing some reforms among middlemen. Speaking of her experience with contractors, one homeworker said:

> Before, it used to be that they wouldn't pay us for 2 months at a time. Three contractors still owe me pay that I have not seen yet. It's from 6 years ago; one owes me Rs. 225, one owes me Rs. 400 and the other Rs. 150. But they don't ever pay up. Even if they see me, they look the other way. And since SEWA came around, they've also had to pay better prices and are on time now because if they don't, then no one will want to work with them.

The middlemen, however, continue to present themselves as competition to SEWA because of their extensive network of homeworkers in the supply chain and SEWA's limited influence. Research revealed that despite a newly instituted minimum wage in Delhi, most suppliers do not follow the pay scale by basing the prices on the origin of the order, outside of Delhi. The National Capital Region, which includes Delhi and areas from four neighboring states, "This is Delhi's minimum wage; this is the time-motion study and so this is the cost," one management member said while simulating a negotiation. "Only then are we able to get our rates." When an order from a company based outside Delhi has a costing lower than the Delhi minimum wage, the organization has no choice but to pay the workers accordingly. The management member continued:

> We have to explain to them that the work has come in from U.P., Noida, and Haryana so we cannot give you Delhi's minimum wage, as it is based on Haryana's wage or Noida's wage.

Among the brands that engage with SEWA Delhi and Ruaab, one management member said the brand Monsoon is the only one currently paying the Delhi minimum wage and added, "They monitor, really monitor whether the workers are getting those benefits or not – the wages that has been increased – they are getting that benefits or not. So they do come and carry on the survey works."

Adherence to minimum wage law is a critical issue that needs attention because minimum wage payments ought to depend on the workers' location and not the suppliers' place of business. SEWA has not been able to answer to this issue, most likely due to its limited leverage over the supplier. By categorizing its role as a vendor in the competitive market, SEWA has limited its influence as a trade union and organizer in this aspect.

While SEWA's stance as a trade union coupled with its CSR procedures ensures direct market linkages and higher pay scales for the homeworkers, an issue that SEWA has very limited control over, however, is that of workers' space, cleanliness, and health conditions. Homeworkers mentioned health issues like back pain and trouble with eyesight due to constant strain, a common feature with the embellishment sector. Sitting in a crouched position and working on a sample in hand, one homeworker shared:

> My eyes have weakened over the years. I also have back pain because of constantly sitting. So I cannot sit for long period anymore like I used to sit for 2–3 hours at a stretch, now I cannot. I have to take breaks now. Sometimes I try to find a backrest but with work like this, you cannot use a backrest.

Ruaab has been making sure that workers understand the importance of proper sitting posture and taking breaks when engaged for long hours. The homeworkers also mentioned they were provided with periodic access to health benefits via SEWA. Management is trying to organize regular health check-ups for the workers and constantly educates them on these topics.

SEWA has instilled CSR procedures that enhance the clarity of its functions and allow for a systemized process. One aspect is the detailed record keeping processed at each stage, which helps in building traceability of the entire process in an organized manner. The other important aspect is the constant monitoring that occurs alongside ongoing engagement with the workers. With an open dialog, the management is able to interact with the workers and address issues and concerns as they arise. The documented costing process also ensures clarity and the workers are aware of the system.

10.5.3 Organizing and Empowering Homeworkers

Through its embroidery centers, SEWA combines its role as a trade union and an NGO working to effectively organize and empower homeworkers. SEWA's organizing skills have been extensively documented in the literature (Spodek 1994; Datta 2003; Bhatt and Jhabvala 2004; Wills and Hale 2005; Bhatt 2006; Kapoor 2007). SEWA's primary role is to organize workers and create empowerment in the long run, especially in groups where it has not existed before. To strengthen this process, SEWA first organizes the women by registering them with the organization as members. Building this sense of community and identity is viewed as crucial to creating a sense of well-being.

In our interviews, external stakeholders noted SEWA's strengths in organizing homeworkers and their ability to empower workers at large. With constant organizing efforts, SEWA is also working to strengthen the homeworkers' outlook of themselves as workers in the industry, an identity that has not existed before. To further their visibility in the supply chain, Ruaab has issued identity cards to its members and has connected 170 workers with a government artisan scheme, bringing them into the mainstream work force.

SEWA management members pointed out that constant organizing effort in the neighborhood helps in building sustained relationships with the workers and the community. Another measure taken by SEWA is embroidery skills training for its members to improve their skill base and improve the quality of work. During the monthly meetings, the workers are also educated and informed about basic homeworker rights and issues. However, one management member spoke about informing homeworkers about various issues at monthly meetings. Even so, it seems the workers do not always grasp the concept of their rights as homeworkers. When asked about whether she was informed by SEWA regarding her rights as a homeworker, one homeworker said, "I don't understand such things."

Overall, SEWA has had a positive impact on the workers' material, social, and psychological well-being. All the homeworkers interviewed mentioned aspects of empowerment and improvement in their material, social, and psychological quality of life as a result of being associated with SEWA's embroidery centers. Examples of empowerment cited in the homeworkers' interviews went beyond having a source of income to include access to constant training and guidance. In response to a question about empowerment, one homeworker said:

> I never used to talk to anyone before, I was so afraid, and now I have so much strength that I can talk to anyone and if someone questions me, I am able to answer. Is this not empowerment? This is all a lot for me.

Additionally, one management member explained, "Once they keep attending meetings and meet people from the outside, their thinking opens up and changes."

10.5.4 Engagement with Brands and Public

Via its livelihood promotion project, SEWA has continuously tried to engage with brands to better the homeworking conditions. The consensus at Ruaab and SEWA Delhi is that if the brands believe in the organization's approach to homework then they will automatically look to Ruaab for the fulfilment of their orders. An external stakeholder said that more and more brands are changing their attitudes about homework and looking to improve their supply chains and, thus, are looking to create ties with organizations like Ruaab.

> I think things have changed a lot [from] . . . say 3-years back or 4-years back when brands were in the whole state of denial. But today, we see more and more brand coming over and saying that they have homeworkers in their supply chain and what exactly we should be doing in order to improve their conditions.

This is a positive sign for the homework sector and also for the success of the model. Only with sustained engagement and support from the leaders in the industry can conditions improve at the lower levels of the supply chain.

From SEWA's point of view, engagement with brands and exporters is crucial to create a level playing field on par with factory workers for the homeworkers. At the same time, SEWA is also focused on improving its business capabilities to remain competitive in the market. This underscores that a key way that SEWA engages with brands is through the business relationship. With this livelihood promotion project, Ruaab is trying to provide brands with a homeworker workforce within a setting of responsible homework practices.

10.6 Discussion

The findings of this study are useful to consider in relationship to the proposed model and to the literature on what types of practices might be best practices in terms of CSR.

10.6.1 Homework Change Model's Influence

As the theoretical model depicts, SEWA has successfully exerted its influence on the homeworkers leading to better terms of employment and an improvement in the overall quality of life. In addition, SEWA has managed to develop systemized processes and negotiate better rates for pay for its workers than if they worked with contractors. SEWA also has attempted to find ways that address industry lead times while not transferring the pressure of short lead times to its workers. However, there remain areas of influence noted in the Homework Change Model that SEWA could further emphasize to heighten its leverage in the homeworkers' cause.

By increasing its engagement with the brands and establishing itself as a successful business case in homework, SEWA stands to exert a higher influence on retailers and brands in the future. Brands could also help SEWA in finding ways that lower the risk for them by funding more orders to Ruaab and tracking effective SEWA CSR procedures that mitigate supply chain issues like child labor. Furthermore, SEWA can further its influence by engaging with the public but the results of this study brought to attention that SEWA does not currently do so. As depicted by the model, exerting influence on the public can establish pressure on the brands to improve their purchasing practices and terms of employment for homeworkers.

10.6.2 SEWA Livelihood Promotion Project – A CSR Best Practice

SEWA's livelihood promotion project is indeed a good example of best CSR practices case in the realm of homework as it currently exists. With a strong background in organizing and empowerment, SEWA has found a way to strengthen the homeworkers' voices and help systemize homework to make it more acceptable in the apparel supply chain.

Management practices. As noted by Dickson and Chang (2015), management systems were the most frequently cited characteristic of apparel manufacturing companies with "world class" CSR programs. With the organization's CSR activity at the centers as the focal point in this homeworker model, Ruaab has revolutionized artisan-based business with their current structure. SEWA's strategy combines several influencers like engagement with brands and CSR procedures like detailed record keeping, tracking work hours, mapping its membership, continuous monitoring, and a systemized process of industry based production practices. As noted by Castka et al. (2004), it is desirable to integrate CSR practices into the business of the organization, which SEWA has done. While the production in this model is centralized, SEWA has managed to attune its system to the needs of these women workers while answering the supply chain's requirements.

Albeit not perfect, SEWA's homework model attempts to bring facets of CSR into homework to better working conditions in the existing supply chain and manages to provide increased visibility to the workers and practices in this sector.

SEWA is not only organizing homeworkers but also including brands and suppliers into its model and attempting to showcase the low risk factor for businesses. Considering the centers were only established in 2005 and Ruaab in 2010, this model is still under a development phase and is constantly being improved as issues surface each production season.

Empowerment. SEWA's livelihood promotion project has immense potential to create long-term empowerment in artisan clusters where such a concept did not exist before. SEWA's livelihood promotion project has not only generated a source of income for these homeworkers by utilizing their traditional skill base but also has created an overall sense of well-being among the women. The empowerment that comes from the establishment of a personal identity, self-worth, and improved quality of life will have a strong impact on the societal structure within settings where it is created. Thus, this homework model has the ability to impact change beyond the supply chain and supports Littrell and Dickson's (2010) assertion that homework can benefit and empower workers.

Engagement with Brands and Retailers. While SEWA manages to engage with brands and exporters to a certain extent, this study revealed that SEWA does not currently engage with the public nor does it carry out public reporting of its activities. SEWA is limited and even restricted in this aspect with Ruaab's role as a "vendor."

SEWA in its unique role as a trade union empowering workers and providing NGO-like social security services was never required to directly engage with the public. But in this case, public engagement could help influence brands' supply chain management decisions. Dickson et al. (2009) note that transparency regarding a company's CSR efforts has become a key factor in stakeholder engagement that adds to the accountability of a company's CSR efforts and builds stronger relationships with stakeholders. Documenting successes of the homework model with a public report could help increase visibility of the homeworkers and engage the general public to play its role in influencing brands. This lack of public engagement also brings to attention SEWA's limited resources as an NGO outfit.

Actively engaging the media would help SEWA to generate interest and educate the public about their cause on a larger scale, both within India and outside. Burchielli and Delaney (2009) mentioned the Fairwear Campaign's success in using media-friendly strategy in furthering the homeworkers' cause. It is important that SEWA enhance their limited online presence and actively engage stakeholders with social media and press exposure to increase their own visibility.

10.7 Practical Implications

While this study revealed SEWA is working to find ways to balance the homeworkers' needs in the future, there remain roadblocks like irregular workflow and the seasonal nature of the work itself that continue to hinder SEWA's efforts. Brands can help alleviate some of these issues by increasing collaboration with SEWA to find ways to improve the process.

Brands and retailers need to increase the purview of their CSR practices to extend beyond the first tier. By acknowledging homework, brands can help bring visibility to the most exploited workers in the supply chain. By doing so, brands will also be able to increasingly map their supply chains and enhance their own image by including homework in their public reporting. Brands need to focus on heightened ethical sourcing by including their design teams in the production planning to accommodate styles that will need to go out to the homework sector and plan accordingly to avoid short lead times and adopt better purchasing practices overall. Brands need to intervene and ensure their suppliers abide by minimum wage laws for the Delhi region. Only when brands and retailers make such an effort and collaborate with SEWA in bringing visibility to homework, this model will have a real chance of bringing about change in the supply chain.

Although our research incorporated perspectives of a limited number of homeworkers as compared with supervisory staff, we identified ways SEWA can improve its processes and strategies to expand its influence on the working conditions of homeworkers.

References

American Society of International Law. (1997). International labour conference: Home work convention, 1996 and recommendation concerning home work. *International Legal Materials, 36*(1), 55–64.

Bhatt, E. R. (2006). *We are poor but so many: The story of self-employed women in India.* Oxford, UK: Oxford University Press.

Bhatt, E., & Jhabvala, R. (2004). The idea of work. *Economic and Political Weekly, 39*(48), 5133–5140.

Boris, E. (1989). Homework and women's rights: The case of the Vermont knitters, 1980–85, in E. Boris & C. R. Daniels (Eds.) *Homework: Historical and contemporary perspectives on paid labor at home* (pp. 233–257). Urbana: University of Illinois Press.

Brill, L. (2002). Can codes of conduct help home-based workers?, in R. Jenkins, R. Pearson, & G. Seyfang (Eds.) *Corporate responsibility and labour rights: Codes of conduct in the global economy* (pp. 113–123). London: Earthscan Publications Ltd.

Burchielli, R., & Delaney, A. (2009). Homework and CSR: Can homeworkers benefit? In: 15th World Congress of the International Industrial Relations Association (IIRA), 24 August 2009–28 August 2009, Sydney Convention and Exhibition Centre.

Buttle, M. (2008, 18 July). *Homeworking in the Indian garment industry: What are the issues and how can homeworkers' lives be improved.* Retrieved 2011, 5 April from impact: http://www.impacttlimited.com/2008/07/18/homeworking-in-the-indian-garment-industry-what-are-the-issues-and-how-can-homeworkers-lives-be-improved/.

Castka, P., & Balzarova, M. A. (2007). A critical look on quality through CSR lenses: Key challenges stemming from the development of ISO 26000. *International Journal of Quality & Reliability Management, 24*(7), 738–752.

Castka, P., Bamber, C. J., Bamber, D. J., & Sharp, J. M. (2004). Integrating corporate social responsibility (CSR) into ISO management systems – in search of a feasible CSR management system framework. *TQM Magazine, 16*(3), 216–224.

Datta, R. (2003). From development to empowerment: The self-employed women's association in India. *International Journal of Politics, Culture, and Society, 16*(3), 351–368.

Delaney, A. (2004). Global trade and home work: Closing the divide. *Gender and Development, 12*(2), 22–28.

Delaney, A. (n.a.). Accounting for corporate social responsibility: Does it benefit workers across the supply chain?

Dickson, M. A., & Chang, R. K. (2015). Apparel manufacturers' path to world class corporate social responsibility: Perspectives of CSR professionals, in T.-M. Choi & T. C. E. Cheng (Eds.) *Sustainable fashion supply chain management* (pp. 107–127). Springer: Switzerland.

Dickson, M. A., Loker, S., & Eckman, M. (2009). *Social responsibility in the global apparel industry*. New York: Fairchild Books.

ETI. (2010). Homeworkers and homeworking: An introduction. Retrieved 2011, 7 April from http://www.ethicaltrade.org/in-action/projects/home workers-project/guidelines.

Freeman, D. (2003). Homeworkers in the global supply chains. *Greener Management International, 43*, 107–118.

Green, N. L. (2003). Fashion, flexible specialization, and the sweatshop: A historical problem, in D. E. Bender & R. A. Greenwald (Eds.) *Sweatshop USA: The American sweatshop in historical and global perspective* (pp. 37–56). Routledge: New York.

Hensman, R. (2005). Defending workers' rights in subcontracted workplaces, in W. W. Worldwide, A. Hale, & J. Wills (Eds.) *Threads of labour garment industry supply chains from the worker's perspectives* (Vol. 1, pp. 189–209). Blackwell Publishing Ltd: Malden, MA.

Hurley, J., & Miller, D. (2005). The changing face of the global garment industry, in W. W. Worldwide, A. Hale, & J. Wills (Eds.) *Threads of labour garment industry supply chains from the worker's perspectives* (Vol. I, pp. 16–39). Blackwell Publishing Ltd: Malden, MA.

Kapoor, A. (2007). The SEWA way: Shaping another future for informal labour. *Futures, 39*: 554–568.

Littrell, M. A., & Dickson, M. A. (2010). *Artisans and fair trade crafting development*. Sterling, VA: Kumarian Press.

Marian, P. (2013, July 1). Harnessing homeworkers in the apparel supply chain. Available from www.just-style.com

McCormick, D., & Schmitz, H. (2001). *Manual for value chain research on homeworkers in the garment industry*. Manual.

SEWA Bharat. (2008–2009). *2008–09* SEWA Bharat. *Annual Report*. Annual Report, SEWA Bharat.

Spodek, H. (1994). The self-employed women's association (SEWA) in India: Feminist, Gandhian power in development. *Economic Development and Cultural Change, 43*(1), 193–202.

Strauss, A. C., & Corbin, J. M. (2008). *Basics of qualitative research: Techniques and procedures for developing grounded theory*. SAGE Publications, Inc: Thousand Oaks, CA.

Wilkinson-Weber, C. M. (1997). Skill, dependency, and differentiation: Artisans and agents in the Lucknow embroidery industry. *Ethnology, 36*(1), 49–65.

Williams, P. (2005). Leveraging change in the working conditions of the UK homeworkers. *Development in Practice, 15*(3/4), 546–558.

Wills, J., & Hale, A. (2005). Threads of labour in the global garment industry, in A. Hale & J. Wills (Eds.) *Threads of Labour: Garment Industry Supply Chains from the Worker's Perspectives* (Vol. 1, p. 266). Malden, MA: Blackwell Publishing.

Archana is a Senior Account Manager at Intertek, where she manages product safety programs for key global accounts. She has worked in design, compliance, and product safety roles in the apparel industry. She has a MS in Fashion Studies from the University of Delaware where she delved into the world of corporate social responsibility. Archana grew up in India surrounded by a plethora of traditional textiles, native crafts, and interaction with artisans and weavers, which she pinpoints as the beginning of her career in the global apparel industry.

Dr Marsha A. Dickson is Irma Ayers Professor of Human Services in the Department of Fashion and Apparel Studies, and co-director of the Sustainable Apparel Initiative at the University of Delaware. Dr Dickson is internationally recognized for her research and teaching on social responsibility in the apparel industry. She is lead author of the book Social Responsibility in the Global Apparel Industry, has co-authored two books on fair trade, and has published on consumer and business practices in social responsibility in peer-reviewed journals such as *Business & Society, Journal of Business Ethics, Journal of Corporate Citizenship*, and the *Clothing and Textiles Research Journal.* She has conducted research on social responsibility in Bangladesh, Cambodia, China, Guatemala, Hong Kong, India, Thailand, Vietnam, and in the UK and Europe. For 14 years Dickson served an executive member of the board of directors of the Fair Labor Association (FLA), a non-governmental organization originally formed by President Clinton to improve working conditions in factories around the world. She is currently on the board of directors of the Fair Factories Clearinghouse. Dr Dickson has received several awards for her academic and industry contributions in social responsibility, including the All Star Award from Apparel Magazine and the International Textile and Apparel Association (ITAA) in 2009, ITAA Distinguished Scholar in 2011, and ITAA Fellow in 2016.

11

User Satisfaction and Dissatisfaction in the App Sharing Economy

An Investigation Into Two-sided Mobile Fashion Reselling and Swapping Markets

Sarah Netter

11.1 Introduction

In recent years, we have witnessed the rise of a phenomenon that we have come to know as the sharing economy. At its core, the sharing economy can be defined as innovative platform businesses, which enable two groups of users to transact or "share" underutilized assets and skills on *two-sided markets* (e.g. Demary 2015; Grinevich et al. 2015; Hagiu and Wright 2015; Li et al. 2015; Rauch and Schleicher 2015; Zervas et al. 2014; Henten and Windekilde 2016). On these *two-sided markets* usually all groups of users benefit from direct and indirect network effects, that is, a growing number of users on the same or opposite side (Codagnone and Martens 2016). While in the case of some platforms, these sharing practices are carried out offline and on an infrequent basis (such as in the case of temporary swap meets), the majority of sharing platforms utilise mobile or online markets, which enables 24/7 sharing.

S. Netter (✉)
Copenhagen Business School, Frederiksberg, Denmark
e-mail: sn.ikl@cbs.dk

C.E. Henninger et al. (eds.), *Sustainability in Fashion*,
DOI 10.1007/978-3-319-51253-2_11

The continual possibility of sharing unwanted goods and services beyond the circle of one's peers, family, and friends, can be regarded as a key distinction, differentiating these new sharing practices from those practices that have been long-established. In the fashion context for instance, the sharing and handing-down of clothes between generations, siblings, or among friends has a long-standing tradition. Docking on to that practice, a number of initiatives have been launched in the past years by start-ups around the globe, enabling the reselling and swapping of unwanted fashion items by means of smartphone enabled applications, hereafter referred to as sharing apps.

In light of the fashion system's sustainability challenges, a throwaway consumer culture, and the increasing scarcity of raw materials, it makes sense to maximize the utilization of unwanted goods by extending their lifespan through sharing (Fletcher 2008; Giesen 2008; Botsman and Rogers 2010). Hence, finding innovative approaches that can facilitate resource optimization on a larger scale has become an ever more pressing issue. While there is a growing number of sharing initiatives enabling consumers to part with their unwanted clothes and fashion items and acquire new ones – both on a short-term and permanent basis – so far, little is known about consumers adopting these practices. This is not only due to the relative infancy of most of these new initiatives but also due to sharing activities historically being part of an informal system (practised on a small scale among families and friends). As such, these systems have traditionally been studied on a small scale by certain academic disciplines such as human geography, sociology, and anthropology (e.g. Gregson and Beale 2004; Benson 2007) and have not been as heavily entwined with practice-oriented business research.

In general, it can be said that verbal or written word-of-mouth testimonials given by others within a particular consumer's direct network about the quality of a product or service can have a significant impact on the formation of that consumer's attitude, that is, the decision-making process in which this consumer adopts or rejects these novelties (Rogers 2003). Parasuraman et al. (1988) suggest that word-of-mouth can provide valuable insight into the quality consumers are expecting from a service or product. This is especially the case in those situations where user evaluations address individual components and are not restricted to overall evaluations of the service quality of any given vendor. According to Song et al. (2015), the "primary purpose of diagnosing service quality is to obtain useful information for improving current service systems towards better customer experiences" (p. 2). There is thus considerable overlap between service quality, attitude formation (e.g. Gönroos 1983), and customer satisfaction, that is the degree to which a purchased product or service meets the expectations that were formulated prior to purchase (Zeithaml et al. 1993).

With the rapid development of the Internet, the proliferation of smartphones and mobile applications, word-of-mouth has been catapulted from the small, personal realm to large-scale networks (e.g. Dellarocas 2003), where information can be communicated faster, easier, with less friction, and with little effort (e.g. Chatterjee 2001; Park and Lee 2009). Recent studies have highlighted the importance of reviews written by users for the overall success of an app (e.g. Li et al. 2010). Not only do apps provide a rich source of data on customer, business and technical issues for app developers and vendors who tend to improve apps in iterative processes (e.g. Chen et al. 2014), the number of downloads and reviews also provides useful indications for potential users regarding the popularity and quality of an app (Finkelstein et al. 2014). Useful app reviews usually contain bug reports (e.g. Pagano and Maalej 2013), feature or enhancement requests (e.g. Iacob and Harrison 2013), testimonials from users about their experience (e.g. Guzman and Maalej 2014), ideas for new features (e.g. Galvis Carreño and Winbladh 2013; Pagano and Maalej 2013), or simply reflect their numeric rating in text form (Pagano and Maalej 2013). With hundreds to thousands of reviews submitted daily (Hoon et al. 2013), app stores are also pervaded by a large number of rather useless reviews, containing slang, spam, insulting comments, and nonsensical information (e.g. Maalej and Nabil 2015). In most cases, app reviews constitute a combination of multiple categories outlined above (e.g. McIlroy et al. 2015). Although the body of literature on app reviews has grown in recent years, still little is known about user satisfaction and service quality in mobile marketplaces.

To the author's knowledge, this chapter is one of the first to study service quality and user satisfaction in *two-sided mobile marketplaces*. The study at hand thus adopts one of the most prominent models for measuring service quality, SERVQUAL (Parasuraman et al. 1988). Gaining a greater understanding of the factors causing satisfaction and dissatisfaction with the service quality delivered by these platforms is crucial, not only from the perspective of initiatives interested in scaling their activities but also from a societal perspective, considering the assumed transformative potential of the sharing economy regarding sustainable development.

Although studied in the context of mobile apps enabling the reselling and swapping of fashion items, the factors causing satisfaction and dissatisfaction appear to be independent of the product being traded and pertain rather to the type of platform. This study contributes to the existing literature in four ways. To the authors' knowledge, it is the first of its kind to (1) explore the applicability of the SERVQUAL measurement in the context of a mobile *two-sided market*, (2) extend its dimensions for the mobile context, (3) provide insights into which factors might prevent interested users from adopting these new mobile-sharing practices, and (4) shed light on the methodological advantages and disadvantages of making use of new forms of natural occurring data, for example app store reviews.

The remainder of this chapter proceeds as follows: Section 11.2 provides an overview of the relevant literature and introduces the adjusted SERVQUAL framework. Section 11.3 describes the data and methodology and is followed by Section 11.4, which presents and discusses the study's findings. Section 11.5 summarizes the conclusion and provides an account of the study's implications and limitations.

11.2 Literature Review and Conceptual Framework

11.2.1 Literature Review

There is a vast body of literature focused on the measures of customer perception of service quality in offline business-to-consumer (B2C) service environments (e.g. Gönroos 1984; Parasuraman et al. 1985, 1988). SERVQUAL, developed by Parasuraman et al. (1988), constitutes one of the most prominent and widely-tested models for measuring service quality across a broad range of industries and service contexts. It is comprised of five dimensions for measuring customer perceptions of service quality, which are presented below (ibid., p. 23): (Table 11.1)

With the growth of the Internet, research has increasingly attempted to employ SERVQUAL in e-commerce settings (e.g. Zeithaml et al. 2001, 2002; Wolfinbarger and Gilly 2002; Yang and Jun 2002). This has proven difficult due to differences between online and offline settings (e.g. Kim and Lee 2002), such as a shift from customer-to-employee interactions (e.g. Lohse and Spiller 1998) to non-human interactions between customers and the web interface (e.g. Jun et al. 2004). Hence, modifications and extensions of established scales and measures of service quality with parameters focusing on information systems quality are required (e.g. Davis et al. 1989).

11.2.2 Conceptual Framework

It can be assumed that mobile and online *two-sided marketplaces* share certain characteristics such as high levels of information asymmetry (e.g. Pavlou et al. 2007), the inability to touch and feel, that is, truthfully assess a product prior to purchasing (Kim and Kim 2004), a time lag in transactions, the transfer of money prior to delivery of the product or service (Utz et al. 2011), the phenomenon of buyers handling complaints, and finally the challenges of wrong product deliveries or delays in delivery (e.g. Utz et al. 2011). While prior experience with online marketplaces might reduce transaction costs (e.g. Teo and Yu 2005), it can be assumed that these costs increase in cases of novel information systems, that is, mobile marketplaces, in which facilitating technologies and communication are frequently prone to failure.

Despite similarities between online and mobile purchasing, there are significant differences between reviews given online and reviews given in a mobile app store. According to Fu et al. (2013), this pertains mainly to the length of review. App reviews tend to be shorter in length and version dependence, that is, apps are frequently updated, which means that reviews are for the most part tied to a specific version. Furthermore, mobile and online reviews influence potential users at different stages of

Table 11.1 Five dimensions to measure customer perceptions of service quality

Tangibles	Reliability	Responsiveness	Assurance	Empathy
Physical facilities, equipment, and appearance of personnel	Ability to perform the promised service dependably and accurately	Willingness to help customers and provide prompt service	Knowledge and courtesy of employees and their ability to inspire trust and confidence	Caring, individualized attention the firm provides its customers

their attitude formation process. Lee and Pee (2013) suggest that consumers firstly select potential products when shopping online before reading reviews. In the mobile context however, users encounter app reviews *before* engaging with the marketplace for the first time, that is, before they download the app. Hence, app reviews do not only influence users in the formation of their attitude towards a certain product or service but can also potentially convince them to shy away from one marketplace in favour of another.

In line with studies suggesting that no universal set of service quality factors exist (e.g. Reeves and Bednar 1994; Carman 1990; Seth et al. 2005), the study at hand adopts the contextualized SERVQUAL measurement by Parasuraman et al. (1988) to study service quality dimensions in a broker facilitated mobile consumer-to-consumer (C2C) marketplace. To pay regard to the special conditions of the mobile context, the first dimension ("tangibles" in the original scale") was rephrased as "app design". The remaining four original dimensions have been retained. It is to be expected that additional contextual dimensions will emerge. Based on the aim of the chapter to identify the factors contributing to user satisfaction and dissatisfaction with sharing apps, the following conceptual framework is proposed (Fig.11.1):

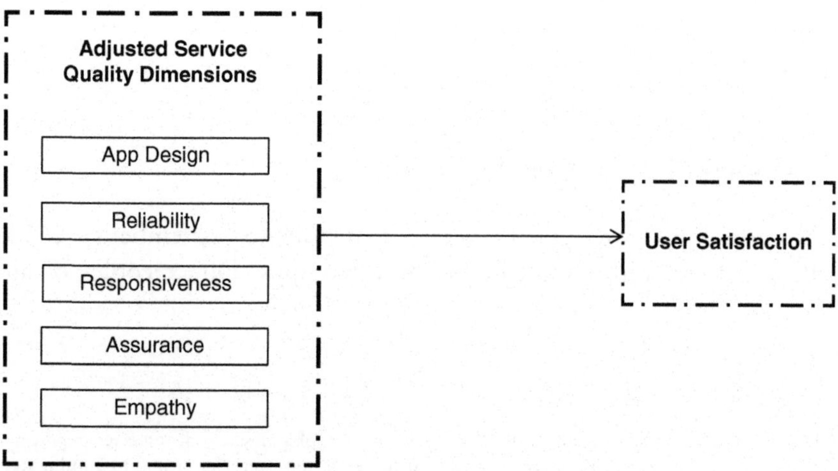

Fig.11.1 Conceptual model

11.3 Data and Methodology

11.3.1 Data Collection

Systematic content analysis of a wide sample of written user app reviews was adopted, with a rigorous cut-off value set at a minimum of 100 textual reviews in the US iTunes (i.e. iOS, the mobile operating system for Apple Inc. devices) app store. This level was set in order to include only those apps that had reached a certain level of maturity with fewer early stage technical struggles.[1]

Data collection took place in September 2014. To identify the apps that met the requirements, a two-step process was applied. In the first step, the app store was reviewed for English speaking *peer-to-peer* platforms which enabled users to buy, sell, or swap used clothing and accessories. Search terms used included combinations of the words "clothing", "fashion", "accessories", "buy", "sell", and "swap". As a second step, those apps that met the cut-off value of 100 reviews were identified, specifically *eBay Fashion, Tradesy*, and *Vinted*. While *eBay Fashion* and *Tradesy* constitute reselling apps, *Vinted* additionally allows users to swap pre-owned garments and fashion accessories. Table 11.2 presents an overview of the sampled apps.

11.3.2 Sample Selection

All written app store reviews were posted prior to September 5, 2014 when samples were collected for the three apps. Direct copies of all

[1] The decision was made in line with the assessment of appFigures, a well-respected reporting platform for mobile app developers, of what constitutes a "top" app. According to AppFigures (2014), an app within the iOS US app store receives 52 reviews on average, whereas the so-called top apps have an average of 144 reviews.

Table 11.2 Overview of sampled reselling and swapping peer-to-peer apps in iTunes

Name	Category	Number of total reviews in iTunes	Number of textual reviews in iTunes
eBay Fashion	Reselling	2.233	206
Tradesy	Reselling	419	350
Vinted	Swapping & Reselling	2.842	631

reviews were made. The sample size of reviews collected totalled 1,187 iOS reviews, of which 206 were from *eBay Fashion*, 350 from *Tradesy*, and 631 from *Vinted*. To ensure an equal group size for all apps, simple random sampling within SPSS was applied to the extracted reviews within each stratum, that is, each app. To control for external influences, such as changes in consumer trends and further development of smartphone technologies, 100 reviews were randomly sampled per app within the years 2013 and 2014. This sampling strategy yielded a final sample of 300 reviews, which were equally distributed over the different platform types. A certain level of representativeness of the studied sample can be assumed, based on the adopted sampling approach.

The average length of the textual reviews was 164 characters with the shortest review comprised of five characters and the longest review comprised of 2,137 characters. The majority of reviews were shorter than 164 characters (72%).

11.3.3 Content Analysis

The app reviews were analysed without the use of computer-assisted qualitative analysis software. The research team adopted an iterative coding process (Flick 2009) to identify, analyse, and report patterns (Braun and Clarke 2006). All members of the research team familiarised themselves with the data by carefully reading through all sampled reviews. As a second step, initial codes were developed, followed by a search for patterns (or categories) among these codes. As a fourth step, these categories were reviewed again, to make sure that they were mutually exclusive. Consequently, the categories were clearly defined and labelled (ibid.), before they were grouped along the lines of the adjusted SERVQUAL measurement outlined in Section 11.3, that is, codes belonging to the categories "app design", "reliability", "responsiveness", "assurance", "empathy", as well as three additional emergent dimensions, "product portfolio", "cost of membership", and "tone".

Each dimension was coded using a dichotomous, positively mentioned ("1")/negatively mentioned ("0"), scale. In cases were dimensions were missing, these were coded with a "99". A coding scheme was developed for each dimension, with keywords to follow. For instance rapid rates for downloading an app, uploading pictures or text, or loading pages resulted in a coding for "speed", which was characterised as part of the "app design" dimension. In line with the experience from previous research carried out on app reviews, it was not possible to code for single issues, due to the unstructured and informal nature of the reviews (e.g. McIlroy et al. 2015).

In addition to coding for the adjusted SERVQUAL measurement and additional dimensions, the reviews were also coded for "tone", which indicated a general liking/disliking of the swapping or reselling idea or app. Positive reviews and constructive critics were coded "1", whereas negative reviews were coded "0". The dimensions "tone" was included, as many reviews contained a purely positive or negative message, without making specific reference to what might have caused this attitude. Table 11.3 provides an overview of the emergent coding scheme.

To reach a high level of inter-coder reliability, two researchers carried out the coding. Initially, both researchers coded a test sample of app reviews. The individual reviews were compared and discussed to minimised future errors and ambiguity. Consequently, the two researchers coded the 300 reviews independently. Disagreement on the coding of any app reviews resulted in another coding round, in which agreement was reached after discussion.

Table 11.3 Overview coding scheme

App Design	Reliability	Responsiveness	Assurance	Empathy	Product portfolio	Cost of Membership	Tone
Ease of use • Convenient • Easy to navigate	**Stability** • Runs smooth/ no crashes • App/functions always available	**Customer service** • Responsive technical issues/trans-action issues	**Up-to-date information** • Up-to-date pictures /item listings, etc.	**Personalisation** • Personalise products/ service /alerts/ editing, payment, delivery, etc.	**General portfolio**	**Transaction fees**	
Speed • Quick download of App/upload of pictures/text/ loading of pages	**Updates** • Frequent updates	**Prompt response** • Prompt response to inquiries	**Confidence** • Instilling confidence in users to solve problems		**Brands**	**Shipping fees**	
Structure • Filter/search functions/well organized	**Trustworthiness** • Keep promises • Truthful offerings • Correct information when agreeing upon transaction	**Prompt problem fixes** • Prompt returns/bug fixes	**Ability** • Knowledge to solve problems		**Sizes**	**Credit** • In-store credit for returns	

(continued)

Table 11.3 (continued)

App Design	Reliability	Responsiveness	Assurance	Empathy	Product portfolio	Cost of Membership	Tone
Visuals • Visually appealing • Nice/clean design			**Safety** • Protection of privacy/ financial information		**Pricing/ deals**		
Compatibility • Compatibility with other systems • Payment integration			**Courtesy** • Friendly com-munication		**Styles**		
					Condition • Condition • Age		

11.4 Findings and Discussion

Overall, this study found that the majority of users who engage in writing app store reviews for smartphone-enabled fashion-sharing platforms have a positive attitude towards the mobile sharing of fashion items, indicated by 76% of the reviews being written in a positive tone.

> This app is quickly taking up all my time because it is so awesome I am completely addicted!!! How could you not be?

According to Lee and Pee (2013) the impact of review tone on consumers' decision-making should not be underestimated, as it interacts with the personal expectations consumers have formulated prior to interaction.

Looking at Table 11.4, which reports the mentioning frequencies and percentages by category on the aggregated level, it can be observed that mentioning frequencies are generally low. However, in light of previous research that suggests that only 31.5% of app reviews contain useful information (Chen et al. 2014), the volume of useful information is actually quite high, with two thirds of all reviews (69%) containing information that allowed for coding along the emergent categories and dimensions, and approximately one third of the reviews (31%) being exclusively coded for tone. One plausible explanation might be that individuals using the studied apps are rather involved in the sharing idea, invested in the app's success and are therefore eager to contribute useful feedback on their experience.

In contrast to previous research suggesting that "responsiveness" constitutes the foremost critical factor for determining user satisfaction and dissatisfaction (e.g. Yang et al. 2004), "responsiveness" in this study turned out to influence the overall service quality assessment to a lesser extent. The factors of "app design", "reliability", as well as "product portfolio" on the other hand were found to be the major causes of user satisfaction and dissatisfaction when reselling or swapping fashion items via these mobile marketplaces. While "app design" (70.32%) and "product portfolio" (85.71%) are overall addressed as sources of satisfaction, "reliability" (81.01%) was highlighted as a source of dissatisfaction.

Table 11.4 Descriptive statistics aggregated level

Type of feedback	N	Positive mention	Negative mention
App Design	**155** (51.67%)	**109** (70.32%)	**46** (29.68%)
Ease of use	70 (23.33%)	65 (92.86%)	5 (7.14%)
Speed	11 (3.67%)	5 (45.45%)	6 (54.55%)
Structure	36 (12.00%)	14 (38.89%)	22 (61.11%)
Visuals	29 (9.67%)	23 (79.31%)	6 (20.69%)
Compatibility	9 (3.00%)	2 (22.22%)	7 (77.78%)
Reliability	**79** (26.33%)	**15** (18.99%)	**64** (81.01%)
Stability	60 (20.00%)	5 (8.33%)	55 (91.67%)
Update	5 (1.67%)	5 (100.00%)	
Trustworthiness	14 (4.67%)	5 (35.71%)	9 (64.29%)
Responsiveness	**27** (9.00%)	**6** (22.22%)	**21** (77.78%)
Customer service	20 (6.67%)	5 (25.00%)	15 (75.00%)
Prompt response	3 (1.00%)	1 (33.33%)	2 (66.67%)
Prompt problem fix	4 (1.33%)		4 (100.00%)
Assurance	**26** (8.67%)	**8** (30.77%)	**18** (69.23%)
Up-to-date information	10 (3.33%)	1 (10.00%)	9 (90.00%)
Confidence	3 (1.00%)	1 (33.33%)	2 (66.67%)
Ability	2 (0.67%)		2 (100.00%)
Safety	9 (3.00%)	4 (44.44%)	5 (55.56%)
Courtesy	2 (0.67%)	2 (100.00%)	
Empathy	**6** (2.00%)	**3** (50.00%)	**3** (50.00%)
Personalisation	6 (2.00%)	3 (50.00%)	3 (50.00%)
Product portfolio	**70** (23.33%)	**60** (85.71%)	**10** (14.29%)
General	19 (6.33%)	18 (94.74%)	1 (5.26%)
Brands	8 (2.67%)	8 (100.00%)	
Sizes	1 (0.33%)		1 (100.00%)
Pricing	30 (10.00%)	27 (90.00%)	3 (10.00%)
Styles	5 (1.67%)	3 (60.00%)	2 (40.00%)
Condition	7 (2.33%)	4 (57.14%)	3 (42.86%)
Cost of membership	**21** (7.00%)	**6** (28.57%)	**15** (71.43%)
Transaction fee	9 (3.00%)	5 (55.56%)	4 (44.44%)
Shipping fee	7 (2.23%)		7 (100.00%)
Credit	5 (1.67%)	1 (20.00%)	4 (80.00%)
Tone	**300** (100.00%)	**228** (76.00%)	**72** (24.00%)
Total	**684** (100%)	**435** (63.60%)	**249** (36.40%)

"App design" was addressed by approximately half of the sample (51.67%), with the majority reviewing the design features of the apps positively (70.32%). "Reliability", mentioned by one fourth of the sample (26.33%), was for the most part addressed in a negative manner, with 81.01% of these reviews expressing dissatisfaction. The "product portfolio" on offer by the reselling and swapping apps was also addressed by approximately one fourth of all reviewers (23.33%). The majority of these reviews (85.71%) mentioned the "product portfolio" as a source of satisfaction.

11.4.1 App Design

While the "tangibles" dimension in the original SERVQUAL measurement pertains to all tangible elements of the service environment, that is, physical facilities, equipment, as well as appearance of the personnel (Parasuraman et al. 1988, p. 23), the tangible elements of the "app design" dimension in the app context relate mainly to the applications' design, that is, their ease of use, speed, structure, visual appeal, as well as their technical feasibility and compatibility. For potential users, the app constitutes the interface and entry point to interaction with the app, its staff, as well as other actors trying to sell or buy things. The applications' design thus plays a vital role in instilling confidence in users regarding the capabilities of the app and convincing them to try this innovative mode of consumption. Shortcomings in the design or absence of certain features might consequently cause the formation of a negative or unfavourable attitude towards the quality of the app, which might result in rejecting the platform altogether and switching to a competing vendor, as can be seen in reviews of the studied which made comparisons between competing apps.

Looking closer at the "app design" dimension, it becomes apparent that reviewers' references to "ease of use", "structure", as well as to the "visuals" of the app constitute the majority of testimonials, with "ease of use" being mentioned most: "Mawmawdog. Love this app!! So easy to use!" "Ease of use", which was mentioned by approximately one quarter of reviewers

(23.33%), pertains primarily to the user-friendliness, convenience, and intuitive navigation of the app. Almost all reviews address "ease of use" (92.86%) of the studied apps as a source of satisfaction:

> Love it. Not much else to say. It's well done and beautifully designed. Looks great on iOS 7

Another source of satisfaction is the aesthetics of the app. Approximately 80% of the reviewers who address the "visuals" (9.67%) of the studied apps regarding them in a positive manner. These findings are in line with previous research on online environments, which suggests that "ease of use" and "visuals" constitute essential features, not only for the attraction of potential new users but also for the retention of existing ones (Yang et al. 2004).

> Needs more options. Nice enough app but needs additional search filters (i.e. size, colour, etc.)

While "ease of use" and "visuals" constitute sources of satisfaction for the users of these sharing apps, the "structure" of the studied apps, that is, search and filter functions, constituted a cause of dissatisfaction, with 61.11% of the reviewers who mentioned this issue (12.00%) addressing this factor in a negative manner. This is in line with the findings of Rice (1997), who discovered that one of the key factors that made consumers revisit a given website were the site's design features, such as layout, but also the ease of locating information and content. As Yang, Peterson and Cai (2003) suggest, "a well-designed navigational structure can facilitate consumers' perceptions of online control and enjoyment" (p. 1166).

11.4.2 Reliability

The "reliability" dimension in the SERVQUAL measurement pertains to a company's ability to perform the promised service in a dependable and accurate manner (Parasuraman et al. 1988). In the mobile context,that is, in absence of direct human interaction with sales staff, it is crucial to instil trust in users that the service vendor will live up to its promise that orders will be delivered promptly and correctly (e.g. Kim and Lee 2002). Besides customer-service vendor interactions, which are primarily of technical and structural nature (i.e. how stable the app runs, the availability of app features), "reliability" also factors into the interactions between different users in the case of broker facilitated mobile C2C marketplaces. These latter interactions pertain primarily to transaction issues between buyers, sellers, or swappers (i.e. whether a user will receive what he or she purchased/bartered).

The "reliability" dimension in an app context addresses issues such as "speed", "updates", as well as "trustworthiness". When looking at this dimension, it becomes apparent that most reviewers (20.00%) address the "stability" of the apps. "Stability" encompasses matters of how smooth the app runs, whether or how frequently it crashes, and whether the app, its functions, or uploaded/edited information are always available. The majority of users who have mentioned the issue of "stability" indicated this to be a source of dissatisfaction, with 91.67% addressing this topic in a negative manner:

> Hate it. It keeps on closing by its one. I'm on the app for like 10 seconds and then it's bam off. I think I would probably enjoy it even more if it would stay open.

These findings are in line with those reported by Khalid et al. (2015), who suggest that users of iOS mobile apps most frequently complain about functional errors, feature requests, and app crashes, with these three types of complaints accounting for more than 50% of all complaints expressed by users. According to Khalid et al. (ibid.), these issues are tremendous sources of frustration for users, especially as they are of developmental nature, that is, outside of the control of users.

While only mentioned by a few (4.67%), reviewers address "trustworthiness" in a similar vein, with a clear majority (64.29%) mentioning this topic as a source of dissatisfaction. "Trustworthiness" pertains to whether promises are kept and offerings are truthful:

> Do NOT BUY ANYTHING SCAM!!!!.... Watch out. I just bought something stated as new!! Got something refurbished!.. I returned for full refund but they made me wait for almost a week and they just want to give me credit!!!...This is Wrong!!!...Where is customer service when you need it!!??? You will regret buying a nothing from here!!!. Trust me!!!...

While technical issues are within the control of the app vendor, transaction issues are for the most part in the hands of other users who act as sellers or buyers in the marketplace. App vendors can set up rules or codes of conduct, which can be enforced by sanctions. Since erratic behaviour is at first subject to interaction between users, app vendors have little influence over this kind of behaviour. With 21.33% of all reviews indicating "reliability" as a key cause of dissatisfaction, and only 5.00% addressing this dimension as a source of satisfaction, it is apparent that "reliability" effectively indicates a hygiene factor: When absent, "reliability" causes a negative evaluation; when present, however, it does not automatically grant a positive performance evaluation. These findings are in line with those of Yang et al. (2003), who suggest that "reliability" constitutes a service dimension that is more likely to lead to dissatisfaction in the case of poor performance than cause satisfaction in case of positive performance.

11.4.3 Product Portfolio

While not addressed in the original SERVQUAL measurement, product portfolio is a service quality dimension that has received attention from a few scholars interested in studying online service quality (e.g. Cho and Park 2001; Yang et al. 2004). Yang et al. (2004) for instance found that a limited range and depth of the product portfolio on offer is most likely preventing interested users from purchasing products and services online. In the study at hand, "product portfolio" refers to the "general portfolio", "brands", "sizes", "pricing", "styles", as well as the "condition" of the clothes shared on the apps:

Great find! This app has such a wide variety of high-end items at very reasonable prices. Such a great find.

Users addressed several facets of this dimension ranging from more general statements regarding the portfolio ("*Love it. The selection is amazing.*"), specific brands, styles, sizing, pricing and deals to the condition of the traded clothes ("*Watch out. I just bought something stated as new!! Got something refurbished!* [...]"). "Pricing" (10.00%) and "general portfolio" (6.33%) were most frequently mentioned. Both factors constitute sources of satisfaction, with 90% addressing the pricing of resold products positively and 94.74% speaking in positive terms about the general selection. These findings are in line with Cho and Park (2001), who identified product merchandising, i.e. variety and newness of products, as a key influence on the satisfaction of Internet shoppers.

11.5 Conclusion

This study contributes to the existing literature in four ways. Firstly, this study tests the applicability of the traditional service quality scale developed by Parasuraman et al. (1988) to the evaluation of quality in the broker-facilitated mobile C2C marketplace. With the emergence of the mobile market, not only for *two-sided sharing economy platforms* but for a wider range of products and services, it is paramount to develop a suitable set of measures for assessing the service quality in these new business environments. Secondly, this exploratory study provides the initial groundwork for the further development of reliable and valid measures by providing a tentative set of additional dimensions. In line with previous research, which is critical towards the universal applicability of the five SERVQUAL dimensions (e.g. Reeves and Bednar 1994; Lee and Lin 2005; Seth et al. 2005), the study at hand adjusted the original measure, with the "tangibles" dimension now pertaining to the "smartphone" app design. Additional dimensions, that is, "product portfolio", "cost of membership", and "tone" emerged while coding the app reviews.

Thirdly, this study casts light on the rather new mobile sharing economy by providing insight into the factors causing satisfaction and dissatisfaction with these new sharing apps. Although studied in the context of the reselling and swapping of fashion items, the identified factors causing satisfaction and dissatisfaction are assumed to be transferrable to the contexts of other *two-sided mobile C2C sharing marketplaces.*

Fourthly, this research provides a methodological contribution on how to make use of a new form of natural occurring data, that is, user app store reviews.

The most striking finding is that the vast majority of reviewers expressed a general appreciation of the sharing of fashion items via the broker-facilitated mobile C2C marketplaces studied. This generally positive evaluation of these sharing apps can be assessed as a crucial step towards changing consumer mind-sets from a throwaway, consumption approach towards one that is focusing on extending the lifespan of products to alter the detrimental course of the current fashion consumption and production system.

With "app design" (i.e. "ease of use" and "visuals") as well as "product portfolio" (i.e. "pricing" and "general portfolio") constituting the major sources of satisfaction, it can be deduced that the studied market operators have a good general understanding of their user base (e.g. what they like and do not like) as well as an ability to connect the right buyers and sellers. However, with "reliability" (i.e. "stability") being the major cause of user dissatisfaction, it can be concluded that the app vendors and developers are not necessarily doing their jobs well in terms of listening and responding to their users' needs and complaints after the initial app development stages. This assumption can be supported by "structure" – an "app design" factor – constituting another source of frustration. This factor pertains to the filter and search functions available for screening through the products on offer. While *two-sided platforms* are assumed to reduce search costs and mitigate coordination problems by bringing together distinct consumer groups (e.g. Rauch and Schleicher 2015), dissatisfaction in terms of "structure" indicate that, on the contrary, facilitators and developers are not doing a good job in reducing search costs in marketplaces that are otherwise valued for their inventory. While these factors as such might not attract users to choose a certain app in the first place, their negative performance might lead to defection in favour of a competitor.

11.6 Limitations

As with any empirical research, the study at hand faced certain threats to its internal and external validity. This study was performed using a sampling of three reselling and swapping C2C apps in iTunes. While the findings might not be generalised to all iOS apps that enable the sharing of clothes, a certain level of representativeness of the sample can be assumed. This was accomplished by (a) sampling all mature apps offering consumers the opportunity to share their clothes mobile within the US iTunes store, and (b) randomly sampling 100 reviews per stratum, that is, apps, written within the years 2013 and 2014, with a final sample size of 300 reviews, which were equally distributed over the different app types.

Additional generalisability issues arise from selection bias and review manipulation by vendors. Firstly, a high selection bias can be assumed, with presumably only highly involved users writing an app review, most likely in cases of extreme satisfaction or dissatisfaction. Hence, few reviews express the average experience. Secondly, while not a dominant behaviour, some companies engage in app review manipulation by purchasing fake reviews, clicks, and likes, which raises questions as to the validity of the reviews (Kornish 2009) and supports the idea that the actual service quality evaluation in the study at hand is in fact less favourable than the reviews might suggest.

Regarding the study's internal validity, there are certain risks connected with manually processing data, which might cause incorrect labelling. Human error might have occurred, for instance, in the sampling of the studied apps by overlooking certain keywords. Besides potential sampling biases, measures were taken by the study's two researchers to mitigate the risks related to the incorrect coding of data such as developing a coding guide and taking an iterative coding approach. However, the possibility of mistakes cannot be excluded due to the length and quality of the reviews as well as the multiple overlapping issues addressed in the reviews.

Finally, it was often a challenge to definitively determine "who" or "what" was being addressed in the app reviews studied. Since many actors were involved in the studied broker-facilitated mobile C2C marketplaces, a multitude of topics and stakeholders were also discussed in the app reviews, including interactions between (1) users and app platform employees, (2) users and the actual app, and most importantly, (3) users taking turns acting in the roles of buyer or seller. With the typical app review being rather short, it is difficult to identify and delimit the different levels of interaction referred to in the reviews. Besides levels of interaction, technical aspects, and traded products, reviews also pertain to the reviewers' own competencies. For instance, a review on instability issues might not necessarily be caused by the defectiveness of the app, but by the reviewer, who is using an outdated version or the reviewer's own technical competencies.

11.7 Future Research

To further develop the SERVQUAL measure for the mobile context, this study also calls for more work on app store reviewing, especially with regard to the generalising quality of this new form of natural occurring data. Further research is needed, including research on apps from additional digital distribution platforms beyond the iPhone operating system (iOS).

Furthermore, since little research has been conducted on which consumer segments actually write reviews, future research could address the following questions: What are the characteristics of those writing app reviews? What are the drivers and barriers for writing a review? What is the impact of user involvement on the decision to write a review(s)? To what extent are app reviews actually read and used by other potential users? What are the effects of fake reviews on users?

11.8 Practical Implications

The findings of this study do not only inform organisations operating in the sharing economy but also those offering products and services in mobile C2C and B2C marketplaces. App reviews provide companies the ability to poll users and gain essential feedback on their products. Although it might make sense in the short-term for businesses to buy fake clicks, reviews, and likes, in the long-run, this will distort any gauge they have for assessing the perceived quality evaluation from users or for identifying aspect of their products that need improvement. As there are many vendors competing in the same marketplace and the costs to users for switching vendors is relatively low, this form of malpractice might have detrimental effects on a company's survival since it is costly and complicated to re-establish one's (damaged) reputation (e.g. Herbig et al. 1994). As with many sharing apps, users constitute not only the demand side but also the supply side – a dynamic which results in organizations being highly dependent on their users and vulnerable to changes in their customers' interests. It can be hypothesised that those sharing organizations will thrive that can navigate this dynamic and blurriness of stakeholder roles and interests.

References

AppFigures. (2014). A deep dive into app store reviews distribution. Retrieved from: http://blog.appfigures.com/a-deep-dive-into-app-store-reviews-distribution/ [accessed on: 15/09/2014]

Benson, S. P. (2007). What goes' round comes' round: Secondhand clothing, furniture, and tools in working-class lives in the interwar United States. *Journal of Women's History, 19*(1): 17–31.

Botsman, R., & Rogers, R. (2010). *What's mine is yours: The rise of collaborative consumption*. Harper Business: New York.

Braun, V., & Clarke, V. (2006). Using thematic analysis in psychology. *Qualitative Research in Psychology, 3*(2): 77–101.

Carman, J. M. (1990). Consumer perceptions of service quality: An assessment of the SERVQUAL dimensions. *Journal of Retailing, 66*(1): 33–55.

Chatterjee, P. (2001). Online reviews – Do consumers use them? *Advances in Consumer Research*, 28: 129–133.

Chen, N., Lin, J., Hoi, S. C., Xiao, X., & Zhang, B. (2014). AR-Miner: Mining informative reviews for developers from mobile app marketplace. In Proceedings of the 36th International Conference on Software Engineering, 767–778.

Cho, N., & Park, S. (2001). Development of electronic commerce user-consumer satisfaction index (ECUSI) for Internet shopping. *Industrial Management & Data Systems, 101*(8): 400–406.

Codagnone, C., & Martens, B. (2016). Scoping the sharing economy: Origins, definitions, impact and regulatory issues. Institute for Prospective Technological Studies Digital Economy Working Paper, 1.

Davis, F. D., Bagozzi, R. P., & Warshaw, P. R. (1989). User acceptance of computer technology: A comparison of two theoretical models. *Management Science, 35*(8): 982–1003.

Dellarocas, C. (2003). The digitization of word of mouth: Promise and challenges of online feedback mechanisms. *Management Science, 49*(10): 1407–1424.

Demary, V. (2015). *Competition in the sharing economy* (No. 19/2015). IW Policy Paper.

Finkelstein, A., Harman, M., Jia, Y., Martin, W., Sarro, F., & Zhang, Y. (2014). *Mining app stores: Extracting technical, business and customer rating information for analysis and prediction.* Research Note RN/14/10, UCL Department of Computer Science.

Fletcher, K. (2008). *Sustainable fashion and textiles: Design journeys*, Earthscan/ James & James: London.

Flick, U. (2009). *Sozialforschung – Methoden und Anwendungen: Ein Überblick für die BA-Studiengänge*, Rowohlt: Reinbek.

Fu, B., Lin, J., Li, L., Faloutsos, C., Hong, J., & Sadeh, N. (2013, August). Why people hate your app: Making sense of user feedback in a mobile app store, In Proceedings of the 19th ACM SIGKDD international conference on Knowledge discovery and data mining, 1276–1284, ACM.

Galvis Carreño, L. V., & Winbladh, K. (2013). *Analysis of user comments: An approach for software requirements evolution*, In ICSE '13 Proceedings of the 2013 International Conference on Software Engineering, 582–591, IEEE Press.

Giesen, B. (2008). *Ethical clothing – New awareness or fading fashion trend.* VDM Verlag, Saarbrücken: Germany.

Gönroos, C. (1983). *Strategic management and marketing in the service sector.* Marketing Science Institution: Cambridge, MA.

Gönroos, C. (1984). A service quality model and its marketing implications. *European Journal of Marketing, 18*(4): 36–44.

Gregson, N., & Beale, V. (2004). Wardrobe matter: The sorting, displacement and circulation of women's clothing. *Geoforum, 35*(6): 689–700.

Grinevich, V., Huber, F., Baines, L., & Eder, M. (2015). *Upscaling in the sharing economy: Insights from the UK*, Research Report, University of Southampton, UK and University Seeburg Castle, Austria.

Guzman, E., & Maalej, W. (2014). *How do users like this feature? A fine grained sentiment analysis of app reviews.* In Requirements Engineering Conference (RE), 2014 IEEE 22nd International, 153–162.

Hagiu, A., & Wright, J. (2015). Multi-sided platforms. *International Journal of Industrial Organization*, 43: 162–174.

Henten, A. H., & Windekilde, I. M. (2016). Transaction costs and the sharing economy. *info*, *18*(1): 1–15.

Herbig, P., Milewicz, J., & Golden, J. (1994). A model of reputation building and destruction. *Journal of Business Research*, *31*(1): 23–31.

Hoon, L., Vasa, R., Schneider, J. G., & Grundy, J. (2013). *An analysis of the mobile app review landscape: Trends and implications.* Faculty of Information and Communication Technologies, Swinburne University of Technology, Technical Report.

Iacob, C., & Harrison, R. (2013). *Retrieving and analyzing mobile apps feature requests from online reviews.* In Mining Software Repositories (MSR), 2013 10th IEEE Working Conference, 41–44.

Jun, M., Yang, Z., & Kim, D. S. (2004). Customers' perceptions of online service quality and their satisfaction. *International Journal of Quality & Reliability Management*, *21*(8): 817–840.

Khalid, H., Shihab, E., Nagappan, M., & Hassan, A. E. (2015). What do mobile app users complain about?. *IEEE Software*, *32*(3): 70–77.

Kim, E. Y., & Kim, Y. K. (2004). Predicting online purchase intentions for clothing products. *European Journal of Marketing*, *38*(7): 883–897.

Kim, J., & Lee, J. (2002). Critical design factors for successful e-commerce systems. *Behaviour and Information Technology*, *21*(3): 185–199.

Kornish, L. J. (2009). *Are user reviews systematically manipulated? Evidence from helpfulness ratings.* Leeds School of Business Working Paper.

Lee, G. G., & Lin, H. F. (2005). Customer perceptions of e-service quality in online shopping. *International Journal of Retail & Distribution Management*, *33*(2): 161–176.

Lee, J., & Pee, L. G. (2013). *Reading consumer reviews to confirm my expectations: The accelerated impact of confirmation under extreme review tones.* PACIS 2013 Proceedings, Paper 76.

Li, H., Zhang, L., Zhang, L., & Shen, J. (2010). *A user satisfaction analysis approach for software evolution.* In Progress in Informatics and Computing (PIC), 2010 IEEE International Conference, 2, 1093–1097.

Li, J., Moreno, A., & Zhang, D. J. (2015). *Agent behavior in the sharing economy: Evidence from Airbnb.* Retrieved from SSRN 2708279.

Lohse, G. L., & Spiller, P. (1998). Electronic shopping. *Communications of the ACM*, 41(7): 81–87.

Maalej, W., & Nabil, H. (2015). *Bug report, feature request, or simply praise? On automatically classifying app reviews*. In Requirements Engineering Conference (RE), 2015 IEEE 23rd International, 116–125.

McIlroy, S., Ali, N., Khalid, H., & Hassan, A. E. (2015). Analyzing and automatically labelling the types of user issues that are raised in mobile app reviews. *Empirical Software Engineering, 21*(3): 1–40.

Pagano, D., & Maalej, W. (2013). *User feedback in the appstore: An empirical study*. In Requirements Engineering Conference (RE), 2013 21st IEEE International, 125–134.

Parasuraman, A., Zeithaml, V. A., & Berry, L. L. (1985). A conceptual model of service quality and its implications for future research. *Journal of Marketing*, 49(Fall): 41–50.

Parasuraman, A., Zeithaml, V. A., & Berry, L. L. (1988). SERVQUAL: A multiple-item scale for measuring consumer perceptions of service quality. *Journal of Retailing*, 64(1): 12–40.

Park, C., & Lee, T. M. (2009). Information direction, website reputation and eWOM effect: A moderating role of product type. *Journal of Business Research*, 62: 61–67.

Pavlou, P. A., Liang, H., & Xue, Y. (2007). Understanding and mitigating uncertainty in online exchange relationships: A principal-agent perspective. *MIS Quarterly, 31*(1): 105–136.

Rauch, D. E., & Schleicher, D. (2015). *Like Uber, but for local governmental policy: The future of local regulation of the "sharing economy"*. George Mason Law & Economics Research Paper (15–01).

Reeves, C. A., & Bednar, D. A. (1994). Defining quality: Alternatives and implications. *Academy of Management Review*, 19(3): 419–445.

Rice, M. (1997). What makes users revisit a Web site. *Marketing News*, 31(6): 12–13.

Rogers, E. M. (2003). *Diffusion of innovations*, 5th edn., Free Press: New York.

Seth, N., Deshmukh, S. G., & Vrat, P. (2005). Service quality models: A review. *International Journal of Quality & Reliability Management*, 22(9): 913–949.

Song, B., Lee, C., Yoon, B., & Park, Y. (2015). Diagnosing service quality using customer reviews: An index approach based on sentiment and gap analyses. *Service Business, 10*(4): 1–24.

Teo, T. S., & Yu, Y. (2005). Online buying behavior: A transaction cost economics perspective. *Omega*, 33(5): 451–465.

Utz, S., Kerkhof, P., & Bos, J. V. D. (2011). Consumers rule: How consumer reviews influence perceived trustworthiness of online stores. *Electronic Commerce Research and Applications*, 11: 49–58.

Wolfinbarger, M., & Gilly, M. (2002). *comQ: Dimensionalizing, measuring, and predicting quality of the e-tail experience*. Marketing Science Institute Report, Cambrigde, MA, No, 02-100, 1–51.

Yang, Z., & Jun, M. (2002). Consumer perception of e-service quality: From Internet purchaser and non-purchaser perspectives. *Journal of Business Strategies*, 19(1): 19–41.

Yang, Z., Jun, M., & Peterson, R. T. (2004). Measuring customer perceived online service quality: Scale development and managerial implications. *International Journal of Operations & Production Management*, 24(11): 1149–1174.

Yang, Z., Peterson, R. T., & Cai, S. (2003). Services quality dimensions of Internet retailing: An exploratory analysis. *Journal of Services Marketing*, 17(7): 685–700.

Zeithaml, V. A., Berry, L. L., & Parasuraman, A. (1993). The nature and determinants of customer expectations of service. *Journal of the Academy of Marketing Science*, 21(1): 1–12.

Zeithaml, V. A., Parasuraman, A., & Malhotra, A. (2001). *A conceptual framework for understanding e-service quality: Implications for future research and managerial practice*. Marketing Science Institute Working Paper Series, No. 00-115, Cambridge, MA, 1–49.

Zeithaml, V. A., Parasuraman, A., & Malhotra, A. (2002). Service quality delivery through web sites: A critical review of extant knowledge. *Journal of the Academy of Marketing Science*, 30(4): 362–375.

Zervas, G., Proserpio, D., & Byers, J. (2014). *The rise of the sharing economy: Estimating the impact of Airbnb on the hotel industry*. Journal of Marketing Research.

Sarah Netter is the Centre Manager at the Centre for Corporate Social Responsibility (cbsCSR) at the Copenhagen Business School (CBS) in Denmark. Prior to her appointment, Sarah has been a PhD fellow and a Post-Doctoral fellow at the Department of Intercultural Communication and Management at CBS. Her research focusses on the sharing economy, sustainable consumer behaviour, business model innovation, and the fashion industry. As part of her research, Sarah has conducted extensive fieldwork on the sharing economy in Europe and the USA. In her research, Sarah aims to explore this new phenomenon and to provide a more nuanced understanding of the opportunities and tensions that characterize the sharing economy. Sarah is affiliated with the MISTRA Future Fashion initiative. MISTRA Future Fashion is a large-scale, cross-disciplinary research initiative, which aims at promoting systemic changes towards sustainability in the fashion industry.

12

A Review of Secondhand Luxury and Vintage Clothing

Daniella Ryding, Menglu Wang, Carly Fox and Yanan Xu

12.1 Introduction

Secondhand luxury fashion consumption is in a state of global growth, with the UK market offering a lucrative market for investment. The global secondhand clothing trade; having been defined as any fashion item that has been "*pre-loved or pre-owned*", has grown as an economic entity and provides a living for in excess of 100,000 people, offering a desirable and essential clothing source in under-developed economies (Hansen 2000; Mhango and Niehm 2005). According to an Oxfam report, global trade in secondhand retailing has grown tenfold since 1990, amounting to a value of approximately $1.5 billion annually (Baden and Barber 2005). Interestingly, the growth in secondhand sales is evidenced foremost within the commodities of secondhand

D. Ryding (✉) · M. Wang · C. Fox · Y. Xu
Manchester University, Manchester, UK
e-mail: Ryding@manchester.ac.uk; annwang0512@gmail.com; carlyfoxx@gmail.com; summerancy@gmail.com

C.E. Henninger et al. (eds.), *Sustainability in Fashion*,
DOI 10.1007/978-3-319-51253-2_12

luxury and vintage (D'Arpizio et al. 2014), the two terms defining garments which offer the consumer brand exclusivity, exceptional craftsmanship, and in vintage terms, unique high-fashion pieces of a specific era (Gerval 2008). Pioneering the new vintage trend for example, are some of Britain's most iconic celebrities, David Beckham, Kate Moss, and Sienna Miller. It is believed that underpinning this overall growth in secondhand sales, entrepreneurs are seeking out new opportunities to capitalise on a market, which is evidencing significant incremental shifts in sustainable consumption behaviour.

Research points to five major challenges facing the fashion industry over the next fifteen years; climate change, resource shortages and rising costs, population change, new technologies and seismic shifts in the global economy will be high on both government and businesses agendas (Levi Strauss & Co 2015). For retailers, the positive relationship and interaction between environment and economy has always been a crucial consideration for safeguarding the future. Companies will need to take responsibility by creating harmonious consumer consumption for sustainable economic development (Goworek et al. 2012). It will be necessary to improve sustainable business practices in a quest for business survival, the fashion industry being no exception to this rule. Clothing manufacturing over the past 20 years has created profound negative impacts on our natural environment; a result of mass garment production in response to frequent changing trends and consumer demands. This chapter makes a contribution to the contemporary debate on sustainable business approaches in fashion, by providing a critical review of a rising new retail concept; secondhand luxury clothing. In particular, the focus of this chapter centres on vintage fashion, this sector having demonstrated significant growth in recent times. Limited studies exist on the thematic of attitudinal and behavioural decision-making in a secondhand clothing context. The trajectory growth of secondhand luxury retailing makes it increasingly important to understand customer expectations and perceptions of both product and service provision, if the outcome of customer satisfaction and profitability is to be sustained. This chapter therefore sets out to (1) critically review fashion retailing and sustainability in context, to identify key drivers for the growth in secondhand luxury clothing within the UK, (2) provide an overview of the secondhand luxury clothing market, identifying some types of secondhand luxury boutiques; their product ranges and unique selling points, (3) examine the attitudinal and behavioural antecedents for secondhand vintage clothing consumption; this particular secondhand sector is chosen due to its increasing popularity amongst high-end fashion consumers and (4) provide suggestions for further research within this growing resellers market. This study thus synthesises the current state of play in regard to secondhand luxury clothing retailing in the UK market and in particular, conceptualises the various consumer decision-making styles of secondhand vintage consumption, bringing forward possible research questions for future studies.

12.2 Fashion Retailing and Sustainability in Context

Fashion retailing forms one of the most important industries worldwide. According to the British Fashion Council (2016), the industry directly contributes £26 billion to the UK economy (GDP). PWC (2015) points out that the retail industry is however becoming more complex and changing at an ever-increasing speed. Changing demographics, household downsizing, more educated consumers, new channel formats – amongst other trends – require that the industry quickly adjusts and modifies existent models, approaches and processes to satisfy the needs of future customers. Retailing will become an industry that realises it must adapt its offerings to select customers, as opposed to the mass appeal approach of the 1980s, to win over customers and foster greater customer loyalty. Consequently, fundamental to retailing success is the formulation of retail strategies which truly incorporate an understanding of changing customer needs, motives and patronage decision-making; marketing research thus playing a central role within this overall process. Retailers must innovate in response to changing trends and become geographically dispersed within omni-channel systems to remain competitive. Ahlert et al. (2010), for example, stipulate that insufficient attention to real needs often leads to a "*copying*" or "*continuation*" of retail formats that instead should be evolved or suspended. Retailers, which pride themselves on being customer orientated; observing strategy as a means to serving real needs, are more likely to embrace new competitive marketing strategies. Ohmae (1988) quotes from the advice of the great Sun Tzu (500BC) who claims:

> *the smartest strategy in war is one that allows you to achieve objectives without having to fight. The highly visible battles involving price, promotions, advertising, formats, are in fact only a part of retail strategy. The largest part, often intentionally invisible, is the quest to find ways of satisfying consumer needs more effectively.*

This traditional retail marketing thought is important for both academics and practitioners alike; S*ustainability* having emerged as a "mega-trend" and one of the most important considerations for millennial corporations and yet a topic very much in its infancy (Mittelstaedt et al. 2014).

Definitions of sustainability range from the popular colour phrasing expression "*green*" which infers some level of ecological and ethical trading practice, to more strategic references such as "*environmental stewardship*", which signifies sustainability is deeply embedded within the organisation. In both cases, striving to engage consumers with more sustainable lifestyles is a key agenda item for many companies and thematic in academic circles. To become truly sustainable, both retailers and manufacturers will need to unlock vertical collaboration within supply chains (PWC 2015). According to a recent report, governments will need to facilitate the development of industry consensus within the context of competition regulation and civil society, and organisational stakeholders will need to network to develop a shared understanding of how sustainability impacts should be measured, incorporated and communicated within the business environment. What will become important is the quest to collaboratively research how organisations can engage consumers to trigger simple behavioural shifts in consumption that enable more sustainable lifestyles, grow demand for sustainable products and create strategic advantage by offering value through a more sustainable customer-orientated approach to business; one which is firmly rooted within the company ethos.

The fashion industry brings many benefits to everyday lives across the globe. Culturally, individuals have demonstrated a greater need for self-expression and according to a study (Kim and Sherman 2007), this need for self-expression is evolving beyond social identity and for some, is being used in a way to actually practise out their social value system and ecological stance within society. Contrary to this positive evolution, is the parallel aftermath of what has become known as consumerism; generated from this outcome is a "throwaway culture", the impacts of which are having detrimental effects on both humanity and our natural environment. Fashion is currently experiencing the "fast fashion" phase (Gabrielli et al. 2013; Runfola and Guercini 2013; Miller 2013; Watson and Yan 2013; Kim et al. 2013), defined as bringing fashion from production to the shop floor in as little as 15 days (Watson and Yan 2013). As a result of increased manufacturing cycles, it has been reported that the fashion industry produces approximately 3.1 million tonnes of CO_2 and 70 million tonnes of water waste each year, and this does not include herbicides, pesticides, and toxic chemicals released into the environment (Minney 2011). Furthermore, according to Levi Strauss & Co (2015), there are estimated to be 1.8 billion people living on the planet by 2030, leading to natural resource scarcity such as water, food, energy and cotton. The United Nations (2015) conducted a proposal for sustainable development, the contents of which stipulate that developed countries were to take the lead and; *"improve progressively through 2030 global resource efficiency in consumption and production, and endeavour to decouple economic growth from environmental degradation in accordance with the 10-year framework of programmes on sustainable consumption and production"*. As a result, it is imperative for organisations to think more sustainably towards product manufacturing and selling for long-term prospects (Choi and Cheng 2015). At the same time, the UK "sustainable product/service" market is still under-developed. It has been reported that 76% of UK adults are aware of *"the ethical and green credentials of products on both manufacturing and distribution processes as well as the reputation of companies or brands"* in 2015, compared with only 35% of adults in the UK having been defined as *"Green and Ethical Crusaders"* in a 2008 study (Mintel 2015). However, despite being under-developed, the UK ethical market, in 2014 was worth £80.26 billion (Ethical Consumer 2015), which shows a significant growth compared with £43.2 billion in 2009; with clothing and cosmetics regarded as the fastest growing sector (Ethical Fashion Forum 2011). This dramatic growth in the size of the sustainable clothing market suggests that whilst an *attitude-behaviour* gap does exist, consumers are beginning to actively pay attention to sustainability (Goworek et al. 2012). Furthermore, secondhand clothing has resurfaced and emerged as a popular alternative to buying newly finished garments; the idea of playing with fashion, using it and then selling it, or donating it for reuse.

12.3 Secondhand Clothing

The emergence of the secondhand clothing industry can be evidenced as early as the 1300s when secondhand clothing was a cheaper substitute to newly finished garments, the latter often being unaffordable to the general population at this time (Frick 2005). This growing phenomenon continued until mass produced clothes were available at more affordable prices. More recently, secondhand retailing in Western cultures has returned in the form of small-scale, unstructured and informal retail formats. Vintage stores, thrift stores, consignment stores, community clothing labels and charities, are amongst some of the specialised types of secondhand retailers on the current retail landscape, with vintage showing the fastest growth (thredUP 2016). These outlets have been classified into what has also become known as a fringe market; a term used in this context, to define buyers and sellers of pre-loved and/or pre-worn clothing; exclusivity and high-quality forming the central unique selling proposition (Gregson and Crewe 2003; Hansen 2000a; Mhango and Niehm 2005). Secondhand luxury is becoming increasingly popular with fashion consumers, and it is estimated that the global secondhand luxury market will be worth $149 billion by 2018 with 24% accounting for luxury sales (Conlumino 2014). Exhibit 12.1–12.6, provide brief case studies of secondhand luxury formats in London, a city renowned as one of the world-leading fashion capitals.

Exhibit 12.1 The Dresser, Dorchester Place, Marble Arch

One of London's leading pre-owned luxury clothing re-sale boutiques, Created in 1986 by an ex-music executive, the Dresser specialises in high-end contemporary couture and vintage handbags, shoes, accessories and clothing in pristine condition. Offering a wide variety of the most sought after and desirable brands, including Chanel, Hermes, Louis Vuitton, Stella McCartney and Alexander McQueen (The Dresser 2013), the boutique attracts fashionistas, magazine editors and celebrities alike, and is unique in catering for the fashion-savvy male by offering an extensive menswear collection. This company does have an online sales and social media presence. In addition, the company is an active charity fundraiser and has a following of celebrities who donate their clothing with all profits from these sales going to charity.

Exhibit 12.2 The Red Cross, Old Church Street, Chelsea

Located on a little side street off Chelsea's famous Kings Road, and only steps away from Manolo Blahnik, this high-end designer charity shop is a favourite amongst locals, Londoners and tourists (TimeOut 2011). There is a community atmosphere within the well-established luxury charity shop with staff taking time to converse and get to know regular faces. This Red Cross store can be quite pricey, price tags of £1000 or more have been known. Evening in-store events and 50% off clearance sales are a regular occurrence. Features women's, men's and children's wear as well as shoes, handbags and accessories. This extremely popular charity shop is stocked with luxury designer brands synonymous with the local Chelsea residents such as Chanel, Armani and Prada, most of which are in great condition and occasionally unworn (British Red Cross 2016).

Exhibit 12.3 Annalena Couture, Fulham Road, Chelsea

Opened in October 2015, Annalena predominantly offers newly designed, beautifully crafted Italian women's wear. It is owned by a young and very knowledgeable Italian couple, Frederica and Andrea, who both grew up in Italy amongst families of high-end designer fashion collectors. You will find a reasonably sized cabinet, offering vintage Chanel (occasionally more recent pieces), sourced from their family collections, other known collectors within their family circle or from international vintage fairs all at attractive prices. This boutique is quickly becoming a local favourite and regularly featured in a well-known television series. The most pleasurable part of the shopping experience is the passion and knowledge that exudes when in conversation with the owners (Annalena, n.d.).

Exhibit 12.4 The Dress Box, Cheval Place, Knightsbridge

Quite possibly London's first luxury resale boutique established after the Second World War by Pam McGraw, this boutique is now run by Stelios, a couturier, avid collector and a man who lives and breathes all things fashion. He has also been Liberty's vintage men's, women's and accessories buyer for over a decade. Stelios carefully selects and sources items for his boutiques and private clients and is well known for stocking rare and unique pieces. The Dress box is actually two boutiques situated side by side. One boutique focuses on high-end European women's wear, shoes and accessories and the other boutique focuses on predominantly vintage Chanel and Hermes. The Dress Box has a long standing, loyal customer base and appeals to more mature women. It offers a couture service as well as an impeccable restoration, conservation and alteration service. Pricing tends to be on the upper end although quality is second to none.

Exhibit 12.5 Salou, Cheval Place, Knightsbridge

Originally situated on the New Kings Road, in the 1980's, it relocated to its exclusive Knightsbridge address in the early 1990's. Patu, the founder, and two of her amazing friends are the heart and soul of this well-established luxury pre-owned fashion agency. A boudoir styled boutique featuring a smorgasbord of delicious luxury brands including recent seasons women's wear, shoes, handbags and accessories from Chanel, Hermes, Christian Louboutin, Hervé Léger and more. Salou is an on-consignment re-seller offering attractively priced pieces in good condition to a young and established client base. They have some online presence although all purchasing must be completed in store.

Exhibit 12.6 The Designer Exchange, Egerton Terrace, Knightsbridge

The Designer Exchange, created by previous Prada employee Angela, has four boutiques in total, a recently opened Madrid location and boutiques in London, Birmingham and Manchester each with differing clients and product styles. The London Designer Exchange attracts the younger and middle-aged housewives of the affluent surrounding areas who are interested in last season's luxury handbags and accessories with vintage pieces mainly being sold in the Manchester boutique. Chanel, Louis Vuitton, Gucci and Mulberry are the most sought after luxury brands within their London location. They have a modern, appealing website with online purchasing possibilities. The Designer Exchange does not use the "on consignment" method of buying that the majority of competitors use, instead they buy items directly and offer the seller either cash or credit (of a greater monetary amount) towards other items in store. No other luxury re-seller is doing this at present (Designer Exchange 2016).

12.4 Vintage – Definitions and Development

Vintage clothing is a sector within the secondhand clothing industry that is showing steady growth and is a popular choice in contemporary fashion circles, with high-end consumers, celebrities and the press, all taking a keen interest in its developments. Today the term "vintage" is used to define "a rare and authentic piece that represents the style of a particular couturier or era" (Gerval 2008). Cornett (2010), provides an alternative definition, and defines vintage as clothing that is "produced in the period between the 1920s and the 1980s". On the other hand, clothing manufactured before the 1920s is classified as antique, whilst clothing produced after the 1980s is not considered to be vintage yet (Cornett 2010). Over the years, the term vintage has been overused in the media, to describe pieces of past collections, without real-time anchorage other than not being of a recent season. Furthermore, capitalising on consumers' craze for vintage style, some secondhand shops have renamed their stocks "*Vintage Clothing*", which creates confusion in the mind of the uninformed consumer. To unravel this confusion, the term secondhand, categorises any piece of clothing which has been used before, notwithstanding the age of the clothes. Vintage on the other hand is determined by the age of the cloth, and not necessarily by the fact that it has been used (Mortara and Ironico 2011).

The vintage trend is on the increase for numerous reasons. Vintage in a fashion sense, represents past style from different eras of the twentieth century, rather than modern day and fast fashion collections (Cassidy and Bennett 2012). To reflect the growing vintage trend, fashion retail expert Mary Portas (2009) states in *The Times* "*The recession means we have all slowed down. We focus more on the value of something*". In addition, we have witnessed a rise in quality secondhand garment sales because fast fashion is seen as "vulgar" by more and more people (Cassidy and Bennett 2012). It is the individuality which comes with vintage style that creates appeal for consumers (Cassidy and Bennett 2012). Similarly, Palmer (2005, p. 197) says, "*vintage has now shifted from subculture to mass culture because of the disappointing fact that, regardless of price, fashion today is rarely exclusive*". The rise of the vintage trend and the factors that are generally assumed responsible for its adoption are further discussed in the next section.

12.5 The Rise of Vintage – Key Influences

John Walsh's article (2010) published in *The Independent* mentions "*vintage is about looking forward through the window of the past*". It seems that nostalgia plays a significant role for most customers when purchasing vintage garments because the past eras can be presented by both the products themselves and the environment in which they are sold (Cassidy and Bennett 2012). Banim and Guy (2001) discuss the notion of historical memories being attached with vintage shopping and the sentimental values these memories hold. One cannot deny that celebrity influence has also instigated a rise in vintage appeal. Since the end of the 2000s, not a typo but from experience I know that street style has been inspired by vintage designs since at least the 1970'. Leading designer brands have also played a role in vintage growth. Luxury fashion brand Louis Vuitton for its 2010/11 winter collection reproduced and reinterpreted vintage clothing. These styles are generally referred to as "*vintage style*", "*vintage inspired*", *or* "*retro*".

As one can evidently see, there are numerous reasons as to why vintage is steadily on the rise and an interesting article written by Cassidy and Bennett (2012) provides a great synthesis of the key impacts. To begin with, the effect of the recession on consumers' finances provides some evidence of a trading down in consumer shopping habits, with some fashion consumers opting for charity shops as an alternative to buying newly finished clothing (Cassidy and Bennett 2012). The "Going Back to Post-war Era" thought, also exists in vintage consumers' minds as they hold the attitude that preferring to repair, reuse and recycle garments rather than throwing them away (ibid). Sladen (1995) mentioned that there was a mass-observation study conducted during 1943 which showed that "women were spending more time on repairs, alterations, [and] generally making-do". Style, quality and individuality also seem to be equally important. Vintage clothing, in fact, is one of the inspirations for designers to produce current collections. Palmer and Clark (2005) state that the massive production of fast fashion clothing results in many people wearing the same garments, whilst vintage provides customers with uniqueness and individuality. In this respect, vintage consumers are able to build their own styles and avoid following the crowd (DeLong et al. 2005). Both Palmer and Clark (2005) and DeLong et al. (2005) mention that vintage fashion provides consumers opportunities to create their own identities by mixing the elements of the past with contemporary clothing.

There is evidence that an additional influence could also be attributed to growing ecological and ethical concerns amongst consumer groups. According to Arnold (2009), consumers' purchasing decisions are more conscientious under the influence of increased media reports on environmental issues. Although it could be argued that the secondhand luxury clothing market could potentially harm the brand image and reputation of luxury fashion houses, D'Arpizio et al. (2014) found the contrary to be the case. The downgraded spending budget led to an increase in secondhand luxury consumption, which in 2014 was worth $17.2 million. *"While this market threatens new product sales, it is simultaneously turning luxury goods into durables with an increasingly defined resell price, thus increasing their value"* (D'Arpizio et al. 2014). This rise in secondhand luxury fashion also fits with the sustainability agenda of governments. To explain, the UK government launched an initiative in 2007, working together with DEFRA (Department of Environment Food and Rural Affairs) and WRAP (Waste and Resource Action Plan) on a Sustainable Clothing Roadmap and Action Plan. The aim was to *"improv[e] the sustainability of clothing across its lifecycle, from the crops [. . .] grown to make the fabrics, to the design and manufacture of the garment, retail, use and end-of-life"* (DEFRA 2011). Examining the extent to which environmentalism plays a fundamental role in decision-making, provides great scope for further research.

12.6 Purchasing Behaviour and Motivation for Opting "Vintage"

Understanding consumer decision making is necessary for determining the effect that the secondhand luxury clothing sector could bring to a brand and how it would benefit the future social, economic and environmental development (Koszewska 2013). Moreover, understanding consumer attitudes and behavioural motivations for secondhand luxury clothing and vintage, provides useful insights for achieving competitive advantage within a lucrative growth industry. Besides, awareness of the key luxury dimensions is a vital aspect for organisations to manage secondhand vintage luxury brands as well as understanding the behavioural motivation of decision-making when purchasing luxury goods (Ghosh and Varshney 2013). Walley et al. (2013) identify five dimensions within the UK context: affect, characteristics, status, gifting and involvement. Additionally, Ghosh and Varshney (2013) proposed that there are three main perspectives regarding luxury goods consumption: characteristics of luxury product/brand, characteristics of luxury buyers and buying motivations of luxury buyers.

12.7 Purchasing Behaviour for Secondhand Vintage Fashion

Cervellon et al. (2010) suggest that there are distinct underlying motivators, as to why women purchase secondhand vintage clothing; nostalgia, price consciousness, fashion involvement, need for status, ecological consciousness, bargain hunting and treasure hunting. Aspects of nostalgia and price consciousness have thus far been reviewed to some extent, but serve as interesting avenues for further research. Bargain hunting and treasure hunting serve as mediators within the overall decision-making process, but equally serve as routes for further research. For this chapter, fashion involvement, the need for uniqueness and status and ecological consciousness are examined; previous studies highlighting these antecedents as important underlying motivators.

Fashion involvement defines the extent to which a consumer is involved with current fashion trends and not necessarily appearance. Demographics are highly related to fashion clothing involvement according to previous studies (Auty and Elliott 1998; O'Cass 2001). It appears that people's attachment and usage of fashion clothing is significantly influenced by age. Cervellon et al. (2012, p. 960) state "as age increases, fashion clothing involvement decreases". Similarly, there is some evidence to suggest that younger people tend to focus more on their appearance than older people (O'Cass 2001, 2004). In a more international context, O'Cass (2000) found that determinants of women's purchase of vintage fashion in Paris are foremost fashion involvement; the extent to which consumers view fashion clothing as personally relevant and being up-to-date with current fashion trends. Vintage consumption is underpinned by the motive to be fashion-involved with garments of a previous era, which offer stylish alternatives to mass fashion, thus allowing fashion conscious consumers to create one's own unique style and identity.

The need for uniqueness, already identified within this chapter as a driver for vintage growth, therefore, forms the next key motivator for vintage consumption. Tian et al. (2001, p. 52) define consumer need for uniqueness as "the trait of pursuing differentness relative to others through the acquisition, utilisation and disposition of consumer goods for the purpose of developing and enhancing one's social and self-image". Jordan and Simpson (2006) add that how an individual defines the level of uniqueness determines her/his need to express uniqueness in a social context. Burns and Warren (1995) have suggested that individuals may take actions to pursue their desirable position in society and improve their perception of uniqueness by such as buying and wearing fashionable clothing if they assume their degree of uniqueness is low. One particular study shows that one of the main reasons for wearing and purchasing vintage garments is personal identity (Gladigau 2008). Respondents from this study said vintage fashion not only helps them express themselves, but also improves their personal uniqueness in public, against mainstream fashion. Compared to regular fashion, vintage clothing is more exclusive and unique (ibid). What is more, Roux and Guiot (2008, 2010) suggested that individuals tend to make non-traditional consumer choices if they have a strong need for uniqueness. For example, they demonstrate their individuality by purchasing clothing in secondhand channels other than conventional channels (Cervellon et al. 2012). Indeed, consumers want to distinguish themselves (snob effect) and value the uniqueness of rare pieces to enhance the exclusivity of their fashion sense (Cervellon et al. 2012). Snyder (1992) pointed out that it has been proven that to establish individuality people keep seeking scarce products. The need for status is the "tendency to purchase goods and services for the status or social prestige value that they confer to the owner" according to Eastman et al. (1999, p. 41). Consumers spend most of their money on products if they have a high need for status, because it serves to enhance status in their view (Eastman et al. 1999). Han et al. (2010) confirmed that to show that they belong to a wealthy group, individuals prefer luxury brands with significant logos. For those consumers with a lower level of wealth but a high need for status, they would buy counterfeit products of luxury brands to show their status; for the consumers with a high need for status and higher level of wealth, they purchase luxury goods to not only show status and connoisseurship, but also to avoid being perceived as an un-wealthy group (Cervellon et al. 2012). According to Belk and Cervellon et al. (2012, p. 961), "in a similar fashion to wine and antiques, vintage connoisseurship and consumption entails a snob appeal which simultaneously attracts and excludes those who do not have the knowledge or the spending power". Identifying high-quality and rarity vintage pieces requires consumers to be "connoisseurs" and have certain levels of knowledge (Cervellon et al. 2012). The couture and boutique items are handed down from generation to generation within old-wealth families to witness the family history (Han et al. 2010).

Over the past few years, there are increasing numbers of consumers who are aware of the influence of the clothes' production on wellbeing, the environment and society. (Cervellon et al. 2010; Cervellon and Carey 2011). Consumers regard the reuse and recycling of clothes as an effective way to positively decrease waste and improve the environment (Bianchi and Birtwistle 2010). For example, the motivation of donating and purchasing secondhand goods are to some extent on the basis of the idea that it is a useful way of extending the lifetime of products thus reduce the waste (Roux and Guiot 2008; Guiot and Roux 2010). The fashion industry tries to give some fascination to recycled clothes by making clothes made out of recycled materials or garments to vintage clothes (Hethorn and Ulasewicz 2008). In the denim industry, some of the retailers encourage consumers to return their old jeans to exchange for a brand new one at half price such as APC and Levi Strauss, moreover, after being cleaned and repaired, the old jeans are resold as vintage (Groves 2008). In addition, Yves Saint Laurent created a collection called "New Vintage" to represent unique pieces, made from recycled cotton drill from the couture house archives.

Also, for a number of consumers, purchasing secondhand clothes is one of the alternatives to fight against a "Kleenex Society" which increase the waste and discard behaviours. From this perspective, buying secondhand clothes buffers the production and selling of unnecessary goods (Roux and Korchia 2006). Thus, consumers try to build and express a socially-conscious concept by purchasing secondhand clothing. "Wearing secondhand clothes by choice can thus be regarded as a sign of opposition to consumerism, associated with voluntary simplicity and various reducing behaviours" (2006, p. 30).

12.8 Conclusion and Recommendations for Future Research

This chapter has provided a critical review of key issues impacting upon the secondhand luxury and vintage clothing market in the UK, drawing together insights into attitudinal and behavioural consumption. A focus on vintage fashion is presented; this sector having evidenced the most significant growth within the secondhand clothing industry in recent years. There has been a growing interest into how companies might trigger simple behavioural shifts in consumption that enable more sustainable lifestyles, grow demand for more sustainable products and create competitive advantage. At organisational level, adopting a more structured approach to sustainable decision-making is important. Retailers and manufacturers will need to unlock vertical collaboration within supply chains and there will be a need for organisational stakeholders to network more effectively to develop a shared understanding of how sustainability impacts should be measured and included within the business environment. This new business requirement has implications for academia, management practitioners and policy makers, and thus, further research into the links between sustainability and organisational culture would be useful. From a demand side perspective, further attitudinal and motivational research into consumer decision making for secondhand clothing within a global context, would also provide meaningful insights into consumption patterns within different cultural and socioeconomic contexts. In particular, bridging this gap in research would serve useful to inform the development of competititive retail marketing strategy for the future.

References

Ahlert, D., Blut, M., & Evanschitzky, H. (2010). *Retailing in the 21st Century – Current Status and Future Evolution of Retail Formats*, 2nd ed., Springer Publishing: US.

Annalena (n.d.). *"Annalena Couture: Italian style into the heart of London"*, Annalena Couture (online), retrieved from: http://www.annalenacouture.london/about-us/, [accessed on: 17/11/2016].

Arnold, C. (2009). *Ethical Marketing and the New Consumer*. Wiley: Chichester.

Auty, S., & Elliott, R. (1998). Fashion involvement, self-monitoring and the meaning of brands. *Journal of Product & Brand Management, 7*(2): 110–112.

Baden, S., & Barber, C. (2005). *The Impact of the second-hand clothing trade on developing countries*. UK: Oxfam.

Banim, M., & Guy, A. (2001). Discontinued Selves: Why Do Women Keep Clothes They No Longer Wear?, in A. Guy, E. Green, & M. Banim (eds) *Through The Wardrobe: Women's Relationships with Their Clothes* (pp. 203–223). Berg: Oxford.

Bianchi, C., & Birtwistle, G. (2010). Sell, give away or donate: An exploratory study of fashion clothing disposal behaviour in two countries. *The International Review of Retail, Distribution and Consumer Research, 20*(3): 353–368.

British Fashion Council (2016), *The British Fashion Industry & London Fashion Week Facts & Figures, BFC* (online), retrieved from: http://britishfashioncouncil.co.uk/pressreleases/The-British-Fashion-Industry–London-Fashion-Week-Facts–Figures [Accessed 25/01/2017].

British Red Cross (2016), *"Vintage clothing and designer charity shops"*, British Red Cross, retrieved from: http://www.redcross.org.uk/Get-involved/Our-shops/Our-specialist-shops/Vintage-clothing-and-designer-charity-shop [accessed on: 17/11/2016].

Burns, D. J., & Warren, H. B. (1995). Need for uniqueness: shopping mall preference and choice activity. *International Journal of Retail & Distribution Management, 23*(12): 4–12.

Butler, S. M., & Francis, S. (1997). The effects of environmental attitudes on apparel purchasing behavior. *Clothing and Textiles Research Journal, 15*(2): 76–85.

Cassidy, T. D., & Bennett, H. R. (2012). The Rise of Vintage Fashion and the Vintage Consumer. *Fashion Practice, 4*: 2, 239–261.

Cervellon, M.-C., Hjerth, H., Ricard, S., & Carey, L. (2010). Green in fashion? An exploratory study of national differences in consumers concern for eco-fashion, Proceedings of the 9th International Marketing Trends Conference, Marketing Trends Association: Venice.

Cervellon, M. C., & Carey, L. (2011). Consumers' perceptions of 'green': why and how consumers use ecofashion and green beauty products. *Critical Issues in Fashion and Beauty, 2*(1–2): 77–95.

Cervellon, M.-C., Carey, L., & Harms, T. (2012). Something old, something used. *International Journal of Retail & Distribution Management, 40*(12): 956–974.

Choi, T. M., & Cheng, T. E. (2015). *Sustainable Fashion Supply Chain Management*. Springer: New York. Retrieved fro:m http://conlumino.com/?p=1583 [accessed on: 05/11/15].

Conlumino. (2014). *UK set to become largest luxury goods market in Europe by 2018. Conlumino*. [Online], retrieved at: http://conlumino.com/?p=1583 [accessed on: 20/03/2016].

Cornett, J. E. (2010), "What is considered vintage clothing?", retrieved from: www.ehow.com/about_6593593_considered-vintage-clothing_.html.

D'Arpizio, C., Levato, F., Zito, D., & De Montolfier, J. (2014). *Luxury goods worldwide market study fall-winter 2014*. Bain & Company [online], retrieved from: http://www.bain.com/publications/articles/luxury-goods-worldwide-market-study-december-2014.aspx [accessed on: 05/11/15].

DEFRA (Department of Environment Food and Rural Affairs). (2011). *Sustainable Clothing Roadmap: Progress Report 2011*, DEFRA [online], retrieved from: https://www.gov.uk/government/uploads/system/uploads/attachment_data/file/69299/pb13461-clothing-actionplan-110518.pdf [accessed on: 05/07/2013].

DeLong, M., Heinemann, B., & Reiley, K. (2005). Hooked on vintage. *Fashion Theory, 9*(1): 23–42.

Eastman, J. K., Goldsmith, R. E., & Flynn, L. R. (1999). Status Consumption in Consumer Behavior: Scale development and validation. *Journal of Marketing Theory and Practice, 7*(3), 41–52.

Ethical Consumer (2015). *UK Ethical Market – Annual Report, Ethical Consumer* (online). retrieved from: http://www.ethicalconsumer.org/researchhub/ukethicalmarket.aspx [accessed on: 24/01/2017].

Ethical Fashion Forum (2011). *The Market for Ethical and Sustainable Fashion Products.* [Online], retrieved from: http://source.ethicalfashionforum.com/assets-uploaded/documents/Market_for_sustainable_fashion_Briefing.pdf [accessed on: 19/03/2016].

Exchange, D. (2016), *"Designer Exchange – About us"*, Designer Exchange (online), retrieved from: https://uk.designerexchange.com/site/aboutus [accessed on: 17/11/2016].

Fletcher, K. (2013). *Sustainable fashion and textiles: design journeys.* Routledge: London, UK.

Frick, C. C. (2005). The Florentine Rigattieri: Second hand clothing dealers and the circulation of goods in the Renaissance, in A. Palmer & H. Clark (Eds) *Old clothes, new looks: second hand fashion*, 13–28, Berg: New York.

Gabrielli, V., Baghi, I., & Codeluppi, V. (2013). Consumption practices of fast fashion products: a consumer-based approach. *Journal of Fashion Marketing and Management, 17*(2): 206–224.

Gerval, O. (2008). *Fashion: Concept to Catwalk.* London: Bloomsbury.

Ghosh, A., & Varshney, S. (2013). Luxury goods consumption: a conceptual framework based on literature review, *South Asian Journal of Management, 20*(2): 146–159.

Gladigau, K. (2008), "Op till you drop: youth, distinction and identity in vintage clothing", retrieved from: www.tasa.org.au.

Goworek, H., Fisher, T., Cooper, T., Woodward, S., & Hiller, A. (2012). The sustainable clothing market: an evaluation of potential strategies for UK retailers. *International Journal of Retail & Distribution Management, 40*(12): 935–955.

Gregson, N., & Crewe, L. (2003). *Second-hand Cultures.* Berg: New York.

Groves, E. (2008). Vintage, green movements spur denim recycling. WWD: Women's Wear Daily, *196*(17): 10.

Guiot, D., & Roux, D. (2010). A second-hand shoppers' motivation scale: Antecedents, consequences, and implications for retailers. *Journal of Retailing, 86*(4): 383–399.

Han, Y. J., Nunes, J. C., & Dre`Ze, X. (2010). Signaling status with luxury goods: The role of brand prominence. *Journal of Marketing, 74*(4): 15–17.

Hansen, K. T. (2000). *Salaula: The world of second-hand clothing and Zambia.* University of Chicago Press: Chicago, IL.

Hethorn, J., & Ulasewicz, C. (2008). *Sustainable fashion: Why now?* Fairchild Books: New York.

Hwang, C. L., & Masud, A. S. M. (2012). *Multiple objective decision making – methods and applications,* Springer Verlag: Berlin.

Jordan, Y., & Simpson, M. N. (2006). Consumer innovativeness among females in specific fashion stores in the Menlyn shopping centre. *Tydskrif vir Gesinsekologie en Verbruikerswetenskappe, 34,* 32–38.

Kim, H., Choo, H. J., & Yoon, N. (2013). The motivational drivers of fast fashion avoidance. *Journal of Fashion Marketing and Management, 17*(2): 243–260.

Kim, H. S., & Sherman, D. K. (2007). 'Express yourself': culture and the effect of self-expression on choice. *Journal of personality and social psychology, 92*(1): 1–11.

Koszweska, M. (2013). A typology of Polish consumers and their behaviours in the market for sustainable textiles and clothing. *International Journal of Consumer Studies, 37*: 507–521.

Levi Strauss & Co. (2015). *Fashion Futures 2025.* [Online], retrieved from: https://www.forumforthefuture.org/sites/default/files/project/downloads/fashionfuturespresentationpdf.pdf [accessed on: 16/03/2016].

Mhango, M. W., & Niehm, L. S. (2005). The second hand clothing distribution channel: Opportunities for retail entrepreneurs in Malawi. *Journal of Fashion Marketing and Management, 9*(3): 342–356.

Miller, K. W. (2013). Hedonic customer responses to fast fashion and replicas. *Journal of Fashion Marketing and Management, 17*(2): 2.

Minney, S. (2011). *Safia Minney: fashion's impact on the earth, Ecologist* (online), retrieved from: http://www.theecologist.org/green_green_living/clothing/1055961/safia_minney_fashions_impact_on_the_earth.html [Accessed: 24/01/2017].

Mintel. (2015). *Consumer Trends 2015.* [Online], retrieved from: http://www.mintel.com/en/uk-consumer-trends-2015/ [accessed on: 19/03/2016].

Mittelstaedt, J. D., Schultz II, C. J., Kilbourne, W. E., & Peterson, M. (2014). Sustainability as a megatrend: Two schools of macromarketing thought. *Journal of Macromarketing, 34*(3): 165–170.

Mortara, A., & Ironico, S. (2011), "Ethical fashion shoppers: Beyond the hedonic/utilitarian motivations dichotomy? An exploratory research", Proceedings of the Congresso de moda ethica.

O'Cass, A. (2000). An assessment of consumers product, purchase decision, advertising and consumption involvement in fashion clothing. *Journal of Economic Psychology, 21*(5): 545–576.

O'Cass, A. (2001). Consumer self-monitoring, materialism and involvement in fashion clothing. *Australasian Marketing Journal, 9*(1): 46–60.

O'Cass, A. (2004). Fashion clothing consumption: Antecedents and consequences of fashion clothing involvement. *European Journal of Marketing, 38*(7): 869–880.

Ohmae, K. (1988) Getting back into strategy. *Harvard Business Review, 66*(6): 149.

Palmer, A., & Clark, H. (2005). *Old clothes, new looks: Second hand fashion.* Berg: New York.

Palmer, A. (2005). Vintage Whores & Vintage Virgins, Second Hand Fashion in the Twenty-first Century, in A. Palmer & H. Clark (eds) *Old Clothes New Looks, Second Hand Fashion*, 197–213, Berg: Oxford.

PWC (2015), *Retailing 2015: New Frontiers, PWC* (online), retrieved: https://www.pwc.com/cl/es/publicaciones/assets/retailing2015.pdf. [accessed: 25/01/2017].

Roux, D., & Guiot, D. (2008). Measuring second-hand shopping motives, antecedents and consequences. *Recherche et Applications en Marketing, 23*(4): 64–84.

Roux, D., & Korchia, M. (2006). Am I what I wear? An exploratory study of symbolic meanings associated with secondhand clothing. *Advances in Consumer Research, 33*: 29–35.

Runfola, A., & Guercini, S. (2013). Fast fashion companies coping with internationalization: Driving the change or changing the model? *Journal of Fashion Marketing and Management, 17*(2): 190–205.

Sladen, C. (1995). *The Conscription of Fashion: Utility Cloth, Clothing and Footwear, 1941–52.* Scholar Press: Aldershot.

Snyder, C. R. (1992). Product scarcity by need for uniqueness interaction: A consumer catch-22 carousel? *Basic and Applied Social Psychology, 13*(1): 9–24.

The Dresser. (2013). *"About us"*, The Dresser (online), retrieved from: http://www.dresseronline.co.uk [accessed on: 17/11/2016].

thredUP (2016). Resale Report 2016, thredUP (online), retrieved: https://www.thredup.com/resale, [accessed on: 24/01/2017].

Tian, K. T., Bearden, W. O., & Hunter, G. L. (2001). Consumers' need for uniqueness: scale development and validation. *Journal of Consumer Research, 28*: 50–66.

TimeOut. (2011). *"British Red Cross"*, TimeOut April 28, 2011, retrieved from: http://www.timeout.com/london/shopping/british-red-cross-1 [accessed on: 17/11/2016]

United Nations (2015). *Sustainable Development Goal 8, UN* (online) retrieved from: https://sustainabledevelopment.un.org/sdg8. [accessed: 24/01/2017].

Walley, K., Custance, P., Copley, P., & Perry, S. (2013). The key dimensions of luxury from a UK consumers' perspective. *Marketing Intelligence & Planning, 31*(7): 823–837.

Walsh, J. (2010). "A Retro Revolution: Why Do We Love All Things Vintage?" *The Independent*, August 28, retrieved from: http://www.independent.co.uk/life-style/fashion/features/a-retro-revolution-why-do-we-love-all-things-vintage-2061798.html.

Watson, M. Z., & Yan, R. N. (2013). An exploratory study of the decision processes of fast versus slow fashion consumers. *Journal of Fashion Marketing and Management, 17*(2): 141–159.

Dr Daniella Ryding is a Lecturer in Fashion Marketing at the University of Manchester in the UK. An active researcher with over with over 40 published articles and several text book contributions, her main research interests focus on consumer behaviour within an international fashion retailing context. The author has more recently been engaged with the psychological cognitive and behavioural mechanisms impacting on consumer decsion-making, contributing to better understandings of memory and the ramifications for business marketing campaigns. Daniella also takes a proactive interest in sustainability and the circular economy, examining further the ecological and ethical principles which drive business strategy.

Ms Menglu Wang is a graduate from the University of Manchester. Her MSc. thesis examines sustainable fashion and its applications to consumer behaviour in the fashion industry by extending the Consumer Style Inventory (CSI) Framework to understand shopper motivations for vintage fashion in the UK market.

Carly Fox has previously studied pattern cutting, fashion and interior design as well as areas of psychology and education. Throughout her career she has gained design, production, sales and manufacturing experience in the UK, Europe, India and China working with both the high-street retail chains and within the luxury fashion market in areas of women's wear, men's wear and accessories. After a stint of being a fashion and lifestyle editor of a London music magazine she was invited to produce fashion shows and events working on projects such as London Fashion Week. Demand was such that she quickly moved into working with a select group of high net worth private clients styling all aspects of their lifestyle.

Ms Yanan Xu is a Marketing Assistant in the fashion industry. She received a distinction in her Masters Degree in Marketing and Management from Loughborough University in 2014, and her MSc. in International Fashion Retailing, awarded from the University of Manchester in 2016. Yanan Xu's MSc. thesis focused on sustainable luxury fashion and consumer behaviour. Her dissertation was entitled *Extending the Consumer Style Inventory (CSI) Framework to Understand Consumer Decision Making for Second-hand Luxury Clothing Consumption: UK Perspective.*

Index

C.E. Henninger et al. (eds.), *Sustainability in Fashion*,
DOI 10.1007/978-3-319-51253-2

M

N

O

P

Q

R

S

Printed by Printforce, the Netherlands

EE